JASHER
INSIGHTS

Book 2

S.N.Strutt

ISBN 978-1-78222-690-1
Book design, layout and production management by Into Print
www.intoprint.net
+44 (0)1604 832149

CONTENTS

BOOK II

BOOK I (Not included in this book)

JASHER INSIGHTS
BOOK 2

The Book of Jasher

Referred to in

Joshua and Second Samuel

Faithfully Translated

FROM THE ORIGINAL HEBREW INTO ENGLISH

"Is not this written in the Book of Jasher?"--*Joshua, x. 13.*
"Behold it is written in the Book of Jasher."--*II. Samuel, i. 18*

SALT LAKE CITY:
PUBLISHED BY J.H. PARRY & COMPANY
1887.

Well, that is what is normally written above the **BOOK OF JASHER**.

It is very important to state that the above-mentioned original Hebrew copy of the Book of Jasher was actually written in pre-Christian times, and eventually was translated into English in the early 1600's and printed in 1613. From what I have studied, the original Book of Jasher, which is a history book, was originally assembled and written in the time of Joshua - 3500 years ago. (**SOURCE**: http:// biblefacts.org/pdf/Jasher_intro.pdf)

Unfortunately, the above traditional description does not do justice to the amazing Book of Jasher.

First of all, I would like to state that I personally, from much study of the book, certainly believe that this book is an inspired writing, although I think that in parts of the book, the stories have been somewhat *embellished*, and some of the *dates are different* than either the Bible or the Septuagint version of the Old Testament. It is likely that the original Book of Jasher, as clearly mentioned in the Old Testament of the Bible has been either altered or tampered with. Nevertheless, it is *still* an excellent book to read. See a lot more about this in the **APPENDIX**.

2PE.1:21 For the prophecy came not in old time by the will of man: but holy men of God spake as they were moved by the Holy Ghost.

Secondly, the above statement '*This text covers much of the same ground as the traditional Mosaic books of the Bible, from the creation of the world to the death of Moses, albeit with several minor variations*' This is somewhat understated. The Book of Jasher in fact, gives a lot more background information to many of the biblical stories than even the Bible itself does.

The Book of Jasher also brings out the supernatural powers of God much more than the Bible does, for example as manifested through the sons of Israel, or Jacob's sons and their constant wars to rid the 'lands of Shem' of the Canaanites and other enemies.

CREDITS: COVER STORY

(**Artwork:** by Suzanne Strutt: www.instagram.com/suzannestruttartist & www.facebook.com/suzannestruttartist)

The cover story describes in great detail, - spread over many chapters in this book, the amazing story of Shechem, to which the cover of this book is dedicated. Just two of Jacob's sons totally destroyed an entire city of the Canaanites called Shechem, because the prince of the city had forcibly taken their only sister and forced himself on her. Later Jacob and all his sons came to live outside of *Shechem*, only to have the whole race of the Canaanites come out to fight against them, numbering in the tens of thousands, against a mere handful. Read what happens in **BOOK I of 'JASHER INSIGHTS'**! It is exciting stuff! The story continues in this **BOOK II OF 'JASHER INSIGHTS'** where the battles and wars continue.

Shechem was where Abraham, grandfather of Jacob was resting under a tree, when the angel of the Lord came to speak with him, and God promised to Abraham that all the lands that he could see to the North and South and East and West his descendants would inherit.

The Story of Joseph and his brethren is even better than the good story in the Bible. It gives amazing details about what exactly happened to poor Joseph when he was sold as a slave into Egypt by his brethren and what happened along the way. There is a very seductive beautiful woman called Zelicah the wife of Potiphar, who is always trying to force Joseph to go to bed with her, when he was only 18 and was her slave. Hardly surprising, as her husband was a eunuch, according to this Book of Jasher. Read what happens. It is an absolutely fascinating story.

This Book of Jasher shows Joseph becoming a 'Warrior King' after getting out of prison, and who led his brethren to fight against all the enemies of Pharaoh and who won time and time again against greatly superior odds.

There are many details about Moses and his calling, that are not mentioned in the Bible and many details of what he did when he was first exiled from Egypt by Pharaoh - for 40 years.

There is also a dubious story about 'Moses being in jail', before being released and having become a king for a long time in the days after he had left Egypt. What did actually happen to Moses in the 40 years that he was away from Egypt? Find out by reading this book. This story is probably the most questionable in the whole Book of Jasher, but interesting anyway.

There is a fascinating description of Moses & the 10 Plagues of Egypt in this book, that is even more descriptive than the story in the Bible, where God calls a Sulanuth, or octopus-like sea creature from the sea, to bring some of His judgments. Quite a fascinating story that children would also like.

Joshua conquers the Promised land overthrowing many cities in the process: It shows how God fulfils His promise to Abraham to drive out all of the Canaanites from the lands of Shem.

There is a good description of other wars that were fought by Angeas, an African king with Zepho the grandson of Esau as his commander in chief. There are many ensuing wars described in detail.

There is a fascinating story of Zepho the grandson of Esau who fought against a large *human - animal chimera* which was described has having 'the top half of a man' and the 'bottom half of a beast'. Zepho killed this monster that was hiding in a cave, because it had decimated the herds and flocks of the local peoples. As a result, Zepho was made king of the land of Chittim (Cyprus).

There is a strange story, a bit similar to Balaam's ass in the Bible, where God opens the mouth of the donkey to actually speak to Balaam; only in this case it is a wolf talking with Jacob concerning his lost son Joseph. Joseph's brothers had told their father Jacob that a wild animal had killed Joseph. See what the wolf had to say about that!

I believe from having studied this book many times, that this book is very valuable, although some of the stories could be *somewhat embellished,* but then who's to say? Some of the miraculous stories in this book may seem far out to us in modern sceptical times, but then I could also argue: Who am I to question God's miraculous ways?

JAM.1:5 If any of you lack wisdom, let him ask of God, that giveth to all men liberally, and upbraideth not; and it shall be given him.

MAT.18:3 And said, Verily I say unto you, 'Except ye be converted, and become as little children, ye shall not enter into (or see and understand) the kingdom of heaven.'

In other words, we must think as a believing little child about things of Faith, and not be of a doubting sceptical & analytical mind, lest the spiritual things of God escape us and sadly pass us by through our unbelief, especially when it comes to outright miracles of God.

1CO.2:14 But the natural man receives not the things of the Spirit of God: for they are foolishness unto him: neither can he know them, because they are spiritually discerned.

You will also find an **APPENDIX** in the back of this book giving many more details and web refs.

THE FORMAT OF THIS BOOK

i) I have decided to divide this book of **JASHER INSIGHTS** into **BOOK I** and **BOOK II** to make for easy reading and greater portability of both books.

ii) I have typed a chapter of the Book of Jasher, and included in each chapter my commentaries, which are just that: my opinions, specula-tions and theories, which are gleaned from much study of the subject matter. Most, if not all of which, could prove to be true, and are written with the express intention to motivate the reader to do a more thorough investigation for him or herself, to prove whether correct or not, as I am sure that some of the ideas, speculations and conjecture will be quite far out there, to some people.

iii) I have also put cross-references to the Bible, and other Apocryphal books where appropriate.

iv) **Details:**

The first '**comment**' in each chapter, will be noted as being '**Comment 1**' & then **C.2, C.3**, etc. The original Text from the Book of Jasher is in slightly larger text than either the 'comments' or 'Bible verses'. Three different types of writing are used. One for the original text, and another type of writing for my comments, and yet another for the Bible verses.

v) The longest commentaries and conclusions are in the '**APPENDICES**' of this book of which there are around 20

The following '**INTRODUCTION**' is to **Book I** for your *interest* only - so that you can be familiar with my first book and what it contains.

INTRODUCTION TO 'JASHER INSIGHTS' BOOK I

In comparing with the Bible, the Book of Jasher describes in great detail about the Garden of Eden, Adam and Eve, Cain and Abel & the 'Origins of Evil'. It also talks about Cainan as the first person to write things down; and later his great grandson Enoch from before the Great Flood also writes things down on tablets of stone.

We will read the infamous **GEN 6** episode in greater detail in this book of Jasher.

GEN.6:2 That the sons of God saw the daughters of men that they were fair; and they took them wives of all which they chose.

GEN.6:4 There were giants in the earth in those days; and also after that, when the sons of God came in unto the daughters of men, and they bare children to them, the same became mighty men which were of old, men of renown.

In the time of Jared - the father of Enoch, **200 of the Watcher class of angels** descended to earth on Mount Hermon in rebellion against God. What was so special about these Watcher class of angels? In this book I will explain about it in detail. One of the reasons for the fall of the Watchers was that they said that they wanted to have their own wives and children. Well that is what most writers of GEN 6 say, but was that the real reason? Find out in this book. The Fallen angels made love to the beautiful women on earth but who was seducing whom? Read all about it in this book. You can also read much more about his topic in my book **ENOCH INSIGHTS**.

In this book gruesome and grisly Giants are born from the offspring of the disobedient Fallen angels and human woman. There were many types of giants which were also of different heights. All incredibly dangerous. What are the possibilities of these same monstrous giants returning one day? You can find a possible answer to that question in this book.

How big were these giants? Read on to find out. Why did the giants become grotesque grisly cannibals who were terrorizing the inhabitants of the earth in Pre-Flood times?

This Book of Jasher portrays Enoch as a sort of King of kings for 243 years; it also talks a lot about Nimrod and Babel in the early times after the Great Flood.

This book describes the Tower of Babel as being at least 9000 feet high and gives many more details of the Tower's structure. It tells us that Nimrod was *'not fully human'*, but that he had the *'blood of the Nephilim'* and was *'becoming one of them'*.

The Book of Jasher helps us to have a much better grip on the time sequence concerning the life of Abraham and his father, where they came from, and what life was really like back then. It shows Abraham as a mighty Warrior King, who was a real Idol Smasher & who totally obliterated all of his enemies.

Abraham is shown to be alive at the same time as Nimrod, and even at the same time as the great Patriarchs Shem and his father Noah. Quite remarkable, when one considers that Abraham was the 10th generation after Noah. Abraham apparently got his spiritual training at the houses of both Noah and Shem, whilst fleeing Nimrod.

Abraham was probably studying and learning from the Book of Noah and the Book of Enoch, which Noah had brought with him on the Ark at the time of the Great Flood.

Concerning Life - right after the Great Flood

There are lots of interesting details in this Book of Jasher that are not given in any other books about Noah and the Great Flood and his life after that; as well as those who were descendants of Noah and what happened to them.

You will read about *Rikayon* who allegedly brought the name of Pharaoh to Egypt. You will also encounter the nasty character of *Satan* himself who is also called *Mastema* in the Book of Jubilees (See my book 'Jubilees Insights'), & who is always lurking around in the background, trying to cause trouble for Abraham and his descendants.

There is a strange story of some of the herdsmen of the descendants of Esau being terrified by hundreds of animal–human chimeras with the top part of their bodies being as a beast and bottom part as a human. These creatures simply rode off with all of their animals. It scared the living daylights out of the men, who then refused to go back to that location.

Stephen Nigel Strutt (May 2019)

Chapter 41

1 And at the revolution of the year the sons of Jacob journeyed from Shechem, and they came to Hebron, to their father Isaac, and they dwelt there, but their flocks and herds they fed daily in Shechem, for there was there in those days good and fat pasture, and Jacob and his sons and all their household dwelt in the valley of Hebron.

2 And it was in those days, in that year, being the hundred and sixth year of the life of Jacob, in the tenth year of Jacob's coming from Padan-aram, that Leah the wife of Jacob died; she was fifty-one years old when she died in Hebron.

C.1 Here are some specifics: Jacob was 106. He died at 146. His wife Leah died being only 51. Her sister Rachel had already died when she was 46. Why did God allow both of his wives to die so young one might ask? What about his two concubines? Rachel's handmaid was raped by Jacob's son Reuben secretly in the darkness of the night, after which Jacob did not go into her anymore. As for Leah's handmaid and Jacob's 2nd concubine, what happened to her? That remains to be seen in this story.

3 And Jacob and his sons buried her in the cave of the field of Machpelah, which is in Hebron, which Abraham had bought from the children of Heth, for the possession of a burial place.

4 And the sons of Jacob dwelt with their father in the valley of Hebron, and all the inhabitants of the land knew their strength and their fame went throughout the land.

5 And Joseph the son of Jacob, and his brother Benjamin, the sons of Rachel, the wife of Jacob, were yet young in those days, and did not go out with their brethren during their battles in all the cities of the Amorites.

6 And when Joseph saw the strength of his brethren, and their greatness, he praised them and extolled them, but he ranked himself greater than them, and extolled himself above them; and Jacob, his father, also loved him more than any of his sons, for he was a son of his old age, and through his love toward him, he made him a coat of many colours.

C.2 FAVOURITISM: [Definition]: the practice of giving unfair preferential treatment to one person or group at the expense of another.

> 7 And when Joseph saw that his father loved him more than his brethren, he continued to exalt himself above his brethren, and he brought unto his father evil reports concerning them.
>
> 8 And the sons of Jacob seeing the whole of Joseph's conduct toward them, and that their father loved him more than any of them, they hated him and could not speak peaceably to him all the days.
>
> 9 And Joseph was seventeen years old, and he was still magnifying himself above his brethren, and thought of raising himself above them.

C.3 SPOILT It is very clear here that Jacob spoiled Joseph because he was the son of his favourite wife Rachel, who had already died. He obviously very much missed his wife Rachel.

> 10 At that time he dreamed a dream, and he came unto his brothers and told them his dream, and he said unto them, I dreamed a dream, and behold we were all binding sheaves in the field, and my sheaf rose and placed itself upon the ground and your sheaves surrounded it and bowed down to it.
>
> 11 And his brethren answered him and said unto him, 'What means this dream that thou didst dream? "Dost thou imagine in thy heart to reign or rule over us'?
>
> 12 And he still came, and told the thing to his father Jacob, and Jacob kissed Joseph when he heard these words from his mouth, and Jacob blessed Joseph.
>
> 13 And when the sons of Jacob saw that their father had blessed Joseph and had kissed him, and that he loved him exceedingly, they became jealous of him and hated him the more.
>
> 14 And after this Joseph dreamed another dream and related the dream to his father in the presence of his brethren, and Joseph said unto his father and brethren, Behold I have again dreamed a dream, and behold the sun and the moon and the eleven stars bowed down to me.

15 And his father heard the words of Joseph and his dream, and seeing that his brethren hated Joseph on account of this matter, Jacob therefore rebuked Joseph before his brethren on account of this thing, saying, What meaneth this dream which thou hast dreamed, and this magnifying thyself before thy brethren who are older than thou art?

16 Dost thou imagine in thy heart that I and thy mother and thy eleven brethren will come and bow down to thee, that thou speakest these things?

C.4 'I and thy mother and thy eleven brethren' Here there seems to be a mistake as Jacob mentions Joseph's mother Rachel as being there with him when she had already died sometime before at the birth of Benjamin her 2nd son? The only explanation could possibly be that Jacob was referring to Bildah the handmaiden of Rachel who was also now one of Jacob's concubine wives.

17 And his brethren were jealous of him on account of his words and dreams, and they continued to hate him, and Jacob reserved the dreams in his heart.

C.5 Joseph at 17 years old, acted like a typical spoilt brat that had no control over his tongue or his pride. It didn't seem to bother him by the fact that his brothers got angry at the things that he related to them. Having the prophetic dreams at this early age of 17 only lifted Joseph up in pride, and he also being obnoxious in his communications with his brethren because his father had allowed him to feel superior to his brothers; the things that he was to have to go through because of being spoiled in eventually being sold as a slave into Egypt by his brethren and ending up as a slave for many years and then in prison for 3 years down in Egypt. A very hard learning process for Joseph and yet it was all part of God's greater plan.

ROM.8:28 And we know that all things work together for good to them that love God, to them who are the called according to his purpose.

18 And the sons of Jacob went one day to feed their father's flock in Shechem, for they were still herdsmen in those days; and whilst the sons of Jacob were that day feeding in Shechem they delayed, and the time of gathering in the cattle was passed, and they had not arrived.

19 And Jacob saw that his sons were delayed in Shechem, and Jacob said within himself, Peradventure the people of Shechem have risen up to fight against them, therefore they have delayed coming this day.

20 And Jacob called Joseph his son and commanded him, saying, Behold thy brethren are feeding in Shechem this day, and behold they have not yet come back; go now therefore and see where they are, and bring me word back concerning the welfare of thy brethren and the welfare of the flock.

21 And Jacob sent his son Joseph to the valley of Hebron, and Joseph came for his brothers to Shechem, and could not find them, and Joseph went about the field which was near Shechem, to see where his brothers had turned, and he missed his road in the wilderness, and knew not which way he should go.

22 And an angel of the Lord found him wandering in the road toward the field, and Joseph said unto the angel of the Lord, I seek my brethren; hast thou not heard where they are feeding? and the angel of the Lord said unto Joseph, I saw thy brethren feeding here, and I heard them say they would go to feed in Dothan.

23 And Joseph hearkened to the voice of the angel of the Lord, and he went to his brethren in Dothan and he found them in Dothan feeding the flock.

24 And Joseph advanced to his brethren, and before he had come nigh unto them, they had resolved to slay him.

25 And Simeon said to his brethren, Behold the man of dreams is coming unto us this day, and now therefore come and let us kill him and cast him in one of the pits that are in the wilderness, and when his father shall seek him from us, we will say an evil beast has devoured him.

26 And Reuben heard the words of his brethren concerning Joseph, and he said unto them, You should not do this thing, for how can we look up to our father Jacob? Cast him into this pit to die there but stretch not forth a hand upon him to spill his blood; and Reuben said this in order to deliver him from their hand, to bring him back to his father.

27 And when Joseph came to his brethren he sat before them, and they rose upon him and seized him and smote him to the earth and stripped the coat of many colours which he had on.

C.6 Think how much hatred Joseph's brothers had towards him. He must have really been a handful always telling his brothers how superior he was to them and how that his father favoured him more than them because he *was* superior. Sounds like he had been deliberately blindly goading on his older brethren not realizing that the fruit of his negative behaviour was to be rewarded upon him this very day.

28 And they took him and cast him into a pit, and in the pit there was no water, but serpents and scorpions. And Joseph was afraid of the serpents and scorpions that were in the pit. And Joseph cried out with a loud voice, and the Lord hid the serpents and scorpions in the sides of the pit, and they did no harm unto Joseph.

C.7 Poor Joseph, he might have been a spoiled brat, but he certainly didn't deserve to be thrown into a pit filled with serpents and scorpions. Neither did he deserve to be killed or sold as a slave. So why did God allow his brethren to react so fiercely? Well, as extreme as these events seem to us today, it was all part of God's much greater purpose as Joseph's dreams would one day come true in the far future when he was destined to become the ruler of Egypt. Notice that God was working in the background all the while in the above verse, as it clearly states that God protected Joseph from the serpents and scorpions.

29 And Joseph called out from the pit to his brethren, and said unto them, What have I done unto you, and in what have I sinned? why do you not fear the Lord concerning me? am I not of your bones and flesh, and is not Jacob your father, my father? why do you do this thing unto me this day, and how will you be able to look up to our father Jacob?

30 And he continued to cry out and call unto his brethren from the pit, and he said, O Judah, Simeon, and Levi, my brethren, lift me up from the place of darkness in which you have placed me, and come this day to have compassion on me, ye children of the Lord, and sons of Jacob my father. And if I have sinned unto you, are you not the sons of Abraham, Isaac, and Jacob? if they saw an orphan they had compassion over him, or one that was hungry, they gave him bread to eat, or one that was thirsty, they gave him water to drink, or one that was naked, they covered him with garments!

C.8 As extreme as this story is the amazing thing is that God had a great purpose in all of this as God wanted to use Joseph's afflictions as a preparation for the forming of the nation of Israel as we shall see in the next chapters.

31 And how then will you withhold your pity from your brother, for I am of your flesh and bones, and if I have sinned unto you, surely you will do this on account of my father!

32 And Joseph spoke these words from the pit, and his brethren could not listen to him, nor incline their ears to the words of Joseph, and Joseph was crying and weeping in the pit.

33 And Joseph said, O that my father knew, this day, the act which my brothers have done unto me, and the words which they have this day spoken unto me.

34 And all his brethren heard his cries and weeping in the pit, and his brethren went and removed themselves from the pit, so that they might not hear the cries of Joseph and his weeping in the pit.

Chapter 42

1 And they went and sat on the opposite side, about the distance of a bow-shot, and they sat there to eat bread, and whilst they were eating, they held counsel together what was to be done with him, whether to slay him or to bring him back to his father.

2 They were holding the counsel, when they lifted up their eyes, and saw, and behold there was a company of Ishmaelites coming at a distance by the road of Gilead, going down to Egypt.

3 And Judah said unto them, What gain will it be to us if we slay our brother? peradventure God will require him from us; this then is the counsel proposed concerning him, which you shall do unto him: Behold this company of Ishmaelites going down to Egypt,

C.1 Judah is stating that perhaps God will require the blood of Joseph at their hands in the same way that God did with Cain and cursed him for murdering his brother.

4 Now therefore, come let us dispose of him to them, and let not our hand be upon him, and they will lead him along with them, and he will be lost amongst the people of the land, and we will not put him to death with our own hands. And the proposal pleased his brethren and they did according to the word of Judah.

C.2 Since what was happening to Joseph was all part of God's greater and long distance plan to bring Israel as a nation into existence, how convenient for God to happen to bring along the company of Ishmaelites just at the right moment so as to make sure that Joseph's brothers didn't kill him, as if they succeeded in killing him it would have effected their own destiny.

5 And whilst they were discoursing about this matter, and before the company of Ishmaelites had come up to them, seven trading men of Midian passed by them, and as they passed they were thirsty, and they lifted up their eyes and saw the pit in which Joseph was immured, and they looked, and behold every species of bird was upon him.

6 And these Midianites ran to the pit to drink water, for they thought that it contained water, and on coming before the pit they heard the voice of Joseph crying and weeping in the pit, and they looked down

into the pit, and they saw and behold there was a youth of comely appearance and well favoured.

7 And they called unto him and said, Who art thou and who brought thee hither, and who placed thee in this pit, in the wilderness? and they all assisted to raise up Joseph and they drew him out, and brought him up from the pit, and took him and went away on their journey and passed by his brethren.

8 And these said unto them, Why do you do this, to take our servant from us and to go away? surely we placed this youth in the pit because he rebelled against us, and you come and bring him up and lead him away; now then give us back our servant.

9 And the Midianites answered and said unto the sons of Jacob, Is this your servant, or does this man attend you? peradventure you are all his servants, for he is more comely and well favoured than any of you, and why do you all speak falsely unto us?

C.3 Not a good move! These Midianites obviously had no idea with whom they were talking. These brothers of Joseph could have easily torn them apart limb from limb. The Midianites really struck the wrong cord this time, especially stating that *'he is more comely and well favoured than any of you'* When one thinks about it, that was the very reason why Joseph was thrown in the well by his brethren in the first place. His brethren were jealous of him for his good looks, and for his having been favoured by his father and spoilt, not to mention his goading them on with his 'superior airs'.

10 Now therefore we will not listen to your words, nor attend to you, for we found the youth in the pit in the wilderness, and we took him; we will therefore go on.

11 And all the sons of Jacob approached them and rose up to them and said unto them, Give us back our servant, and why will you all die by the edge of the sword? And the Midianites cried out against them, and they drew their swords, and approached to fight with the sons of Jacob.

12 And behold Simeon rose up from his seat against them, and sprang upon the ground and drew his sword and approached the Midianites and he gave a terrible shout before them, so that his shouting was heard at a distance, and the earth shook at Simeon's shouting.

13 And the Midianites were terrified on account of Simeon and the noise of his shouting, and they fell upon their faces, and were excessively alarmed.

14 And Simeon said unto them, Verily I am Simeon, the son of Jacob the Hebrew, who have, only with my brother, destroyed the city of Shechem and the cities of the Amorites; so shall God moreover do unto me, that if all your brethren the people of Midian, and also the kings of Canaan, were to come with you, they could not fight against me.

C.4 Who was this Simeon character, who could utter a ghastly shriek, which could scare the living daylights out of others? How was it possible that as he said, 'Even if all your brethren the people of Midian, and also the kings of Canaan, were to come with you, they could not fight against me.' How is that even physically possible? The only explanation if this story is to be believed, is that Jacob's sons had been supernaturally empowered by God Himself, in order to protect them from their many enemies round about them and in particular the cursed Canaanites with their Giants.

C.5 Here's a thought: If God had not supernaturally empowered Jacob's sons then perhaps Jacob and his sons never would have survived to fulfil God's promise to their great-grandfather Abraham that He would make a special and great nation from the lineage of Abraham. If Jacob's sons had not been so strong then perhaps the nation of Israel would never have happened. Another character mentioned in the Bible, who had supernatural strength was Samson. Samson came on the scene after the children of Israel had come out of the '400 years Captivity' down in Egypt. He was to be the last of the Judges of Israel. (See: Judges 16)

15 Now therefore give us back the youth whom you have taken, lest I give your flesh to the birds of the skies and the beasts of the earth.

16 And the Midianites were more afraid of Simeon, and they approached the sons of Jacob with terror and fright, and with pathetic words, saying,

17 Surely you have said that the young man is your servant, and that he rebelled against you, and therefore you placed him in the pit; what then will you do with a servant who rebels against his master? Now therefore sell him unto us, and we will give you all that you require for him; and the Lord was pleased to do this in order that the sons of Jacob should not slay their brother.

C.6 Here God is making absolutely sure that Joseph's brothers would not end up killing him, so His Spirit put the idea into their hearts to indeed sell Joseph to the Midianites.

18 And the Midianites saw that Joseph was of a comely appearance and well-favoured; they desired him in their hearts and were urgent to purchase him from his brethren.

19 And the sons of Jacob hearkened to the Midianites and they sold their brother Joseph to them for twenty pieces of silver, and Reuben their brother was not with them, and the Midianites took Joseph and continued their journey to Gilead.

20 They were going along the road, and the Midianites repented of what they had done, in having purchased the young man, and one said to the other, What is this thing that we have done, in taking this youth from the Hebrews, who is of comely appearance and well favoured.

21 Perhaps this youth is stolen from the land of the Hebrews, and why then have we done this thing? and if he should be sought for and found in our hands we shall die through him.

22 Now surely hardy and powerful men have sold him to us, the strength of one of whom you saw this day; perhaps they stole him from his land with their might and with their powerful arm, and have therefore sold him to us for the small value which we gave unto them.

23 And whilst they were thus discoursing together, they looked, and behold the company of Ishmaelites which was coming at first, and which the sons of Jacob saw, was advancing toward the Midianites, and the Midianites said to each other, Come let us sell this youth to the company of Ishmaelites who are coming toward us, and we will take for him the little that we gave for him, and we will be delivered from his evil.

C.7 Apparently the Midianites realized that they had very 'hot merchandise' for which they might be held accountable, get themselves killed, so they quickly repented of their deeds, and decided to sell Joseph to the Ishmaelites, who were travelling down to Egypt.

24 And they did so, and they reached the Ishmaelites, and the Midianites sold Joseph to the Ishmaelites for twenty pieces of silver which they had given for him to his brethren.

25 And the Midianites went on their road to Gilead, and the Ishmaelites took Joseph and they let him ride upon one of the camels, and they were leading him to Egypt.

26 And Joseph heard that the Ishmaelites were proceeding to Egypt, and Joseph lamented and wept at this thing that he was to be so far removed from the land of Canaan, from his father, and he wept bitterly whilst he was riding upon the camel, and one of their men observed him, and made him go down from the camel and walk on foot, and notwithstanding this Joseph continued to cry and weep, and he said, O my father, my father.

27 And one of the Ishmaelites rose up and smote Joseph upon the cheek, and still he continued to weep; and Joseph was fatigued in the road, and was unable to proceed on account of the bitterness of his soul, and they all smote him and afflicted him in the road, and they terrified him in order that he might cease from weeping.

C.8 Poor Joseph! Such a terrible thing to happen to any human being. Sold into slavery and treated like dirt! Well it turned out that God was willing for Joseph to suffer for a little while but not to be unduly tormented so that he smote the Ishmaelites with darkness and confusion and caused their hands to become withered when they smote Joseph..

28 And the Lord saw the ambition of Joseph and his trouble, and the Lord brought down upon those men darkness and confusion, and the hand of every one that smote him became withered.

29 And they said to each other, What is this thing that God has done to us in the road? and they knew not that this befell them on account of Joseph. And the men proceeded on the road, and they passed along the road of Ephrath where Rachel was buried.

30 And Joseph reached his mother's grave, and Joseph hastened and ran to his mother's grave, and fell upon the grave and wept.

C.9 A very unusual story here. Joseph happens to ride by the very tomb of his mother Rachel and stops to cry out to his dead mother at her graveside. Why would he do that? After all she is already dead and gone! But gone where? Is it actually possible to call up the dead or the spirits of the dead who have already passed on to the spirit world and have them come and speak with us directly upon occasion? The story of Saul calling up the spirit of Samuel the prophet would indicate that it is indeed supernaturally possible upon occasion if God Himself warrants it.

1SA.28:3 Now Samuel was dead, and all Israel had lamented him, and buried him in Ramah, even in his own city. And Saul had put away those that had familiar spirits, and the wizards, out of the land.

1SA.28:9 And the woman said unto him, Behold, thou know what Saul hath done, how he hath cut off those that have familiar spirits, and the wizards, out of the land: wherefore then lay thou a snare for my life, to cause me to die?

1SA.28:10 And Saul sware to her by the LORD, saying, As the LORD lives, there shall no punishment happen to thee for this thing.

1SA.28:11 Then said the woman, Whom shall I bring up unto thee? And he said, Bring me up Samuel.

1SA.28:12 And when the woman saw Samuel, she cried with a loud voice: and the woman spoke to Saul, saying, Why hast thou deceived me? for thou art Saul.

1SA.28:13 And the king said unto her, Be not afraid: for what saw thou? And the woman said unto Saul, I saw gods ascending out of the earth.

1SA.28:14 And he said unto her, What form is he of? And she said, An old man cometh up; and he is covered with a mantle. And Saul perceived that it was Samuel, and he stooped with his face to the ground, and bowed himself.

1SA.28:15 And Samuel said to Saul, 'Why hast thou disquieted me, to bring me up'? And Saul answered, I am sore distressed; for the Philistines make war against me, and God is departed from me, and answers me no more, neither by prophets, nor by dreams: therefore I have called thee, that thou mayest make known unto me what I shall do.

---

31 And Joseph cried aloud upon his mother's grave, and he said, O my mother, my mother, O thou who didst give me birth, awake now, and rise and see thy son, how he has been sold for a slave, and no one to pity him.

32 O rise and see thy son, weep with me on account of my troubles, and see the heart of my brethren.

> 33 Arouse my mother, arouse, awake from thy sleep for me, and direct thy battles against my brethren. O how have they stripped me of my coat, and sold me already twice for a slave, and separated me from my father, and there is no one to pity me.
>
> 34 Arouse and lay thy cause against them before God, and see whom God will justify in the judgment, and whom he will condemn.
>
> 35 Rise, O my mother, rise, awake from thy sleep and see my father how his soul is with me this day, and comfort him and ease his heart.
>
> 36 And Joseph continued to speak these words, and Joseph cried aloud and wept bitterly upon his mother's grave; and he ceased speaking, and from bitterness of heart he became still as a stone upon the grave.

C.10 Joseph was so full of grief and sorrow & so self-occupied at this particular time, he was weeping at the grave of his mother and 'talked to her'. From his reaction, when he actually did get a response, he didn't really take it seriously. This is a lot how most people would react today, if someone started talking to them from the spirit world in their very thoughts, they would simply dismiss it, especially if the instructions from the spirit world went against their own plans. God's Spirit is always faithfully trying to instruct the sons of men, but the Holy Spirit is rejected more and more these days, until people become hardened and calloused against hearing the very voice of God.

C.11 In general people today are largely just like Satan before them: they prefer to do things their own way and not God's way and are often in direct rebellion against God by their very actions and words. It takes a lot of concentration and meditation and quietness to learn 'the ways of the Lord' as well as constantly meditating upon His word.

> 37 And Joseph heard a voice speaking to him from beneath the ground, which answered him with bitterness of heart, and with a voice of weeping and praying in these words:

C.12 An unusual part of the story where the 'voice of the dead' is heard from the grave. It is true that this part of the story is rather unusual, but not uncommon. In the Bible we see Saul the night before a great battle at which he was to die, talking with Samuel the prophet a few days after he had died with the help of a woman psychic at Endor who called up the spirit of Samuel from the grave.

1SA.28:15 And Samuel said to Saul, 'Why hast thou disquieted me, to bring me up'? And Saul answered, I am sore distressed; for the Philistines make war against me, and God is departed from me, and answers me no more, neither by prophets, nor by dreams: therefore I have called thee, that thou mayest make known unto me what I shall do.

1SA.28:16 Then said Samuel, 'Wherefore then dost thou ask of me, seeing the LORD is departed from thee, and is become thine enemy'?

1SA.28:17 And the LORD hath done to him, as he spake by me: for the LORD hath rent the kingdom out of thine hand, and given it to thy neighbour, even to David:

1SA.28:19 Moreover the LORD will also deliver Israel with thee into the hand of the Philistines: and tomorrow shalt thou and thy sons be with me: the LORD also shall deliver the host of Israel into the hand of the Philistines.

C.13 Note that just as Samuel predicted, the *very next day Saul and his sons were killed in battle.*

---

38 My son, my son Joseph, I have heard the voice of thy weeping and the voice of thy lamentation; I have seen thy tears; I know thy troubles, my son, and it grieves me for thy sake, and abundant grief is added to my grief.

39 Now therefore my son, Joseph my son, hope to the Lord, and wait for him and do not fear, for the Lord is with thee, he will deliver thee from all trouble.

40 Rise my son, go down unto Egypt with thy masters, and do not fear, for the Lord is with thee, my son. And she continued to speak like unto these words unto Joseph, and she was still.

C.14 Here we see that the spirit of Joseph's dead mother Rachel actually did come to speak to him and told him not to worry but to trust the Lord & that he was in God's hands, therefore he should not be afraid and to go down to Egypt and that everything would work out. Did it turn out to be true what Rachel the mother of Joseph told him? Yes, it turned out that Rachel's counsel was 100% accurate.

---

41 And Joseph heard this, and he wondered greatly at this, and he continued to weep; and after this one of the Ishmaelites observed him crying and weeping upon the grave, and his anger was kindled against him, and he drove him from there, and he smote him and cursed him.

C.15 It would seem that although Joseph did hear from his mother from the realms beyond, that initially he wasn't too happy with her advice, as he was still learning to hear from the Spirit of the Lord. His heart was set on going back to his father. But God knew that he had to grow up and be 'kicked out of the nest' evenly forcibly, so that he could fulfil God's greater purpose: That of saving Israel's family; for the famine that would come in the future whilst Joseph was down in Egypt.

> 42 And Joseph said unto the men, May I find grace in your sight to take me back to my father's house, and he will give you abundance of riches.

C.16 We see here that Joseph was not wanting to follow the counsel of his dead mother from beyond the grave! Why? Because he still was acting like a spoiled 17-year-old rich kid who was wanting to go back to the 'easy way' to the comfort of his father and stepmother, and the wealth of this family. Someone has wisely said, 'The most uncomfortable place for a true follower of God is a 'too comfortable place.' Because Joseph was not listening to God's counsel through the spirit of his dead mother Rachel, therefore he started to get even more chastisements:

> 43 And they answered him, saying, Art thou not a slave, and where is thy father? and if thou hadst a father thou wouldst not already twice have been sold for a slave for so little value; and their anger was still roused against him, and they continued to smite him and to chastise him, and Joseph wept bitterly.

C.17 Even though Joseph hadn't yet learned to both listen and obey God fully, God would not suffer the Ishmaelites to chastise him further, so God Himself started to chastise them even more than previously:

> 44 And the Lord saw Joseph's affliction, and Lord again smote these men, and chastised them, and the Lord caused darkness to envelope them upon the earth, and the lightning flashed and the thunder roared, and the earth shook at the voice of the thunder and of the mighty wind, and the men were terrified and knew not where they should go.
>
> 45 And the beasts and camels stood still, and they led them, but they would not go, they smote them, and they crouched upon the ground; and the men said to each other, What is this that God has done to us? what are our transgressions, and what are our sins that this thing has thus befallen us?

C.18 Even the beasts of the Ishmaelites had more sense and would not move because they knew the Spirit of God was angry and they were scared to move. There a perfect example of this in the Bible called Balaam's Ass:

NUM.22:23 And the ass saw the angel of the LORD standing in the way, and his sword drawn in his hand: and the ass turned aside out of the way and went into the field: and Balaam smote the ass, to turn her into the way.

NUM.22:25 And when the ass saw the angel of the LORD, she thrust herself unto the wall, and crushed Balaam's foot against the wall: and he smote her again.

NUM.22:27 And when the ass saw the angel of the LORD, she fell down under Balaam: and Balaam's anger was kindled, and he smote the ass with a staff.

NUM.22:28 And the LORD opened the mouth of the ass, and she said unto Balaam, What have I done unto thee, that thou hast smitten me these three times?

NUM.22:29 And Balaam said unto the ass, Because thou hast mocked me: I would there were a sword in mine hand, for now would I kill thee.

NUM.22:30 And the ass said unto Balaam, Am not I thine ass, upon which thou hast ridden ever since I was thine unto this day? was I ever wont to do so unto thee? And he said, Nay.

NUM.22:31 Then the LORD opened the eyes of Balaam, and he saw the angel of the LORD standing in the way, and his sword drawn in his hand: and he bowed down his head, and fell flat on his face.

---

46 And one of them answered and said unto them, Perhaps on account of the sin of afflicting this slave has this thing happened this day to us; now therefore implore him strongly to forgive us, and then we shall know on whose account this evil befalleth us, and if God shall have compassion over us, then we shall know that all this cometh to us on account of the sin of afflicting this slave.

C.19 It is good to see that the Ishmaelites, who were also descended from Abraham, were yet God-fearing men, and knew that God was dealing with them, on account of their mistreating Joseph.

---

47 And the men did so, and they supplicated Joseph and pressed him to forgive them; and they said, 'We have sinned to the Lord and to thee, now therefore vouchsafe to request of thy God that he shall put away this death from amongst us, for we have sinned to him.'

48 And Joseph did according to their words, and the Lord hearkened to Joseph, and the Lord put away the plague which he had inflicted upon those men on account of Joseph, and the beasts rose up from the ground and they conducted them, and they went on, and the raging storm abated and the earth became tranquilized, and the men proceeded on their journey to go down to Egypt, and the men knew that this evil had befallen them on account of Joseph.

31

C.20 Joseph prayed for God to take away the judgements against the Ishmaelites including the raging storm and the plague which had afflicted them, and God heard the prayer of Joseph and took away both the storm and their afflictions.

---

49 And they said to each other, 'Behold we know that it was on account of his affliction that this evil befell us; now therefore why shall we bring this death upon our souls? Let us hold counsel what to do to this slave'.

50 And one answered and said, 'Surely he told us to bring him back to his father; now therefore come, let us take him back and we will go to the place that he will tell us, and take from his family the price that we gave for him and we will then go away.'

C.21 First of all. the Ishmaelites considered taking Joseph back to his father, but then realised that the distance was too far. and so they then decided it would be better to sell him down in Egypt for a high price, and thus be rid of the 'evil curse' now associated with chastising Joseph.

C.22 Joseph probably kept remembering what his mother Rachel had just told him from the spirit world, about having faith in God: *'Now therefore my son, Joseph, hope in the Lord, and wait for him and do not fear, for the Lord is with thee, he will deliver thee from all trouble.'* And so, Joseph finally calmed down and learned to trust in God and to wait on His instructions: *'Rise my son, go down unto Egypt with thy masters, and do not fear, for the Lord is with thee, my son.'*

---

51 And one answered again and said, 'Behold this counsel is very good, but we cannot do so for the way is very far from us, and we cannot go out of our road'.

52 And one more answered and said unto them, 'This is the counsel to be adopted, we will not swerve from it; behold we are this day going to Egypt, and when we shall have come to Egypt, we will sell him there at a high price, and we will be delivered from his evil.'

53 And this thing pleased the men and they did so, and they continued their journey to Egypt with Joseph.

Chapter 43

1 And when the sons of Jacob had sold their brother Joseph to the Midianites, their hearts were smitten on account of him, and they repented of their acts, and they sought for him to bring him back, but could not find him.

Comment:1: '*repented of their acts*'. This very important part is not mentioned in the Bible. Why so important? As on many other occasions this Book of Jasher gives many more details than the Bible does about the Story of Joseph.

1JN.1:9 If we confess our sins, he is faithful and just to forgive us our sins, and to cleanse us from all unrighteousness.

C.2 God had an important plan in getting Joseph into Egypt. As he had the 'gift of telling dreams' it would eventually enable his family to be nourished by Pharaoh once Jacob's family had moved down to Egypt, where they could both grow and prosper, before it was time for God to bring them out of Egypt once again.

2 And Reuben returned to the pit in which Joseph had been put, in order to lift him out, and restore him to his father, and Reuben stood by the pit, and he heard not a word, and he called out Joseph! Joseph! and no one answered or uttered a word.

3 And Reuben said, Joseph has died through fright, or some serpent has caused his death; and Reuben descended into the pit, and he searched for Joseph and could not find him in the pit, and he came out again.

4 And Reuben tore his garments and he said, The child is not there, and how shall I reconcile my father about him if he be dead? and he went to his brethren and found them grieving on account of Joseph, and counselling together how to reconcile their father about him, and Reuben said unto his brethren, I came to the pit and behold Joseph was not there, what then shall we say unto our father, for my father will only seek the lad from me.

5 And his brethren answered him saying, Thus and thus we did, and our hearts afterward smote us on account of this act, and we now sit to seek a pretext how we shall reconcile our father to it.

C.3 *'our hearts afterward smote us on account of this act'.* As super-humanly strong and tough as these men were, they were not entirely hardened against God's Spirit. Now they all felt great remorse, but it was too late to go and find out what had happened to Joseph. They must have felt like complete jerks for having sold their own brother into slavery. Because they were sorry, God eventually blessed them with a re-uniting with their long-lost brother some 20 years later down in Egypt, once he had become 2nd to Pharaoh.

6 And Reuben said unto them, 'What is this you have done to bring down the grey hairs of our father in sorrow to the grave? the thing is not good, that you have done'.

7 And Reuben sat with them, and they all rose up and swore to each other not to tell this thing unto Jacob, and they all said, 'The man who will tell this to our father or his household, or who will report this to any of the children of the land, we will all rise up against him and slay him with the sword'.

8 And the sons of Jacob feared each other in this matter, from the youngest to the oldest, and no one spoke a word, and they concealed the thing in their hearts.

9 And they afterward sat down to determine and invent something to say unto their father Jacob concerning all these things.

10 And Issachar said unto them, Here is an advice for you if it seem good in your eyes to do this thing, take the coat which belongs to Joseph and tear it, and kill a kid of the goats and dip it in its blood.

11 And send it to our father and when he sees it he will say an evil beast has devoured him, therefore tear ye his coat and behold his blood will be upon his coat, and by your doing this we shall be free of our father's murmurings.

12 And Issachar's advice pleased them, and they hearkened unto him and they did according to the word of Issachar which he had counselled them.

13 And they hastened and took Joseph's coat and tore it, and they killed a kid of the goats and dipped the coat in the blood of the kid, and then

trampled it in the dust, and they sent the coat to their father Jacob by the hand of Naphtali, and they commanded him to say these words:

14 We had gathered in the cattle and had come as far as the road to Shechem and farther, when we found this coat upon the road in the wilderness dipped in blood and in dust; now therefore know whether it be thy son's coat or not.

15 And Naphtali went and he came unto his father and he gave him the coat, and he spoke unto him all the words which his brethren had commanded him.

16 And Jacob saw Joseph's coat and he knew it and he fell upon his face to the ground, and became as still as a stone, and he afterward rose up and cried out with a loud and weeping voice and he said, It is the coat of my son Joseph!

17 And Jacob hastened and sent one of his servants to his sons, who went to them and found them coming along the road with the flock.

18 And the sons of Jacob came to their father about evening, and behold their garments were torn and dust was upon their heads, and they found their father crying out and weeping with a loud voice.

19 And Jacob said unto his sons, Tell me truly what evil have you this day suddenly brought upon me? and they answered their father Jacob, saying, We were coming along this day after the flock had been gathered in, and we came as far as the city of Shechem by the road in the wilderness, and we found this coat filled with blood upon the ground, and we knew it and we sent unto thee if thou could know it.

20 And Jacob heard the words of his sons and he cried out with a loud voice, and he said, It is the coat of my son, an evil beast has devoured him; Joseph is rent in pieces, for I sent him this day to see whether it was well with you and well with the flocks and to bring me word again from you, and he went as I commanded him, and this has happened to him this day whilst I thought my son was with you.

21 And the sons of Jacob answered and said, He did not come to us, neither have we seen him from the time of our going out from thee until now.

22 And when Jacob heard their words he again cried out aloud, and he rose up and tore his garments, and he put sackcloth upon his loins, and he wept bitterly and he mourned and lifted up his voice in weeping and exclaimed and said these words,

C.4 We know that God talked clearly to the Patriarchs. In the above verse, it begs the question as to why God didn't speak to Jacob in one form or the other either by vision or by dream to inform him that his son was not dead, so that he didn't have to endlessly grieve? Especially when we realize that his endless grief caused the death of his daughter Dinah and of Rachel's nurse and Jacob's concubine Bildah? I know, the circumstances were very extreme! Well, the answer is simple. If God had told Jacob that Joseph was still alive, and that he was down in Egypt, then Jacob would have sent his sons down to Egypt right away and tried to rescue Joseph when God had a long-term plan. So, in hindsight, it was best that Jacob didn't know the truth about his son Joseph having been sold into slavery. Many times, God has to hide things from us for our own good. At other times He speaks with us freely, as evidenced by God's many conversations with Jacob, Isaac & Abraham.

23 Joseph my son, O my son Joseph, I sent thee this day after the welfare of thy brethren and behold thou hast been torn in pieces; through my hand has this happened to my son.

24 It grieves me for thee Joseph my son, it grieves me for thee; how sweet wast thou to me during life, and now how exceedingly bitter is thy death to me.

25 that I had died in thy stead Joseph my son, for it grieves me sadly for thee my son, O my son, my son. Joseph my son, where art thou, and where hast thou been drawn? arouse, arouse from thy place, and come and see my grief for thee, O my son Joseph.

26 Come now and number the tears gushing from my eyes down my cheeks, and bring them up before the Lord, that his anger may turn from me.

27 Joseph my son, how didst thou fall, by the hand of one by whom

no one had fallen from the beginning of the world unto this day; for thou hast been put to death by the smiting of an enemy, inflicted with cruelty, but surely I know that this has happened to thee, on account of the multitude of my sins.

28 Arouse now and see how bitter is my trouble for thee my son, although I did not rear thee, nor fashion thee, nor give thee breath and soul, but it was God who formed thee and built thy bones and covered them with flesh, and breathed in thy nostrils the breath of life, and then he gave thee unto me.

29 Now truly God who gave thee unto me, he has taken thee from me, and such then has befallen thee

30 And Jacob continued to speak like unto these words concerning Joseph, and he wept bitterly; he fell to the ground and became still.

31 And all the sons of Jacob seeing their father's trouble, they repented of what they had done, and they also wept bitterly.

32 And Judah rose up and lifted his father's head from the ground, and placed it upon his lap, and he wiped his father's tears from his cheeks, and Judah wept an exceeding great weeping, whilst his father's head was reclining upon his lap, still as a stone.

33 And the sons of Jacob saw their father's trouble, and they lifted up their voices and continued to weep, and Jacob was yet lying upon the ground still as a stone.

34 And all his sons and his servants and his servant's children rose up and stood round him to comfort him, and he refused to be comforted.

C.5 *'he refused to be comforted'*. This was a serious mistake on the part of Jacob as he was resisting the Spirit of God, which is the spirit of comfort. As a result of over a year of sorrow and weeping over Joseph, according to the book of Jubilees, both his daughter Dinah died of grief over the loss of her half-brother Joseph, so also did Jacob's concubine, Rachel's handmaiden Bildah also died of grief. It does not pay to get so bent out of shape with grief as in Jacob's case it actually turned out to be a lack of faith and trust in God. Because God had a better plan for the safety of all of Jacob's children and descendants, but he had to get them down to Egypt first of all.

35 And the whole household of Jacob rose up and mourned a great mourning on account of Joseph and their father's trouble, and the intelligence reached Isaac, the son of Abraham, the father of Jacob, and he wept bitterly on account of Joseph, he and all his household, and he went from the place where he dwelt in Hebron, and his men with him, and he comforted Jacob his son, and he refused to be comforted.

36 And after this, Jacob rose up from the ground, and his tears were running down his cheeks, and he said unto his sons, Rise up and take your swords and your bows, and go forth into the field, and seek whether you can find my son's body and bring it unto me that I may bury it.

37 Seek also, I pray you, among the beasts and hunt them, and that which shall come the first before you seize and bring it unto me, perhaps the Lord will this day pity my affliction, and prepare before you that which did tear my son in pieces, and bring it unto me, and I will avenge the cause of my son.

38 And his sons did as their father had commanded them, and they rose up early in the morning, and each took his sword and his bow in his hand, and they went forth into the field to hunt the beasts.

39 And Jacob was still crying aloud and weeping and walking to and fro in the house, and smiting his hands together, saying, Joseph my son, Joseph my son.

40 And the sons of Jacob went into the wilderness to seize the beasts, and behold a wolf came toward them, and they seized him, and brought him unto their father, and they said unto him, This is the first we have found, and we have brought him unto thee as thou didst command us, and thy son's body we could not find.

41 And Jacob took the beast from the hands of his sons, and he cried out with a loud and weeping voice, holding the beast in his hand, and he spoke with a bitter heart unto the beast, Why didst thou devour my son Joseph, and how didst thou have no fear of the God of the earth, or of my trouble for my son Joseph?

42 And thou didst devour my son for naught, because he committed no violence, and didst thereby render me culpable on his account, therefore God will require him that is persecuted.

43 And the Lord opened the mouth of the beast in order to comfort Jacob with its words, and it answered Jacob and spoke these words unto him,

C.6 *'opened the mouth of the beast'* A very unusual situation where God actually opens the mouth of an animal to speak in a human language. This also happened in the Bible when Balaam's ass suddenly started talking to him in a time of great anguish.

NUM.22:28 And the LORD opened the mouth of the ass, and she said unto Balaam, 'What have I done unto thee, that thou hast smitten me these three times?'

C.7 It also mentioned in the above verse that God had opened the mouth of the wolf to actually speak to Jacob in order to be a comfort to him. However, we notice that Jacob refuses to be comforted which is a form of rebellion against the Spirit of God and as a direct result he caused the death of his daughter Dinah (According to the book of Jubilees) and his concubine because of excessive grief which wasn't a good example to those younger and weaker than himself.

44 As God lives who created us in the earth, and as thy soul lives, my lord, I did not see thy son, neither did I tear him to pieces, but from a distant land I also came to seek my son who went from me this day, and I know not whether he be living or dead.

45 And I came this day into the field to seek my son, and your sons found me, and seized me and increased my grief, and have this day brought me before thee, and I have now spoken all my words to thee.

46 And now therefore, O son of man, I am in thy hands, and do unto me this day as it may seem good in thy sight, but by the life of God who created me, I did not see thy son, nor did I tear him to pieces, neither has the flesh of man entered my mouth all the days of my life.

47 And when Jacob heard the words of the beast, he was greatly astonished, and sent forth the beast from his hand, and she went her way.

48 And Jacob was still crying aloud and weeping for Joseph day after day, and he mourned for his son many days.

JUBILEES 34.13-17 And he mourned all that night, for they had brought it to him in the evening, and he became feverish with mourning for his death, and he said: 'An evil beast hath devoured Joseph'; and all the members of his house [mourned with him that day, and they] were grieving and mourning with him all that day. And his sons and his daughter rose up to comfort him, but he refused to be comforted for his son. And on that day Bilhah heard that Joseph had perished, and she died mourning him, and she was living in Qafratef, and Dinah also, his daughter, died after Joseph had perished. And there came these three mournings upon Israel in one month. And they buried Bilhah over against the tomb of Rachel, and Dinah also, his daughter, they buried there. And he mourned for Joseph one year, and did not cease, for he said, 'Let me go down to the grave mourning for my son'.

C.8 Dinah, the only daughter of Jacob had already suffered and been abused by Shechem when she was only 12- years old.

Now, Dinah had to put up with having to see her father Jacob in such continued sorrow over something that wasn't even true (The supposed death of her half-brother Joseph).

As a direct result, God didn't bless that rebellion and lack of trust in God, so that a real tragedy emerged out of a seeming tragedy.

C.9 This story clearly shows the importance of not getting all bent out of shape about anything but to trust God much more. Of course, it is much easier for us today to see that in hindsight that God had deliberately allowed Joseph to be sold into slavery and that He had a greater plan.

C.10 Why was Joseph so hated by his brethren in the first place? He was obviously a very spoilt brat, who thumbed his nose up at this brothers with his superior airs.

C.11 Why was Joseph so spoiled? Because Jacob obviously didn't discipline him. Why? Favouritism! Jacob loved Joseph extra much because he was the son of Jacob's favourite wife Rachel. Even God didn't like the fact the Jacob loved Rachel more than his wife Leah. As it is stated that when God saw that Rachel was loved and Leah hated, then God allowed Leah to have 4 sons and Rachel didn't conceive for a long season. God was trying to teach Jacob to also love Leah, and not show favouritism to either his wives, or certainly not to give preference to any of his sons, by treating one better than the others. He really learned the hard way, by bitter experience. This was the root of the whole problem in the first place,

C.12 Nevertheless, 'all things work together for good' to those that love God. God's longer vision was for Jacob and his sons to move to Egypt and to be protected by Pharaoh, and to be bountifully supplied for by Joseph, Jacob's son, who would become 2nd to Pharaoh himself.

C.13 Jacob did get to see his long-lost son Joseph again some 20 years later when the famine started.

ROM.8:28 And we know that all things work together for good to them that love God, to them who are the called according to his purpose.

Chapter 44

1 And the sons of Ishmael who had bought Joseph from the Midianites, who had bought him from his brethren, went to Egypt with Joseph, and they came upon the borders of Egypt, and when they came near unto Egypt, they met four men of the sons of Medan the son of Abraham, who had gone forth from the land of Egypt on their journey.

2 And the Ishmaelites said unto them, Do you desire to purchase this slave from us? and they said, Deliver him over to us, and they delivered Joseph over to them, and they beheld him, that he was a very comely youth and they purchased him for twenty shekels.

3 And the Ishmaelites continued their journey to Egypt and the Medanim also returned that day to Egypt, and the Medanim said to each other, Behold we have heard that Potiphar, an officer of Pharaoh, captain of the guard, seeketh a good servant who shall stand before him to attend him, and to make him overseer over his house and all belonging to him.

4 Now therefore come let us sell him to him for what we may desire, if he be able to give unto us that which we shall require for him.

5 And these Medanim went and came to the house of Potiphar, and said unto him, We have heard that thou seekest a good servant to attend thee, behold we have a servant that will please thee, if thou canst give unto us that which we may desire, and we will sell him unto thee.

6 And Potiphar said, Bring him before me, and I will see him, and if he please me I will give unto you that which you may require for him.

7 And the Medanim went and brought Joseph and placed him before Potiphar, and he saw him, and he pleased him exceedingly, and Potiphar said unto them, Tell me what you require for this youth?

8 And they said, Four hundred pieces of silver we desire for him, and Potiphar said, I will give it you if you bring me the record of his sale to you, and will tell me his history, for perhaps he may be stolen, for this

youth is neither a slave, nor the son of a slave, but I observe in him the appearance of a goodly and handsome person.

9 And the Medanim went and brought unto him the Ishmaelites who had sold him to them, and they told him, saying, He is a slave and we sold him to them.

10 And Potiphar heard the words of the Ishmaelites in his giving the silver unto the Medanim, and the Medanim took the silver and went on their journey, and the Ishmaelites also returned home.

11 And Potiphar took Joseph and brought him to his house that he might serve him, and Joseph found favour in the sight of Potiphar, and he placed confidence in him, and made him overseer over his house, and all that belonged to him he delivered over into his hand.

12 And the Lord was with Joseph and he became a prosperous man, and the Lord blessed the house of Potiphar for the sake of Joseph.

13 And Potiphar left all that he had in the hand of Joseph, and Joseph was one that caused things to come in and go out, and everything was regulated by his wish in the house of Potiphar.

14 And Joseph was eighteen years old, a youth with beautiful eyes and of comely appearance, and like unto him was not in the whole land of Egypt.

15 At that time whilst he was in his master's house, going in and out of the house and attending his master, Zelicah, his master's wife, lifted up her eyes toward Joseph and she looked at him, and behold he was a youth comely and well favoured.

16 And she coveted his beauty in her heart, and her soul was fixed upon Joseph, and she enticed him day after day, and Zelicah persuaded Joseph daily, but Joseph did not lift up his eyes to behold his master's wife.

17 And Zelicah said unto him, How goodly are thy appearance and

form, truly I have looked at all the slaves, and have not seen so beautiful a slave as thou art; and Joseph said unto her, Surely he who created me in my mother's womb created all mankind.

18 And she said unto him, How beautiful are thine eyes, with which thou hast dazzled all the inhabitants of Egypt, men and women; and he said unto her, How beautiful they are whilst we are alive, but shouldst thou behold them in the grave, surely thou wouldst move away from them.

19 And she said unto him, How beautiful and pleasing are all thy words; take now, I pray thee, the harp which is in the house, and play with thy hands and let us hear thy words.

20 And he said unto her, How beautiful and pleasing are my words when I speak the praise of my God and his glory; and she said unto him, How very beautiful is the hair of thy head, behold the golden comb which is in the house, take it I pray thee, and curl the hair of thy head.

21 And he said unto her, How long wilt thou speak these words? cease to utter these words to me, and rise and attend to thy domestic affairs.

22 And she said unto him, There is no one in my house, and there is nothing to attend to but to thy words and to thy wish; yet notwithstanding all this, she could not bring Joseph unto her, neither did he place his eye upon her, but directed his eyes below to the ground.

23 And Zelicah desired Joseph in her heart, that he should lie with her, and at the time that Joseph was sitting in the house doing his work, Zelicah came and sat before him, and she enticed him daily with her discourse to lie with her, or ever to look at her, but Joseph would not hearken to her.

C.1 It sounds like the poor woman didn't have enough to do or to occupy her mind. Also, it doesn't seem too promising for a woman if your husband is a eunuch like Potiphar. A sad situation for Zelicah. She has money and influence, but she can't have everything that she might desire, and she wasn't able to entice Joseph as he knew that according to Hebrew laws of his own family that he could face death if he committed adultery against Potiphar.

24 And she said unto him, If thou wilt not do according to my words, I will chastise thee with the punishment of death, and put an iron yoke upon thee.

25 And Joseph said unto her, Surely God who created man looseth the fetters of prisoners, and it is he who will deliver me from thy prison and from thy judgment.

26 And when she could not prevail over him, to persuade him, and her soul being still fixed upon him, her desire threw her into a grievous sickness.

27 And all the women of Egypt came to visit her, and they said unto her, Why art thou in this declining state? thou that lack nothing; surely thy husband is a great and esteemed prince in the sight of the king, should thou lack anything of what thy heart desires?

28 And Zelicah answered them, saying, This day it shall be made known to you, whence this disorder springs in which you see me, and she commanded her maid servants to prepare food for all the women, and she made a banquet for them, and all the women ate in the house of Zelicah.

29 And she gave them knives to peel the citrons to eat them, and she commanded that they should dress Joseph in costly garments, and that he should appear before them, and Joseph came before their eyes and all the women looked on Joseph, and could not take their eyes from off him, and they all cut their hands with the knives that they had in their hands, and all the citrons that were in their hands were filled with blood.

30 And they knew not what they had done but they continued to look at the beauty of Joseph, and did not turn their eyelids from him.

31 And Zelicah saw what they had done, and she said unto them, What is this work that you have done? behold I gave you citrons to eat and you have all cut your hands.

32 And all the women saw their hands, and behold they were full of

blood, and their blood flowed down upon their garments, and they said unto her, this slave in your house has overcome us, and we could not turn our eyelids from him on account of his beauty.

33 And she said unto them, Surely this happened to you in the moment that you looked at him, and you could not contain yourselves from him; how then can I refrain when he is constantly in my house, and I see him day after day going in and out of my house? how then can I keep from declining or even from perishing on account of this?

34 And they said unto her, the words are true, for who can see this beautiful form in the house and refrain from him, and is he not thy slave and attendant in thy house, and why dost thou not tell him that which is in thy heart, and suffer thy soul to perish through this matter?

35 And she said unto them, I am daily endeavouring to persuade him, and he will not consent to my wishes, and I promised him everything that is good, and yet I could meet with no return from him; I am therefore in a declining state as you see.

36 And Zelicah became very ill on account of her desire toward Joseph, and she was desperately lovesick on account of him, and all the people of the house of Zelicah and her husband knew nothing of this matter, that Zelicah was ill on account of her love to Joseph.

37 And all the people of her house asked her, saying, Why art thou ill and declining, and lackest nothing? and she said unto them, I know not this thing which is daily increasing upon me.

38 And all the women and her friends came daily to see her, and they spoke with her, and she said unto them, This can only be through the love of Joseph; and they said unto her, Entice him and seize him secretly, perhaps he may hearken to thee, and put off this death from thee.

39 And Zelicah became worse from her love to Joseph, and she continued to decline, till she had scarce strength to stand.

40 And on a certain day Joseph was doing his master's work in the house, and Zelicah came secretly and fell suddenly upon him, and Joseph rose

up against her, and he was more powerful than she, and he brought her down to the ground.

41 And Zelicah wept on account of the desire of her heart toward him, and she supplicated him with weeping, and her tears flowed down her cheeks, and she spoke unto him in a voice of supplication and in bitterness of soul, saying,

42 Hast thou ever heard, seen or known of so beautiful a woman as I am, or better than myself, who speak daily unto thee, fall into a decline through love for thee, confer all this honor upon thee, and still thou wilt not hearken to my voice?

43 And if it be through fear of thy master lest he punish thee, as the king lives no harm shall come to thee from thy master through this thing; now, therefore pray listen to me, and consent for the sake of the honour which I have conferred upon thee, and put off this death from me, and why should I die for thy sake? and she ceased to speak.

44 And Joseph answered her, saying, Refrain from me, and leave this matter to my master; behold my master knows not what there is with me in the house, for all that belongs to him he has delivered into my hand, and how shall I do these things in my master's house?

45 For he hath also greatly honoured me in his house, and he hath also made me overseer over his house, and he hath exalted me, and there is no one greater in this house than I am, and my master hath refrained nothing from me, excepting thee who art his wife, how then canst thou speak these words unto me, and how can I do this great evil and sin to God and to thy husband?

46 Now therefore refrain from me, and speak no more such words as these, for I will not hearken to thy words. But Zelicah would not hearken to Joseph when he spoke these words unto her, but she daily enticed him to listen to her.

47 And it was after this that the brook of Egypt was filled above all its sides, and all the inhabitants of Egypt went forth, and also the king and

princes went forth with timbrels and dances, for it was a great rejoicing in Egypt, and a holiday at the time of the inundation of the sea Sihor, and they went there to rejoice all the day.

48 And when the Egyptians went out to the river to rejoice, as was their custom, all the people of the house of Potiphar went with them, but Zelicah would not go with them, for she said, I am indisposed, and she remained alone in the house, and no other person was with her in the house.

49 And she rose up and ascended to her temple in the house, and dressed herself in princely garments, and she placed upon her head precious stones of onyx stones, inlaid with silver and gold, and she beautified her face and skin with all sorts of women's purifying liquids, and she perfumed the temple and the house with cassia and frankincense, and she spread myrrh and aloes, and she afterward sat in the entrance of the temple, in the passage of the house, through which Joseph passed to do his work, and behold Joseph came from the field, and entered the house to do his master's work.

50 And he came to the place through which he had to pass, and he saw all the work of Zelicah, and he turned back.

51 And Zelicah saw Joseph turning back from her, and she called out to him, saying What aileth thee Joseph? come to thy work, and behold I will make room for thee until thou shalt have passed to thy seat.

52 And Joseph returned and came to the house, and passed from thence to the place of his seat, and he sat down to do his master's work as usual and behold Zelicah came to him and stood before him in princely garments, and the scent from her clothes was spread to a distance.

53 And she hastened and caught hold of Joseph and his garments, and she said unto him, As the king lives if thou wilt not perform my request thou shalt die this day, and she hastened and stretched forth her other hand and drew a sword from beneath her garments, and she placed it upon Joseph's neck, and she said, Rise and perform my request, and if not thou diest this day.

54 And Joseph was afraid of her at her doing this thing, and he rose up to flee from her, and she seized the front of his garments, and in the terror of his flight the garment which Zelicah seized was torn, and Joseph left the garment in the hand of Zelicah, and he fled and got out, for he was in fear.

C.2 One thing comes to mind in this situation: If Potiphar's wife had been trying to entice Joseph for such a long time, then why hadn't he reported it to Potiphar himself. Wouldn't that have been the correct thing to do under the circumstances. So why didn't he? I would guess that it would still be only his word (the word of a slave against a high-level citizen) of Egypt, such as his wife. So, if Joseph had reported the incident to Potiphar, he would probably have been thrown into prison all the sooner! Joseph must have realized this and decided not to tell Potiphar.

55 And when Zelicah saw that Joseph's garment was torn, and that he had left it in her hand, and had fled, she was afraid of her life, lest the report should spread concerning her, and she rose up and acted with cunning, and put off the garments in which she was dressed, and she put on her other garments.

56 And she took Joseph's garment, and she laid it beside her, and she went and seated herself in the place where she had sat in her illness, before the people of her house had gone out to the river, and she called a young lad who was then in the house, and she ordered him to call the people of the house to her.

57 And when she saw them she said unto them with a loud voice and lamentation, See what a Hebrew your master has brought to me in the house, for he came this day to lie with me.

58 For when you had gone out he came to the house, and seeing that there was no person in the house, he came unto me, and caught hold of me, with intent to lie with me.

59 And I seized his garments and tore them and called out against him with a loud voice, and when I had lifted up my voice he was afraid of his life and left his garment before me and fled.

60 And the people of her house spoke nothing, but their wrath was very

much kindled against Joseph, and they went to his master and told him the words of his wife.

61 And Potiphar came home enraged, and his wife cried out to him, saying, What is this thing that thou hast done unto me in bringing a He. brew servant into my house, for he came unto me this day to sport with me; thus did he do unto me this day.

62 And Potiphar heard the words of his wife, and he ordered Joseph to be punished with severe stripes, and they did so to him.

63 And whilst they were smiting him, Joseph called out with a loud voice, and he lifted up his eyes to heaven, and he said, O Lord God, thou know that I am innocent of all these things, and why shall I die this day through falsehood, by the hand of these uncircumcised wicked men, whom thou know?

64 And whilst Potiphar's men were beating Joseph, he continued to cry out and weep, and there was a child there eleven months old, and the Lord opened the mouth of the child, and he spoke these words before Potiphar's men, who were smiting Joseph, saying,

65 What do you want of this man, and why do you do this evil unto him? My mother speaks falsely and utter lies; thus was the transaction.

66 And the child told them accurately all that happened, and all the words of Zelicah to Joseph day after day did he declare unto them.

67 And all the men heard the words of the child and they wondered greatly at the child's words, and the child ceased to speak and became still.

68 And Potiphar was very much ashamed at the words of his son, and he commanded his men not to beat Joseph any more, and the men ceased beating Joseph.

69 And Potiphar took Joseph and ordered him to be brought to justice

before the priests, who were judges belonging to the king, in order to judge him concerning this affair.

70 And Potiphar and Joseph came before the priests who were the king's judges, and he said unto them, Decide I pray you, what judgment is due to a servant, for thus has he done.

71 And the priests said unto Joseph, Why didst thou do this thing to thy master? and Joseph answered them, saying, Not so my lords, thus was the matter; and Potiphar said unto Joseph, Surely I entrusted in thy hands all that belonged to me, and I withheld nothing from thee but my wife, and how could thou do this evil?

72 And Joseph answered saying, Not so my lord, as the Lord lives, and as thy soul lives, my lord, the word which thou didst hear from thy wife is untrue, for thus was the affair this day.

73 A year has elapsed to me since I have been in thy house; hast thou seen any iniquity in me, or anything which might cause thee to demand my life?

74 And the priests said unto Potiphar, Send, we pray thee, and let them bring before us Joseph's torn garment, and let us see the tear in it, and if it shall be that the tear is in front of the garment, then his face must have been opposite to her and she must have caught hold of him, to come to her, and with deceit did thy wife do all that she has spoken.

75 And they brought Joseph's garment before the priests who were judges, and they saw and behold the tear was in front of Joseph, and all the judging priests knew that she had pressed him, and they said, The judgment of death is not due to this slave for he has done nothing, but his judgment is, that he be placed in the prison house on account of the report, which through him has gone forth against thy wife.

76 And Potiphar heard their words, and he placed him in the prison house, the place where the king's prisoners are confined, and Joseph was in the house of confinement twelve years.

77 And notwithstanding this, his master's wife did not turn from him, and she did not cease from speaking to him day after day to hearken to her, and at the end of three months Zelicah continued going to Joseph to the house of confinement day by day, and she enticed him to hearken to her, and Zelicah said unto Joseph, How long wilt thou remain in this house? but hearken now to my voice, and I will bring thee out of this house.

C.3 It is very odd how that Potiphar did nothing against his wife even though she was obviously unfaithful to him. We know that she was really continually after Joseph and only God knows how many other young men that she had desired? So why didn't Potiphar do something about his wife and why did he still place Joseph in the prison, knowing that Joseph was innocent? Well I suspect that the Egyptians had a different standard of ethics as to what is considered right and wrong. It would seem that Potiphar was afraid of his wife for one reason or the other. Zelicah was obviously an important woman, and from a very good family and had a lot of influence with many other influential women as noted in the story above. Her influential women friends advised her to keep trying to 'get Joseph into her bed'. This shows that the women didn't think much about committing adultery when it suited their purpose. The fact that they all advised that as they had all seen Joseph and noted that he was indeed a handsome fellow and her friends also desired Joseph.

78 And Joseph answered her, saying, It is better for me to remain in this house than to hearken to thy words, to sin against God; and she said unto him, If thou wilt not perform my wish, I will pluck out thine eyes, add fetters to thy feet, and will deliver thee into the hands of them whom thou didst not know before.

79 And Joseph answered her and said, Behold the God of the whole earth is able to deliver me from all that thou canst do unto me, for he opens the eyes of the blind, and looses those that are bound, and preserves all strangers who are unacquainted with the land.

80 And when Zelicah was unable to persuade Joseph to hearken to her, she left off going to entice him; and Joseph was still confined in the house of confinement. And Jacob the father of Joseph, and all his brethren who were in the land of Canaan still mourned and wept in those days on account of Joseph, for Jacob refused to be comforted for his son Joseph, and Jacob cried aloud, and wept and mourned all those days.

C.4 The fact that Jacob refused to be comforted and kept mourning for his lost son Joseph, shows that he could find no 'closure' in the situation of Joseph's supposed death. I propose that part of Jacob knew that something was wrong with the situation, but he didn't know exactly what. Why? Because God had deliberately withheld this information from Jacob because he a had a much great purpose with Jacob's son Joseph. It was almost as if Jacob sensed that this long-lost son was still alive and that he must do something and get up and go and find him. But he couldn't prove it, so he continued to grieve and mourn for his son. This is clearly the reason that he 'refused to be comforted' for so long a time period as he suspected that something simply just did not add up!

Chapter 45

1 And it was at that time in that year, which is the year of Joseph's going down to Egypt after his brothers had sold him, that Reuben the son of Jacob went to Timnah and took unto him for a wife Eliuram, the daughter of Avi the Canaanite, and he came to her.

2 And Eliuram the wife of Reuben conceived and bare him Hanoch, Palu, Chetzron and Carmi, four sons; and Simeon his brother took his sister Dinah for a wife, and she bare unto him Memuel, Yamin, Ohad, Jachin and Zochar, five sons. Why would Simeon take his own sister as a wife?

Comment:1: It sounds very unlikely that Simeon would marry his sister! and was against the laws given by God to Abraham or at least the Laws of Moses which came later on? I don't know which story is in correct This story account in Jasher or the one in Jubilees? According to the Book of Jubilees it is stated that Dinah died when she heard the news that Joseph had supposedly been killed by a wild animal, when his brothers secretly sold Joseph into slavery. However, I think it very unlikely that Dinah would have died, just because of the rumour that Joseph had died. I think it more likely that the Book of Jubilees, being a very religious book, full of laws of 'do's and 'don'ts' and dire punishments, so much so that if one didn't adhere to the laws, one could be burned at the stake or stoned. I think it therefore very likely that some unpleasant stories were altered in the book of Jubilees. Anything that shed a bad light on Jacob and his sons or other famous biblical characters. In effect hiding their crimes as by the later Mosaic laws, they could have been burned at the stake or stoned.

3 And he afterward came to Bunah the Canaanitish woman, the same is Bunah whom Simeon took captive from the city of Shechem, and Bunah was before Dinah and attended upon her, and Simeon came to her, and she bare unto him Saul.

C.2 The following verse above is an example of disobedience to God's command to Abraham for his descendants not to marry Canaanites. One could be stoned for marrying a Canaanite woman under the Mosaic law. Personally, I would think that the stories in the Book of Jasher are the ones closer to the actual truth, as this book is more like a record of History whilst the book of Jubilees is a deeply religious book where any unsavoury references to the heroes has probably been altered for convenience as is often the case with religions. They tell the people what they want to know and not the unsavoury parts that could reflect badly on the 'heroes of the books'

The Bible itself is an excellent book as by large it doesn't hide the sins of the heroes and even points them out which is a good thing, as long as people get forgiven by God for their sins.

4 And Judah went at that time to Adulam, and he came to a man of Adulam, and his name was Hirah, and Judah saw there the daughter of a man from Canaan, and her name was Aliyath, the daughter of Shua, and he took her, and came to her, and Aliyath bare unto Judah, Er, Onan and Shiloh; three sons.

5 And Levi and Issachar went to the land of the east, and they took unto themselves for wives the daughters of Jobab the son of Yoktan, the son of Eber; and Jobab the son of Yoktan had two daughters; the name of the elder was Adinah, and the name of the younger was Aridah.

6 And Levi took Adinah, and Issachar took Aridah, and they came to the land of Canaan, to their father's house, and Adinah bare unto Levi, Gershon, Kehath and Merari; three sons.

7 And Aridah bare unto Issachar Tola, Puvah, Job and Shomron, four sons; and Dan went to the land of Moab and took for a wife Aphlaleth, the daughter of Chamudan the Moabite, and he brought her to the land of Canaan.

8 And Aphlaleth was barren, she had no offspring, and God afterward remembered Aphlaleth the wife of Dan, and she conceived and bare a son, and she called his name Chushim.

9 And Gad and Naphtali went to Haran and took from thence the daughters of Amuram the son of Uz, the son of Nahor, for wives.

10 And these are the names of the daughters of Amuram; the name of the elder was Merimah, and the name of the younger Uzith; and Naphtali took Merimah, and Gad took Uzith; and brought them to the land of Canaan, to their father's house.

11 And Merimah bare unto Naphtali Yachzeel, Guni, Jazer and Shalem, four sons; and Uzith bare unto Gad Zephion, Chagi, Shuni, Ezbon, Eri, Arodi and Arali, seven sons.

12 And Asher went forth and took Adon the daughter of Aphlal, the son of Hadad, the son of Ishmael, for a wife, and he brought her to the land of Canaan.

13 And Adon the wife of Asher died in those days: she had no offspring; and it was after the death of Adon that Asher went to the other side of the river and took for a wife Hadurah the daughter of Abimael, the son of Eber, the son of Shem.

14 And the young woman was of a comely appearance, and a woman of sense, and she had been the wife of Malkiel the son of Elam, the son of Shem.

15 And Hadurah bare a daughter unto Malkiel, and he called her name Serach, and Malkiel died after this, and Hadurah went and remained in her father's house.

16 And after the death of the wife at Asher he went and took Hadurah for a wife, and brought her to the land of Canaan, and Serach her daughter he also brought with them, and she was three years old, and the damsel was brought up in Jacob's house.

17 And the damsel was of a comely appearance, and she went in the sanctified ways of the children of Jacob; she lacked nothing, and the Lord gave her wisdom and understanding.

18 And Hadurah the wife of Asher conceived and bare unto him Yimnah, Yishvah, Yishvi and Beriah; four sons.

19 And Zebulun went to Midian, and took for a wife Merishah the daughter of Molad, the son of Abida, the son of Midian, and brought her to the land of Canaan.

20 And Merushah bare unto Zebulun Sered, Elon and Yachleel; three sons.

21 And Jacob sent to Aram, the son of Zoba, the son of Terah, and he took for his son Benjamin Mechalia the daughter of Aram, and she came to the land of Canaan to the house of Jacob; and Benjamin was ten years old when he took Mechalia the daughter of Aram for a wife.

22 And Mechalia conceived and bare unto Benjamin Bela, Becher, Ashbel, Gera and Naaman, five sons; and Benjamin went afterward and took for a wife Aribath, the daughter of Shomron, the son of Abraham, in addition to his first wife, and he was eighteen years old; and Aribath bare unto Benjamin Achi, Vosh, Mupim, Chupim, and Ord; five sons.

23 And in those days Judah went to the house of Shem and took Tamar the daughter of Elam, the son of Shem, for a wife for his first born Er.

24 And Er came to his wife Tamar, and she became his wife, and when he came to her he outwardly destroyed his seed, and his work was evil in the sight of the Lord, and the Lord slew him.

25 And it was after the death of Er, Judah's first born, that Judah said unto Onan, go to thy brother's wife and marry her as the next of kin, and raise up seed to thy brother.

26 And Onan took Tamar for a wife and he came to her, and Onan also did like unto the work of his brother, and his work was evil in the sight of the Lord, and he slew him also.

27 And when Onan died, Judah said unto Tamar, Remain in thy father's house until my son Shiloh shall have grown up, and Judah did no more delight in Tamar, to give her unto Shiloh, for he said, Peradventure he will also die like his brothers.

28 And Tamar rose up and went and remained in her father's house, and Tamar was in her father's house for some time.

29 And at the revolution of the year, Aliyath the wife of Judah died; and Judah was comforted for his wife, and after the death of Aliyath, Judah went up with his friend Hirah to Timnah to shear their sheep.

30 And Tamar heard that Judah had gone up to Timnah to shear the sheep, and that Shiloh was grown up, and Judah did not delight in her.

31 And Tamar rose up and put off the garments of her widowhood, and she put a vail upon her, and she entirely covered herself, and she went and sat in the public thoroughfare, which is upon the road to Timnah.

32 And Judah passed and saw her and took her and he came to her, and she conceived by him, and at the time of being delivered, behold, there were twins in her womb, and he called the name of the first Perez, and the name of the second Zarah.

C.3 In this Book of Jasher, Judah ends up marrying his 'daughter in law' after the death of both his own wife and the death of his son who was Tamar's husband. Again, this would have been against the law and we read in the Book of Jubilees, that Judah had a great repentance for having lain with Tamar, but the Book of Jubilees does not state that Judah ended up marrying Tamar and having many children with her. In the Book of Jubilees that story has been altered as it refects badly on Judah according to the Mosaic law.

C.4 Because of the obvious disobediences by the sons of Jacob of 1) Simeon marrying his sister Dinah. 2) Several of the other sons of Jacob marrying Canaanite women 3) Judah marrying his daughter in law. This would explain why God had to give very lengthly and detailed laws to Moses some few hundred years later so that the Children of Israel could remember what was right and what was wrong and get it down pat! All the above sins were punishable by death according the Mosaic laws.

C.5 I like this Book of Jasher very much, as it doesn't try to hide things, but reveals the full truth and just states what happened both good and bad, no matter how incredible some of the stories may sound like. The writer of the Book of Jasher knew that he was dealing with a world, where supernatural things occurred, and he wasn't ashamed to write about it in full. He simply did not try to hide away the unexplainable or the inconvenient truths, but simply told it like it was as if he was a reporter just doing his job.

Chapter 46

1 In those days Joseph was still confined in the prison house in the land of Egypt.

2 At that time the attendants of Pharaoh were standing before him, the chief of the butlers and the chief of the bakers which belonged to the king of Egypt.

C.1 Here we see the exact same story as is related in Genesis 40

3 And the butler took wine and placed it before the king to drink, and the baker placed bread before the king to eat, and the king drank of the wine and ate of the bread, he and his servants and ministers that ate at the king's table.

4 And whilst they were eating and drinking, the butler and the baker remained there, and Pharaoh's ministers found many flies in the wine, which the butler had brought, and stones of nitre were found in the baker's bread.

5 And the captain of the guard placed Joseph as an attendant on Pharaoh's officers, and Pharaoh's officers were in confinement one year.

6 And at the end of the year, they both dreamed dreams in one night, in the place of confinement where they were, and in the morning Joseph came to them to attend upon them as usual, and he saw them, and behold their countenances were dejected and sad.

7 And Joseph asked them, Why are your countenances sad and dejected this day? and they said unto him, We dreamed a dream, and there is no one to interpret it; and Joseph said unto them, Relate, I pray you, your dream unto me, and God shall give you an answer of peace as you desire.

8 And the butler related his dream unto Joseph, and he said, I saw in my dream, and behold a large vine was before me, and upon that vine I saw three branches, and the vine speedily blossomed and reached a great height, and its clusters were ripened and became grapes.

9 And I took the grapes and pressed them in a cup and placed it in Pharaoh's hand and he drank; and Joseph said unto him, The three branches that were upon the vine are three days.

10 Yet within three days, the king will order thee to be brought out and he will restore thee to thy office, and thou shalt give the king his wine to drink as at first when thou wast his butler; but let me find favour in thy sight, that thou shalt remember me to Pharaoh when it will be well with thee, and do kindness unto me, and get me brought forth from this prison, for I was stolen away from the land of Canaan and was sold for a slave in this place.

11 And also that which was told thee concerning my master's wife is false, for they placed me in this dungeon for naught; and the butler answered Joseph, saying, If the king deal well with me as at first, as thou last interpreted to me, I will do all that thou desires, and get thee brought out of this dungeon.

12 And the baker, seeing that Joseph had accurately interpreted the butler's dream, also approached, and related the whole of his dream to Joseph.

13 And he said unto him, In my dream I saw and behold three white baskets upon my head, and I looked, and behold there were in the upper-most basket all manner of baked meats for Pharaoh, and behold the birds were eating them from off my head.

14 And Joseph said unto him, The three baskets which thou didst see are three days, yet within three days Pharaoh will take off thy head, and hang thee upon a tree, and the birds will eat thy flesh from off thee, as thou saw in thy dream.

15 In those days the queen was about to be delivered, and upon that day she bare a son unto the king of Egypt, and they proclaimed that the king had gotten his first born son and all the people of Egypt together with the officers and servants of Pharaoh rejoiced greatly.

16 And upon the third day of his birth Pharaoh made a feast for his officers and servants, for the hosts of the land of Zoar and of the land of Egypt.

17 And all the people of Egypt and the servants of Pharaoh came to eat and drink with the king at the feast of his son, and to rejoice at the king's rejoicing.

18 And all the officers of the king and his servants were rejoicing at that time for eight days at the feast, and they made merry with all sorts of musical instruments, with timbrels and with dances in the king's house for eight days.

19 And the butler, to whom Joseph had interpreted his dream, forgot Joseph, and he did not mention him to the king as he had promised, for this thing was from the Lord in order to punish Joseph because he had trusted in man.

20 And Joseph remained after this in the prison house two years, until he had completed twelve years.

Chapter 47

1 And Isaac the son of Abraham was still living in those days in the land of Canaan; he was very aged, one hundred and eighty years old, and Esau his son, the brother of Jacob, was in the land of Edom, and he and his sons had possessions in it amongst the children of Seir.

2 And Esau heard that his father's time was drawing nigh to die, and he and his sons and household came unto the land of Canaan, unto his father's house, and Jacob and his sons went forth from the place where they dwelt in Hebron, and they all came to their father Isaac, and they found Esau and his sons in the tent.

3 And Jacob and his sons sat before his father Isaac, and Jacob was still mourning for his son Joseph.

4 And Isaac said unto Jacob, Bring me hither thy sons and I will bless them; and Jacob brought his eleven children before his father Isaac.

5 And Isaac placed his hands upon all the sons of Jacob, and he took hold of them and embraced them, and kissed them one by one, and Isaac blessed them on that day, and he said unto them, May the God of your fathers bless you and increase your seed like the stars of heaven for number.

6 And Isaac also blessed the sons of Esau, saying, May God cause you to be a dread and a terror to all that will behold you, and to all your enemies.

7 And Isaac called Jacob and his sons, and they all came and sat before Isaac, and Isaac said unto Jacob, The Lord God of the whole earth said unto me, Unto thy seed will I give this land for an inheritance if thy children keep my statutes and my ways, and I will perform unto them the oath which I swore unto thy father Abraham.

8 Now therefore my son, teach thy children and thy children's children to fear the Lord, and to go in the good way which will please the Lord thy God, for if you keep the ways of the Lord and his statutes the Lord

will also keep unto you his covenant with Abraham, and will do well with you and your seed all the days.

9 And when Isaac had finished commanding Jacob and his children, he gave up the ghost and died, and was gathered unto his people.

10 And Jacob and Esau fell upon the face of their father Isaac, and they wept, and Isaac was one hundred and eighty years old when he died in the land of Canaan, in Hebron, and his sons carried him to the cave of Machpelah, which Abraham had bought from the children of Heth for a possession of a burial place.

11 And all the kings of the land of Canaan went with Jacob and Esau to bury Isaac, and all the kings of Canaan showed Isaac great honor at his death.

12 And the sons of Jacob and the sons of Esau went barefooted round about, walking and lamenting until they reached Kireath-arba.

13 And Jacob and Esau buried their father Isaac in the cave of Machpelah, which is in Kireath-arba in Hebron, and they buried him with very great honor, as at the funeral of kings.

14 And Jacob and his sons, and Esau and his sons, and all the kings of Canaan made a great and heavy mourning, and they buried him and mourned for him many days.

15 And at the death of Isaac, he left his cattle and his possessions and all belonging to him to his sons; and Esau said unto Jacob, Behold I pray thee, all that our father has left we will divide it in two parts, and I will have the choice, and Jacob said, We will do so.

16 And Jacob took all that Isaac had left in the land of Canaan, the cattle and the property, and he placed them in two parts before Esau and his sons, and he said unto Esau, Behold all this is before thee, choose thou unto thyself the half which thou wilt take.

17 And Jacob said unto Esau, Hear thou I pray thee what I will speak

unto thee, saying, The Lord God of heaven and earth spoke unto our fathers Abraham and Isaac, saying, Unto thy seed will I give this land for an inheritance forever.

18 Now therefore all that our father has left is before thee and behold all the land is before thee; choose thou from them what thou desires.

19 If thou desire the whole land take it for thee and thy children forever, and I will take this riches, and it thou desires the riches take it unto thee, and I will take this land for me and for my children to inherit it forever.

20 And Nebayoth, the son of Ishmael, was then in the land with his children, and Esau went on that day and consulted with him, saying.

21 Thus has Jacob spoken unto me, and thus has he answered me, now give thy advice and we will hear.

22 And Nebayoth said, What is this that Jacob hath spoken unto thee? behold all the children of Canaan are dwelling securely in their land, and Jacob sayeth he will inherit it with his seed all the days.

C.1 Nebayoth is giving Esau the wrong counsel in saying that *'all the children of Canaan are dwelling securely in their land.* Well, they might have been secure in Nebayoth's time, but later in time when Moses & the children of Israel came out of Egypt, the Israelites practically eradicated the Canaanites from the land:

JASHER 91.13 And all the elders also fought the battles of Israel against the Canaanites and the Lord drove the Canaanites from before the children of Israel, in order to place the Israelites in their land.

23 Go now therefore and take all thy father's riches and leave Jacob thy brother in the land, as he has spoken.

24 And Esau rose up and returned to Jacob, and did all that Nebayoth the son of Ishmael had advised; and Esau took all the riches that Isaac had left, the souls, the beasts, the cattle and the property, and all the riches; he gave nothing to his brother Jacob; and Jacob took all the land of Canaan, from the brook of Egypt unto the river Euphrates, and he took it for an everlasting possession, and for his children and for his seed after him forever.

25 Jacob also took from his brother Esau the cave of Machpelah, which is in Hebron, which Abraham had bought from Ephron for a possession of a burial place for him and his seed forever.

26 And Jacob wrote all these things in the book of purchase, and he signed it, and he testified all this with four faithful witnesses.

27 And these are the words which Jacob wrote in the book, saying: The land of Canaan and all the cities of the Hittites, the Hivites, the Jebusites, the Amorites, the Perizzites, and the Gergashites, all the seven nations from the river of Egypt unto the river Euphrates.

28 And the city of Hebron Kireath-arba, and the cave which is in it, the whole did Jacob buy from his brother Esau for value, for a possession and for an inheritance for his seed after him forever.

29 And Jacob took the book of purchase and the signature, the command and the statutes and the revealed book, and he placed them in an earthen vessel in order that they should remain for a long time, and he delivered them into the hands of his children.

30 Esau took all that his father had left him after his death from his brother Jacob, and he took all the property, from man and beast, camel and ass, ox and lamb, silver and gold, stones and bdellium, and all the riches which had belonged to Isaac the son of Abraham; there was nothing left which Esau did not take unto himself, from all that Isaac had left after his death.

31 And Esau took all this, and he and his children went home to the land of Seir the Horite, away from his brother Jacob and his children.

32 And Esau had possessions amongst the children of Seir, and Esau returned not to the land of Canaan from that day forward.

33 And the whole land of Canaan became an inheritance to the children of Israel for an everlasting inheritance, and Esau with all his children inherited the mountain of Seir.

Chapter 48

1 In those days, after the death of Isaac, the Lord commanded and caused a famine upon the whole earth.

2 At that time Pharaoh king of Egypt was sitting upon his throne in the land of Egypt, and lay in his bed and dreamed dreams, and Pharaoh saw in his dream that he was standing by the side of the river of Egypt.

Comment:1: This story about Pharaoh and his dreams is also recorded in the Bible in a very similar way in Genesis

GEN.41:1 And it came to pass at the end of two full years, that Pharaoh dreamed: and, behold, he stood by the river.

3 And whilst he was standing, he saw and behold seven fat fleshed and well favoured kine came up out of the river.

4 And seven other kine, lean fleshed and ill favoured, came up after them, and the seven ill-favoured ones swallowed up the well-favoured ones, and still their appearance was ill as at first.

5 And he awoke, and he slept again and he dreamed a second time, and he saw and behold seven ears of corn came up upon one stalk, rank and good, and seven thin ears blasted with the east wind sprang, up after them, and the thin ears swallowed up the full ones, and Pharaoh awoke out of his dream.

6 And in the morning the king remembered his dreams, and his spirit was sadly troubled on account of his dreams, and the king hastened and sent and called for all the magicians of Egypt, and the wise men, and they came and stood before Pharaoh.

7 And the king said unto them, I have dreamed dreams, and there is none to interpret them; and they said unto the king, relate thy dreams to thy servants and let us hear them.

8 And the king related his dreams to them, and they all answered and said with one voice to the king, may the king live forever; and this is the interpretation of thy dreams.

9 The seven good kine which thou didst see denote seven daughters that will be born unto thee in the latter days, and the seven kine which thou saw come up after them, and swallowed them up, are for a sign that the daughters which will be born unto thee will all die in the life-time of the king.

10 And that which thou didst see in the second dream of seven full good ears of corn coming up upon one stalk, this is their interpretation, that thou wilt build unto thyself in the latter days seven cities throughout the land of Egypt; and that which thou saw of the seven blasted ears of corn springing up after them and swallowing them up whilst thou didst behold them with thine eyes, is for a sign that the cities which thou wilt build will all be destroyed in the latter days, in the life-time of the king.

11 And when they spoke these words the king did not incline his ear to their words, neither did he fix his heart upon them, for the king knew in his wisdom that they did not give a proper interpretation of the dreams; and when they had finished speaking before the king, the king answered them, saying, What is this thing that you have spoken unto me? surely you have uttered falsehood and spoken lies; therefore now give the proper interpretation of my dreams, that you may not die.

12 And the king commanded after this, and he sent and called again for other wise men, and they came and stood before the king, and the king related his dreams to them, and they all answered him according to the first interpretation, and the king's anger was kindled and he was very wroth, and the king said unto them, Surely you speak lies and utter falsehood in what you have said.

13 And the king commanded that a proclamation should be issued throughout the land of Egypt, saying, It is resolved by the king and his great men, that any wise man who knows and understands the interpretation of dreams, and will not come this day before the king, shall die.

14 And the man that will declare unto the king the proper interpretation of his dreams, there shall be given unto him all that he will require from the king. And all the wise men of the land of Egypt came before the king, together with all the magicians and sorcerers that were in

Egypt and in Goshen, in Rameses, in Tachpanches, in Zoar, and in all the places on the borders of Egypt, and they all stood before the king.

15 And all the nobles and the princes, and the attendants belonging to the king, came together from all the cities of Egypt, and they all sat before the king, and the king related his dreams before the wise men, and the princes, and all that sat before the king were astonished at the vision.

16 And all the wise men who were before the king were greatly divided in their interpretation of his dreams; some of them interpreted them to the king, saying, The seven good kine are seven kings, who from the king's issue will be raised over Egypt.

17 And the seven bad kine are seven princes, who will stand up against them in the latter days and destroy them; and the seven ears of corn are the seven great princes belonging to Egypt, who will fall in the hands of the seven less powerful princes of their enemies, in the wars of our lord the king.

18 And some of them interpreted to the king in this manner, saying, The seven good kine are the strong cities of Egypt, and the seven bad kine are the seven nations of the land of Canaan, who will come against the seven cities of Egypt in the latter days and destroy them.

19 And that which thou saw in the second dream, of seven good and bad ears of corn, is a sign that the government of Egypt will again return to thy seed as at first.

20 And in his reign the people of the cities of Egypt will turn against the seven cities of Canaan who are stronger than they are, and will destroy them, and the government of Egypt will return to thy seed.

21 And some of them said unto the king, This is the interpretation of thy dreams; the seven good kine are seven queens, whom thou wilt take for wives in the latter days, and the seven bad kine denote that those women will all die in the lifetime of the king.

22 And the seven good and bad ears of corn which thou didst see in the second dream are fourteen children, and it will be in the latter days that they will stand up and fight amongst themselves, and seven of them will smite the seven that are more powerful.

23 And some of them said these words unto the king, saying, The seven good kine denote that seven children will be born to thee, and they will slay seven of thy children's children in the latter days; and the seven good ears of corn which thou didst see in the second dream, are those princes against whom seven other less powerful princes will fight and destroy them in the latter days, and avenge thy children's cause, and the government will again return to thy seed.

24 And the king heard all the words of the wise men of Egypt and their interpretation of his dreams, and none of them pleased the king.

25 And the king knew in his wisdom that they did not altogether speak correctly in all these words, for this was from the Lord to frustrate the words of the wise men of Egypt, in order that Joseph might go forth from the house of confinement, and in order that he should become great in Egypt.

26 And the king saw that none amongst all the wise men and magicians of Egypt spoke correctly to him, and the king's wrath was kindled, and his anger burned within him.

27 And the king commanded that all the wise men and magicians should go out from before him, and they all went out from before the king with shame and disgrace.

28 And the king commanded that a proclamation be sent throughout Egypt to slay all the magicians that were in Egypt, and not one of them should be suffered to live.

29 And the captains of the guards belonging to the king rose up, and each man drew his sword, and they began to smite the magicians of Egypt, and the wise men.

30 And after this Merod, chief butler to the king, came and bowed down before the king and sat before him.

31 And the butler said unto the king, May the king live forever, and his government be exalted in the land.

32 Thou wast angry with thy servant in those days, now two years past, and didst place me in the ward, and I was for some time in the ward, I and the chief of the bakers.

33 And there was with us a Hebrew servant belonging to the captain of the guard, his name was Joseph, for his master had been angry with him and placed him in the house of confinement, and he attended us there.

34 And in some time after when we were in the ward, we dreamed dreams in one night, I and the chief of the bakers; we dreamed, each man according to the interpretation of his dream.

35 And we came in the morning and told them to that servant, and he interpreted to us our dreams, to each man according to his dream, did he correctly interpret.

36 And it came to pass as he interpreted to us, so was the event; there fell not to the ground any of his words.

37 And now therefore my lord and king do not slay the people of Egypt for naught; behold that slave is still confined in the house by the captain of the guard his master, in the house of confinement.

38 If it pleaseth the king let him send for him that he may come before thee and he will make known to thee, the correct interpretation of the dream which thou didst dream.

39 And the king heard the words of the chief butler, and the king ordered that the wise men of Egypt should not be slain.

40 And the king ordered his servants to bring Joseph before him, and the king said unto them, Go to him and do not terrify him lest he be confused and will not know to speak properly.

41 And the servants of the king went to Joseph, and they brought him hastily out of the dungeon, and the king's servants shaved him, and he changed his prison garment and he came before the king.

42 And the king was sitting upon his royal throne in a princely dress girt around with a golden ephod, and the fine gold which was upon it sparkled, and the carbuncle and the ruby and the emerald, together with all the precious stones that were upon the king's head, dazzled the eye, and Joseph wondered greatly at the king.

43 And the throne upon which the king sat was covered with gold and silver, and with onyx stones, and it had seventy steps.

44 And it was their custom throughout the land of Egypt, that every man who came to speak to the king, if he was a prince or one that was estimable in the sight of the king, he ascended to the king's throne as far as the thirty-first step, and the king would descend to the thirty-sixth step, and speak with him.

45 If he was one of the common people, he ascended to the third step, and the king would descend to the fourth and speak to him, and their custom was, moreover, that any man who understood to speak in all the seventy languages, he ascended the seventy steps, and went up and spoke till he reached the king.

46 And any man who could not complete the seventy, he ascended as many steps as the languages which he knew to speak in.

47 And it was customary in those days in Egypt that no one should reign over them, but who understood to speak in the seventy languages.

C.2 I admit that I have always thought this particular story to be very unlikely. How could anyone know 70 languages?

48 And when Joseph came before the king he bowed down to the ground before the king, and he ascended to the third step, and the king sat upon the fourth step and spoke with Joseph.

49 And the king said unto Joseph, I dreamed a dream, and there is no interpreter to interpret it properly, and I commanded this day that all

the magicians of Egypt and the wise men thereof, should come before me, and I related my dreams to them, and no one has properly interpreted them to me.

50 And after this I this day heard concerning thee, that thou art a wise man, and canst correctly interpret every dream that thou hearest.

51 And Joseph answered Pharaoh, saying, Let Pharaoh relate his dreams that he dreamed; surely the interpretations belong to God; and Pharaoh related his dreams to Joseph, the dream of the kine, and the dream of the ears of corn, and the king left off speaking.

52 And Joseph was then clothed with the spirit of God before the king, and he knew all the things that would befall the king from that day forward, and he knew the proper interpretation of the king's dream, and he spoke before the king.

53 And Joseph found favour in the sight of the king, and the king inclined his ears and his heart, and he heard all the words of Joseph. And Joseph said unto the king, Do not imagine that they are two dreams, for it is only one dream, for that which God has chosen to do throughout the land he has shown to the king in his dream, and this is the proper interpretation of thy dream:

54 The seven good kine and ears of corn are seven years, and the seven bad kine and ears of corn are also seven years; it is one dream.

55 Behold the seven years that are coming there will be a great plenty throughout the land, and after that the seven years of famine will follow them, a very grievous famine; and all the plenty will be forgotten from the land, and the famine will consume the inhabitants of the land.

56 The king dreamed one dream, and the dream was therefore repeated unto Pharaoh because the thing is established by God, and God will shortly bring it to pass.

57 Now therefore I will give thee counsel and deliver thy soul and the souls of the inhabitants of the land from the evil of the famine, that thou seek throughout thy kingdom for a man very discreet and wise,

who knows all the affairs of government, and appoint him to superintend over the land of Egypt.

58 And let the man whom thou place over Egypt appoint officers under him, that they gather in all the food of the good years that are coming and let them lay-up corn and deposit it in thy appointed stores.

59 And let them keep that food for the seven years of famine, that it may be found for thee and thy people and thy whole land, and that thou and thy land be not cut off by the famine.

60 Let all the inhabitants of the land be also ordered that they gather in, every man the produce of his field, of all sorts of food, during the seven good years, and that they place it in their stores, that it may be found for them in the days of the famine and that they may live upon it.

61 This is the proper interpretation of thy dream, and this is the counsel given to save thy soul and the souls of all thy subjects.

62 And the king answered and said unto Joseph, Who sayeth and who knows that thy words are correct? And he said unto the king, This shall be a sign for thee respecting all my words, that they are true and that my advice is good for thee.

C.3 Here is a story not mentioned anywhere else:

63 Behold thy wife sits this day upon the stool of delivery, and she will bear thee a son and thou wilt rejoice with him; when thy child shall have gone forth from his mother's womb, thy first born son that has been born these two years back shall die, and thou wilt be comforted in the child that will be born unto thee this day.

64 And Joseph finished speaking these words to the king, and he bowed down to the king and he went out, and when Joseph had gone out from the king's presence, those signs which Joseph had spoken unto the king came to pass on that day.

65 And the queen bare a son on that day and the king heard the glad tidings about his son, and he rejoiced, and when the reporter had gone

forth from the king's presence, the king's servants found the first born son of the king fallen dead upon the ground.

66 And there was great lamentation and noise in the king's house, and the king heard it, and he said, What is the noise and lamentation that I have heard in the house? and they told the king that his first born son had died; then the king knew that all Joseph's words that he had spoken were correct, and the king was consoled for his son by the child that was born to him on that day as Joseph had spoken.

Chapter 49

1 After these things the king sent and assembled all his officers and servants, and all the princes and nobles belonging to the king, and they all came before the king.

2 And the king said unto them, Behold you have seen and heard all the words of this Hebrew man, and all the signs which he declared would come to pass, and not any of his words have fallen to the ground.

3 You know that he has given a proper interpretation of the dream, and it will surely come to pass, now therefore take counsel, and know what you will do and how the land will be delivered from the famine.

4 Seek now and see whether the like can be found, in whose heart there is wisdom and knowledge, and I will appoint him over the land.

5 For you have heard what the Hebrew man has advised concerning this to save the land therewith from the famine, and I know that the land will not be delivered from the famine but with the advice of the Hebrew man, him that advised me.

6 And they all answered the king and said, The counsel which the Hebrew has given concerning this is good; now therefore, our lord and king, behold the whole land is in thy hand, do that which seems good in thy sight.

7 Him whom thou chooses, and whom thou in thy wisdom know to be wise and capable of delivering the land with his wisdom, him shall the king appoint to be under him over the land.

8 And the king said to all the officers: I have thought that since God has made known to the Hebrew man all that he has spoken, there is none so discreet and wise in the whole land as he is; if it seem good in your sight I will place him over the land, for he will save the land with his wisdom.

9 And all the officers answered the king and said, But surely it is written in the laws of Egypt, and it should not be violated, that no man shall

reign over Egypt, nor be the second to the king, but one who has knowledge in all the languages of the sons of men.

10 Now therefore our lord and king, behold this Hebrew man can only speak the Hebrew language, and how then can he be over us the second under government, a man who not even know our language?

11 Now we pray thee send for him, and let him come before thee, and prove him in all things, and do as thou see fit.

12 And the king said, It shall be done tomorrow, and the thing that you have spoken is good; and all the officers came on that day before the king.

13 And on that night the Lord sent one of his ministering angels, and he came into the land of Egypt unto Joseph, and the angel of the Lord stood over Joseph, and behold Joseph was lying in the bed at night in his master's house in the dungeon, for his master had put him back into the dungeon on account of his wife.

14 And the angel roused him from his sleep, and Joseph rose up and stood upon his legs, and behold the angel of the Lord was standing opposite to him; and the angel of the Lord spoke with Joseph, and he taught him all the languages of man in that night, and he called his name Jehoseph.

Comment:1: I suppose that it is possible for the angel of God to have taught Joseph 70 languages in one night in order to fulfil God's supernatural purpose with Joseph, so that Israel and all the sons of Jacob would end up living In Egypt in the fair land of Goshen?

15 And the angel of the Lord went from him, and Joseph returned and lay upon his bed, and Joseph was astonished at the vision which he saw.

16 And it came to pass in the morning that the king sent for all his officers and servants, and they all came and sat before the king, and the king ordered Joseph to be brought, and the king's servants went and brought Joseph before Pharaoh.

17 And the king came forth and ascended the steps of the throne, and

Joseph spoke unto the king in all languages, and Joseph went up to him and spoke unto the king until he arrived before the king in the seventieth step, and he sat before the king.

18 And the king greatly rejoiced on account of Joseph, and all the king's officers rejoiced greatly with the king when they heard all the words of Joseph.

19 And the thing seemed good in the sight of the king and the officers, to appoint Joseph to be second to the king over the whole land of Egypt, and the king spoke to Joseph, saying,

20 Now thou didst give me counsel to appoint a wise man over the land of Egypt, in order with his wisdom to save the land from the famine; now therefore, since God has made all this known to thee, and all the words which thou hast spoken, there is not throughout the land a discreet and wise man like unto thee.

21 And thy name no more shall be called Joseph, but Zaphnath Paaneah shall be thy name; thou shalt be second to me, and according to thy word shall be all the affairs of my government, and at thy word shall my people go out and come in.

22 Also from under thy hand shall my servants and officers receive their salary which is given to them monthly, and to thee shall all the people of the land bow down; only in my throne will I be greater than thou.

23 And the king took off his ring from his hand and put it upon the hand of Joseph, and the king dressed Joseph in a princely garment, and he put a golden crown upon his head, and he put a golden chain upon his neck.

24 And the king commanded his servants, and they made him ride in the second chariot belonging to the king, that went opposite to the king's chariot, and he caused him to ride upon a great and strong horse from the king's horses, and to be conducted through the streets of the land of Egypt.

25 And the king commanded that all those that played upon timbrels, harps and other musical instruments should go forth with Joseph; one thousand timbrels, one thousand mecholoth, and one thousand nebalim went after him.

26 And five thousand men, with drawn swords glittering in their hands, and they went marching and playing before Joseph, and twenty thousand of the great men of the king girt with girdles of skin covered with gold, marched at the right hand of Joseph, and twenty thousand at his left, and all the women and damsels went upon the roofs or stood in the streets playing and rejoicing at Joseph, and gazed at the appearance of Joseph and at his beauty.

27 And the king's people went before him and behind him, perfuming the road with frankincense and with cassia, and with all sorts of fine perfume, and scattered myrrh and aloes along the road, and twenty men proclaimed these words before him throughout the land in a loud voice:

28 Do you see this man whom the king has chosen to be his second? all the affairs of government shall be regulated by him, and he that transgresses his orders, or that does not bow down before him to the ground, shall die, for he rebels against the king and his second.

29 And when the heralds had ceased proclaiming, all the people of Egypt bowed down to the ground before Joseph and said, May the king live, also may his second live; and all the inhabitants of Egypt bowed down along the road, and when the heralds approached them, they bowed down, and they rejoiced with all sorts of timbrels, mechol and nebal before Joseph.

30 And Joseph upon his horse lifted up his eyes to heaven, and called out and said, He raiseth the poor man from the dust, He lifteth up the needy from the dunghill. O Lord of Hosts, happy is the man who trusteth in thee.

31 And Joseph passed throughout the land of Egypt with Pharaoh's servants and officers, and they showed him the whole land of Egypt and all the king's treasures.

32 And Joseph returned and came on that day before Pharaoh, and the king gave unto Joseph a possession in the land of Egypt, a possession of fields and vineyards, and the king gave unto Joseph three thousand talents of silver and one thousand talents of gold, and onyx stones and bdellium and many gifts.

33 And on the next day the king commanded all the people of Egypt to bring unto Joseph offerings and gifts, and that he that violated the command of the king should die; and they made a high place in the street of the city, and they spread out garments there, and whoever brought anything to Joseph put it into the high place.

34 And all the people of Egypt cast something into the high place, one man a golden ear-ring, and the other rings and ear-rings, and different vessels of gold and silver work, and onyx stones and bdellium did he cast upon the high place; every one gave something of what he possessed.

35 And Joseph took all these and placed them in his treasuries, and all the officers and nobles belonging to the king exalted Joseph, and they gave him many gifts, seeing that the king had chosen him to be his second.

36 And the king sent to Potiphera, the son of Ahiram priest of On, and he took his young daughter Osnath and gave her unto Joseph for a wife.

37 And the damsel was very comely, a virgin, one whom man had not known, and Joseph took her for a wife; and the king said unto Joseph, I am Pharaoh, and beside thee none shall dare to lift up his hand or his foot to regulate my people throughout the land of Egypt.

38 And Joseph was thirty years old when he stood before Pharaoh, and Joseph went out from before the king, and he became the king's second in Egypt.

39 And the king gave Joseph a hundred servants to attend him in his house, and Joseph also sent and purchased many servants and they remained in the house of Joseph.

40 Joseph then built for himself a very magnificent house like unto the houses of kings, before the court of the king's palace, and he made in the house a large temple, very elegant in appearance and convenient for his residence; three years was Joseph in erecting his house.

41 And Joseph made unto himself a very elegant throne of abundance of gold and silver, and he covered it with onyx stones and bdellium, and he made upon it the likeness of the whole land of Egypt, and the likeness of the river of Egypt that watereth the whole land of Egypt; and Joseph sat securely upon his throne in his house and the Lord increased Joseph's wisdom.

42 And all the inhabitants of Egypt and Pharaoh's servants and his princes loved Joseph exceedingly, for this thing was from the Lord to Joseph.

43 And Joseph had an army that made war, going out in hosts and troops to the number of forty thousand six hundred men, capable of bearing arms to assist the king and Joseph against the enemy, besides the king's officers and his servants and inhabitants of Egypt without number.

C.2 JOSEPH – THE SUPER-WARRIOR KING. Here we see Joseph with an army of 46,000 men fighting the wars on behalf of Pharaoh. All the sons of Jacob would have been in that army, and woe betide any country that tried to fight against Pharaoh in those days.

C.3 This whole book is about incessant wars in the Middle East in ancient times. First of all, in the times of Abraham and then then the times of his grandson Jacob, and then incessantly in the times of Jacob's sons.

C.4 There were wars made by Chittim (Cyprus), Lebanon, the lands of the Canaanites and the Amorites. Wars made by Tarshish, Africa and by Egypt and all the nations in between. In other words, a very sizeable area indeed was constantly at war for one reason or the other.

C.5 Some nations were just waiting for an excuse to go to war- even a flimsy excuse. The story of Troy, which used to be known as a mere fictitious story which came much later in time, and happened near Greece, could have indeed been true. Men *will fight* for a beautiful woman!

C.6 Two nations went to war as to who should marry the daughter of the King of Chittim – Angeas of Africa and Turnus from the land of the Canaanites. Other times the wars were to enslave other nations and to put them under tribute.

C.7 There were also the relatives of Jacob, such as the descendants of his brother Esau. His son Eliphaz and much more importantly his grandson Zepho who ended up becoming a very powerful general of armies and also the king of Chittim for 40 years.

C.8 Jacob's relatives such as both the descendants of Esau, and the descendants of Ishmael, Abraham's son by Sarah's bond-woman Hagar, were always trying to fight against Jacob and his sons wherever they were and even when they were living down in Egypt in captivity.

C.9 Nations would align with their relatives one minute and go to war against them on another occasion. A very barbaric existence back then.

C.10 No wonder God Himself 'fought for Israel', otherwise they never would have survived and budded and grew as a nation being originally so small in number at the time of Jacob. God used Egypt to be the 'cocoon' for the 'budding new nation of Israel'. and He used Pharaoh to both protect and provide for the sons of Jacob until they had grown into a nation. Then it was time for the Exodus under Moses.

C.11 You will find in reading the rest of the chapters of this book, that many try to fight against the sons of Jacob for one reason or another, and even come against them with massive and seemingly invincible armies, and yet none of the many nations were able to defeat Israel, because God fought on their side as long as they obeyed him. Occasionally someone would disobey in the army of Israel, and they would be typically punished by losing the next battle in war.

C.12 God would use Israel time and time again 'As a Sword in the hands of the Living God' 'YAHWEY' This you see even more in the latter chapters of this interesting book in the times of Moses & Joshua.

JOS.10:14 And there was no day like that before it or after it, that the LORD hearkened unto the voice of a man: for the LORD fought for Israel.

C.13 The meaning of YAHWEY or the name for God told to Moses whom we will read about in later chapters which means *'I am that I am'*, which has many meanings: https://www.desiringgod.org/articles/10-things-yahweh-means

---

44 And Joseph gave unto his mighty men, and to all his host, shields and javelins, and caps and coats of mail and stones for slinging.

Chapter 50

1 At that time the children of Tarshish came against the sons of Ishmael, and made war with them, and the children of Tarshish spoiled the Ishmaelites for a long time.

2 And the children of Ishmael were small in number in those days, and they could not prevail over the children of Tarshish, and they were sorely oppressed.

3 And the old men of the Ishmaelites sent a record to the king of Egypt, saying, Send I pray thee unto thy servants officers and hosts to help us to fight against the children of Tarshish, for we have been consuming away for a long time.

4 And Pharaoh sent Joseph with the mighty men and host which were with him, and also his mighty men from the king's house.

5 And they went to the land of Havilah to the children of Ishmael, to assist them against the children of Tarshish, and the children of Ishmael fought with the children of Tarshish, and Joseph smote the Tarshishites and he subdued all their land, and the children of Ishmael dwell therein unto this day.

6 And when the land of Tarshish was subdued, all the Tarshishites ran away, and came on the border of their brethren the children of Javan, and Joseph with all his mighty men and host returned to Egypt, not one man of them missing.

7 And at the revolution of the year, in the second year of Joseph's reigning over Egypt, the Lord gave great plenty throughout the land for seven years as Joseph had spoken, for the Lord blessed all the produce of the earth in those days for seven years, and they ate and were greatly satisfied.

8 And Joseph at that time had officers under him, and they collected all the food of the good years, and heaped corn year by year, and they placed it in the treasuries of Joseph.

9 And at any time when they gathered the food Joseph commanded that they should bring the corn in the ears, and also bring with it some of the soil of the field, that it should not spoil.

10 And Joseph did according to this year by year, and he heaped up corn like the sand of the sea for abundance, for his stores were immense and could not be numbered for abundance.

11 And also all the inhabitants of Egypt gathered all sorts of food in their stores in great abundance during the seven good years, but they did not do unto it as Joseph did.

12 And all the food which Joseph and the Egyptians had gathered during the seven years of plenty, was secured for the land in stores for the seven years of famine, for the support of the whole land.

13 And the inhabitants of Egypt filled each man his store and his concealed place with corn, to be for support during the famine.

14 And Joseph placed all the food that he had gathered in all the cities of Egypt, and he closed all the stores and placed sentinels over them.

15 And Joseph's wife Osnath the daughter of Potiphera bare him two sons, Manasseh and Ephraim, and Joseph was thirty-four years old when he begat them.

16 And the lads grew up and they went in his ways and in his instructions, they did not deviate from the way which their father taught them, either to the right or left.

17 And the Lord was with the lads, and they grew up and had understanding and skill in all wisdom and in all the affairs of government, and all the king's officers and his great men of the inhabitants of Egypt exalted the lads, and they were brought up amongst the king's children.

18 And the seven years of plenty that were throughout the land were at an end, and the seven years of famine came after them as Joseph had spoken, and the famine was throughout the land.

19 And all the people of Egypt saw that the famine had commenced in the land of Egypt, and all the people of Egypt opened their stores of corn for the famine prevailed over them.

20 And they found all the food that was in their stores, full of vermin and not fit to eat, and the famine prevailed throughout the land, and all the inhabitants of Egypt came and cried before Pharaoh, for the famine was heavy upon them.

21 And they said unto Pharaoh, Give food unto thy servants, and wherefore shall we die through hunger before thy eyes, even we and our little ones?

22 And Pharaoh answered them, saying, And wherefore do you cry unto me? did not Joseph command that the corn should be laid up during the seven years of plenty for the years of famine? and wherefore did you not hearken to his voice?

23 And the people of Egypt answered the king, saying, As thy soul liveth, our lord, thy servants have done all that Joseph ordered, for thy servants also gathered in all the produce of their fields during the seven years of plenty and laid it in the stores unto this day.

24 And when the famine prevailed over thy servants we opened our stores, and behold all our produce was filled with vermin and was not fit for food.

25 And when the king heard all that had befallen the inhabitants of Egypt, the king was greatly afraid on account of the famine, and he was much terrified; and the king answered the people of Egypt, saying, Since all this has happened unto you, go unto Joseph, do whatever he shall say unto you, transgress not his commands.

26 And all the people of Egypt went forth and came unto Joseph, and said unto him, Give unto us food, and wherefore shall we die before thee through hunger? for we gathered in our produce during the seven years as thou didst command, and we put it in store, and thus has it befallen us.

27 And when Joseph heard all the words of the people of Egypt and what had befallen them, Joseph opened all his stores of the produce and he sold it unto the people of Egypt.

28 And the famine prevailed throughout the land, and the famine was in all countries, but in the land of Egypt there was produce for sale.

29 And all the inhabitants of Egypt came unto Joseph to buy corn, for the famine prevailed over them, and all their corn was spoiled, and Joseph daily sold it to all the people of Egypt.

30 And all the inhabitants of the land of Canaan and the Philistines, and those beyond the Jordan, and the children of the east and all the cities of the lands far and nigh heard that there was corn in Egypt, and they all came to Egypt to buy corn, for the famine prevailed over them.

31 And Joseph opened the stores of corn and placed officers over them, and they daily stood and sold to all that came.

32 And Joseph knew that his brethren also would come to Egypt to buy corn, for the famine prevailed throughout the earth. And Joseph commanded all his people that they should cause it to be proclaimed throughout the land of Egypt, saying,

33 It is the pleasure of the king, of his second and of their great men, that any person who wishes to buy corn in Egypt shall not send his servants to Egypt to purchase, but his sons, and also any Egyptian or Canaanite, who shall come from any of the stores from buying corn in Egypt, and shall go and sell it throughout the land, he shall die, for no one shall buy but for the support of his household.

34 And any man leading two or three beasts shall die, for a man shall only lead his own beast.

35 And Joseph placed sentinels at the gates of Egypt, and commanded them, saying, Any person who may come to buy corn, suffer him not to enter until his name, and the name of his father, and the name of

his father's father be written down, and whatever is written by day, send their names unto me in the evening that I may know their names.

36 And Joseph placed officers throughout the land of Egypt, and he commanded them to do all these things.

37 And Joseph did all these things, and made these statutes, in order that he might know when his brethren should come to Egypt to buy corn; and Joseph's people caused it daily to be proclaimed in Egypt according to these words and statutes which Joseph had commanded.

38 And all the inhabitants of the east and west country, and of all the earth, heard of the statutes and regulations which Joseph had enacted in Egypt, and the inhabitants of the extreme parts of the earth came and they bought corn in Egypt day after day, and then went away.

39 And all the officers of Egypt did as Joseph had commanded, and all that came to Egypt to buy corn, the gate keepers would write their names, and their fathers' names, and daily bring them in the evening before Joseph.

Chapter 51

1 And Jacob afterward heard that there was corn in Egypt, and he called unto his sons to go to Egypt to buy corn, for upon them also did the famine prevail, and he called unto his sons, saying,

Comment:1: This story is similar in Genesis 42 but there are more details in this Book of Jasher.

GEN.42:1 Now when Jacob saw that there was corn in Egypt, Jacob said unto his sons, Why do ye look one upon another?

GEN.42:2 And he said, Behold, I have heard that there is corn in Egypt: get you down thither, and buy for us from thence; that we may live, and not die.

GEN.42:3 And Joseph's ten brethren went down to buy corn in Egypt.

2 Behold I hear that there is corn in Egypt, and all the people of the earth go there to purchase, now therefore why will you show yourselves satisfied before the whole earth? go you also down to Egypt and buy us a little corn amongst those that come there, that we may not die.

3 And the sons of Jacob hearkened to the voice of their father, and they rose up to go down to Egypt in order to buy corn amongst the rest that came there.

4 And Jacob their father commanded them, saying, When you come into the city do not enter together in one gate, on account of the inhabitants of the land.

5 And the sons of Jacob went forth and they went to Egypt, and the sons of Jacob did all as their father had commanded them, and Jacob did not send Benjamin, for he said, Lest an accident might befall him on the road like his brother; and ten of Jacob's sons went forth.

6 And whilst the sons of Jacob were going on the road, they repented of what they had done to Joseph, and they spoke to each other, saying, We know that our brother Joseph went down to Egypt, and now we will seek him where we go, and if we find him we will take him from his master for a ransom, and if not, by force, and we will die for him.

7 And the sons of Jacob agreed to this thing and strengthened them-selves on account of Joseph, to deliver him from the hand of his master, and the sons of Jacob went to Egypt; and when they came near to Egypt they separated from each other, and they came through ten gates of Egypt, and the gate keepers wrote their names on that day, and brought them to Joseph in the evening.

8 And Joseph read the names from the hand of the gate-keepers of the city, and he found that his brethren had entered at the ten gates of the city, and Joseph at that time commanded that it should be proclaimed throughout the land of Egypt, saying,

9 Go forth all ye store guards, close all the corn stores and let only one remain open, that those who come may purchase from it.

10 And all the officers of Joseph did so at that time, and they closed all the stores and left only one open.

11 And Joseph gave the written names of his brethren to him that was set over the open store, and he said unto him, Whosoever shall come to thee to buy corn, ask his name, and when men of these names shall come before thee, seize them and send them, and they did so.

12 And when the sons of Jacob came into the city, they joined together in the city to seek Joseph before they bought themselves corn.

13 And they went to the walls of the harlots, and they sought Joseph in the walls of the harlots for three days, for they thought that Joseph would come in the walls of the harlots, for Joseph was very comely and well favoured, and the sons of Jacob sought Joseph for three days, and they could not find him.

14 And the man who was set over the open store sought for those names which Joseph had given him, and he did not find them.

15 And he sent to Joseph, saying, These three days have passed, and those men whose names thou didst give unto me have not come; and Joseph sent servants to seek the men in all Egypt, and to bring them before Joseph.

16 And Joseph's servants went and came into Egypt and could not find them, and went to Goshen and they were not there, and then went to the city of Rameses and could not find them.

17 And Joseph continued to send sixteen servants to seek his brothers, and they went and spread themselves in the four corners of the city, and four of the servants went into the house of the harlots, and they found the ten men there seeking their brother.

18 And those four men took them and brought them before him, and they bowed down to him to the ground, and Joseph was sitting upon his throne in his temple, clothed with princely garments, and upon his head was a large crown of gold, and all the mighty men were sitting around him.

19 And the sons of Jacob saw Joseph, and his figure and comeliness and dignity of countenance seemed wonderful in their eyes, and they again bowed down to him to the ground.

20 And Joseph saw his brethren, and he knew them, but they knew him not, for Joseph was very great in their eyes, therefore they knew him not.

21 And Joseph spoke to them, saying, From whence come ye? and they all answered and said, Thy servants have come from the land of Canaan to buy corn, for the famine prevails throughout the earth, and thy servants heard that there was corn in Egypt, so they have come amongst the other comers to buy corn for their support.

22 And Joseph answered them, saying, If you have come to purchase as you say, why do you come through ten gates of the city? it can only be that you have come to spy through the land.

23 And they all together answered Joseph, and said, Not so my lord, we are right, thy servants are not spies, but we have come to buy corn, for thy servants are all brothers, the sons of one man in the land of Canaan, and our father commanded us, saying, When you come to the city do not enter together at one gate on account of the inhabitants of the land.

24 And Joseph again answered them and said, That is the thing which I spoke unto you, you have come to spy through the land, therefore you all came through ten gates of the city; you have come to see the nakedness of the land.

25 Surely every one that cometh to buy corn goeth his way, and you are already three days in the land, and what do you do in the walls of harlots in which you have been for these three days? surely spies do like unto these things.

26 And they said unto Joseph, Far be it from our lord to speak thus, for we are twelve brothers, the sons of our father Jacob, in the land of Canaan, the son of Isaac, the son of Abraham, the Hebrew, and behold the youngest is with our father this day in the land of Canaan, and one is not, for he was lost from us, and we thought perhaps he might be in this land, so we are seeking him throughout the land, and have come even to the houses of harlots to seek him there.

27 And Joseph said unto them, And have you then sought him throughout the earth, that there only remained Egypt for you to seek him in? And what also should your brother do in the houses of harlots, although he were in Egypt? have you not said, That you are from the sons of Isaac, the son of Abraham, and what shall the sons of Jacob do then in the houses of harlots?

28 And they said unto him, Because we heard that Ishmaelites stole him from us, and it was told unto us that they sold him in Egypt, and thy servant, our brother, is very comely and well favoured, so we thought he would surely be in the houses of harlots, therefore thy servants went there to seek him and give ransom for him.

29 And Joseph still answered them, saying, Surely you speak falsely and utter lies, to say of yourselves that you are the sons of Abraham; as Pharaoh liveth you are spies, therefore have you come to the houses of harlots that you should not be known.

30 And Joseph said unto them, And now if you find him, and his master requireth of you a great price, will you give it for him? and they said, It shall be given.

31 And he said unto them, And if his master will not consent to part with him for a great price, what will you do unto him on his account? and they answered him, saying, If he will not give him unto us we will slay him, and take our brother and go away.

32 And Joseph said unto them, That is the thing which I have spoken to you; you are spies, for you are come to slay the inhabitants of the land, for we heard that two of your brethren smote all the inhabitants of Shechem, in the land of Canaan, on account of your sister, and you now come to do the like in Egypt on account of your brother.

33 Only hereby shall I know that you are true men; if you will send home one from amongst you to fetch your youngest brother from your father, and to bring him here unto me, and by doing this thing I will know that you are right.

34 And Joseph called to seventy of his mighty men, and he said unto them, Take these men and bring them into the ward.

35 And the mighty men took the ten men, they laid hold of them and put them into the ward, and they were in the ward three days.

36 And on the third day Joseph had them brought out of the ward, and he said unto them, Do this for yourselves if you be true men, so that you may live, one of your brethren shall be confined in the ward whilst you go and take home the corn for your household to the land of Canaan, and fetch your youngest brother, and bring him here unto me, that I may know that you are true men when you do this thing.

37 And Joseph went out from them and came into the chamber, and wept a great weeping, for his pity was excited for them, and he washed his face, and returned to them again, and he took Simeon from them and ordered him to be bound, but Simeon was not willing to be done so, for he was a very powerful man and they could not bind him.

38 And Joseph called unto his mighty men and seventy valiant men came before him with drawn swords in their hands, and the sons of Jacob were terrified at them.

39 And Joseph said unto them, Seize this man and confine him in prison until his brethren come to him, and Joseph's valiant men hastened and they all laid hold of Simeon to bind him, and Simeon gave a loud and terrible shriek and the cry was heard at a distance.

40 And all the valiant men of Joseph were terrified at the sound of the shriek, that they fell upon their faces, and they were greatly afraid and fled.

41 And all the men that were with Joseph fled, for they were greatly afraid of their lives, and only Joseph and Manasseh his son remained there, and Manassah the son of Joseph saw the strength of Simeon, and he was exceedingly wroth.

42 And Manassah the son of Joseph rose up to Simeon, and Manassah smote Simeon a heavy blow with his fist against the back of his neck, and Simeon was stilled of his rage.

43 And Manassah laid hold of Simeon and he seized him violently and he bound him and brought him into the house of confinement, and all the sons of Jacob were astonished at the act of the youth.

C.2 Here was a situation that Joseph's brothers were not accustomed to, that someone else was as strong as they were; not realizing that Joseph was their brother and that Manassah was their nephew who had inherited the same supernatural strength.

44 And Simeon said unto his brethren, 'None of you must say that this is the smiting of an Egyptian, but it is the smiting of the house of my father'.

C.3 Notice how Simeon simply can't grasp the thought that the reason that Manassah could bind him was because he was his brother's son. Amazing how God kept that knowledge from Simeon and his brethren until it was the correct time for Joseph to reveal to them all that he was indeed their long-lost brother whom they had sold into slavery over 20 years earlier.

45 And after this Joseph ordered him to be called who was set over the storehouse, to fill their sacks with corn as much as they could carry, and to restore every man's money into his sack, and to give them provision for the road, and thus did he unto them.

46 And Joseph commanded them, saying, Take heed lest you transgress my orders to bring your brother as I have told you, and it shall be when you bring your brother hither unto me, then will I know that you are true men, and you shall traffic in the land, and I will restore unto you your brother, and you shall return in peace to your father.

47 And they all answered and said, According as our lord speaketh so will we do, and they bowed down to him to the ground.

48 And every man lifted his corn upon his ass, and they went out to go to the land of Canaan to their father; and they came to the inn and Levi spread his sack to give provender to his ass, when he saw and behold his money in full weight was still in his sack.

49 And the man was greatly afraid, and he said unto his brethren, My money is restored, and lo, it is even in my sack, and the men were greatly afraid, and they said, What is this that God hath done unto us?

50 And they all said, And where is the Lord's kindness with our fathers, with Abraham, Isaac, end Jacob, that the Lord has this day delivered us into the hands of the king of Egypt to contrive against us?

51 And Judah said unto them, Surely we are guilty sinners before the Lord our God in having sold our brother, our own flesh, and wherefore do you say, Where is the Lord's kindness with our fathers?

52 And Reuben said unto them, Said I not unto you, do not sin against the lad, and you would not listen to me? now God requireth him from us, and how dare you say, Where is the Lord's kindness with our fathers, whilst you have sinned unto the Lord?

53 And they tarried overnight in that place, and they rose up early in the morning and laded their asses with their corn, and they led them and went on and came to their father's house in the land of Canaan.

54 And Jacob and his household went out to meet his sons, and Jacob saw and behold their brother Simeon was not with them, and Jacob said unto his sons, Where is your brother Simeon, whom I do not see? and his sons told him all that had befallen them in Egypt.

Chapter 52

1 And they entered their house, and every man opened his sack and they saw and behold every man's bundle of money was there, at which they and their father were greatly terrified.

Comment:1: The evil deeds of Jacob's sons against his younger son Joseph are now returning on their own heads. There is a similar story in the Bible, but again there are many more details in this Book of Jasher.

GEN.42:35 And it came to pass as they emptied their sacks, that, behold, every man's bundle of money was in his sack: and when both they and their father saw the bundles of money, they were afraid.

2 And Jacob said unto them, What is this that you have done to me? I sent your brother Joseph to inquire after your welfare and you said unto me. A wild beast did devour him.

3 And Simeon went with you to buy food and you say the king of Egypt hath confined him in prison, and you wish to take Benjamin to cause his death also, and bring down my grey hairs with sorrow to the grave on account of Benjamin and his brother Joseph.

4 Now therefore my son shall not go down with you, for his brother is dead and he is left alone, and mischief may befall him by the way in which you go, as it befell his brother.

5 And Reuben said unto his father, Thou shalt slay my two sons if I do not bring thy son and place him before thee; and Jacob said unto his sons, Abide ye here and do not go down to Egypt, for my son shall not go down with you to Egypt, nor die like his brother.

6 And Judah said unto them, refrain ye from him until the corn is finished, and he will then say, Take down your brother, when he will find his own life and the life of his household in danger from the famine.

7 And in those days the famine was sore throughout the land, and all the people of the earth went and came to Egypt to buy food, for the famine prevailed greatly amongst them, and the sons of Jacob remained in Canaan a year and two months until their corn was finished.

8 And it came to pass after their corn was finished, the whole house-hold of Jacob was pinched with hunger, and all the infants of the sons of Jacob came together and they approached Jacob, and they all surrounded him, and they said unto him, Give unto us bread, and wherefore shall we all perish through hunger in thy presence?

9 Jacob heard the words of his son's children, and he wept a great weeping, and his pity was roused for them, and Jacob called unto his sons and they all came and sat before him.

10 And Jacob said unto them, And have you not seen how your children have been weeping over me this day, saying, Give unto us bread, and there is none? now therefore return and buy for us a little food.

11 And Judah answered and said unto his father, If thou wilt send our brother with us we will go down and buy corn for thee, and if thou wilt not send him then we will not go down, for surely the king of Egypt particularly enjoined us, saying, You shall not see my face unless your brother be with you, for the king of Egypt is a strong and mighty king, and behold if we shall go to him without our brother we shall all be put to death.

12 Dost thou not know and hast thou not heard that this king is very powerful and wise, and there is not like unto him in all the earth? behold we have seen all the kings of the earth and we have not seen one like that king, the king of Egypt; surely amongst all the kings of the earth there is none greater than Abimelech king of the Philistines, yet the king of Egypt is greater and mightier than he, and Abimelech can only be compared to one of his officers.

13 Father, thou hast not seen his palace and his throne, and all his servants standing before him; thou hast not seen that king upon his throne in his pomp and royal appearance, dressed in his kingly robes with a large golden crown upon his head; thou hast not seen the honor and glory which God has given unto him, for there is not like unto him in all the earth.

14 Father, thou hast not seen the wisdom, the understanding and the knowledge which God has given in his heart, nor heard his sweet voice when he spake unto us.

15 We know not, father, who made him acquainted with our names and all that befell us, yet he asked also after thee, saying, Is your father still living, and is it well with him?

16 Thou hast not seen the affairs of the government of Egypt regulated by him, without inquiring of Pharaoh his lord; thou hast not seen the awe and fear which he impressed upon all the Egyptians.

17 And also when we went from him, we threatened to do unto Egypt like unto the rest of the cities of the Amorites, and we were exceedingly wroth against all his words which he spoke concerning us as spies, and now when we shall again come before him his terror will fall upon us all, and not one of us will be able to speak to him either a little or a great thing.

18 Now therefore father, send we pray thee the lad with us, and we will go down and buy thee food for our support, and not die through hunger. And Jacob said, Why have you dealt so ill with me to tell the king you had a brother? what is this thing that you have done unto me?

19 And Judah said unto Jacob his father, Give the lad into my care and we will rise up and go down to Egypt and buy corn, and then return, and it shall be when we return if the lad be not with us, then let me bear thy blame forever.

20 Hast thou seen all our infants weeping over thee through hunger and there is no power in thy hand to satisfy them? now let thy pity be roused for them and send our brother with us and we will go.

21 For how will the Lord's kindness to our ancestors be manifested to thee when thou sayest that the king of Egypt will take away thy son? as the Lord liveth I will not leave him until I bring him and place him before thee; but pray for us unto the Lord, that he may deal kindly with us, to cause us to be received favourably and kindly before the king of

Egypt and his men, for had we not delayed surely now we had returned a second time with thy son.

22 And Jacob said unto his sons, I trust in the Lord God that he may deliver you and give you favour in the sight of the king of Egypt, and in the sight of all his men.

23 Now therefore rise up and go to the man, and take for him in your hands a present from what can be obtained in the land and bring it before him, and may the Almighty God give you mercy before him that he may send Benjamin and Simeon your brethren with you.

24 And all the men rose up, and they took their brother Benjamin, and they took in their hands a large present of the best of the land, and they also took a double portion of silver.

25 And Jacob strictly commanded his sons concerning Benjamin, Saying, Take heed of him in the way in which you are going, and do not separate yourselves from him in the road, neither in Egypt.

26 And Jacob rose up from his sons and spread forth his hands and he prayed unto the Lord on account of his sons, saying, O Lord God of heaven and earth, remember thy covenant with our father Abraham, remember it with my father Isaac and deal kindly with my sons and deliver them not into the hands of the king of Egypt; do it I pray thee O God for the sake of thy mercies and redeem all my children and rescue them from Egyptian power, and send them their two brothers.

27 And all the wives of the sons of Jacob and their children lifted up their eyes to heaven and they all wept before the Lord and cried unto him to deliver their fathers from the hand of the king of Egypt.

28 And Jacob wrote a record to the king of Egypt and gave it into the hand of Judah and into the hands of his sons for the king of Egypt, saying,

29 From thy servant Jacob, son of Isaac, son of Abraham the Hebrew,

the prince of God, to the powerful and wise king, the revealer of secrets, king of Egypt, greeting.

30 Be it known to my lord the king of Egypt, the famine was sore upon us in the land of Canaan, and I sent my sons to thee to buy us a little food from thee for our support.

31 For my sons surrounded me and I being very old cannot see with my eyes, for my eyes have become very heavy through age, as well as with daily weeping for my son, for Joseph who was lost from before me, and I commanded my sons that they should not enter the gates of the city when they came to Egypt, on account of the inhabitants of the land.

32 And I also commanded them to go about Egypt to seek for my son Joseph, perhaps they might find him there, and they did so, and thou didst consider them as spies of the land.

33 Have we not heard concerning thee that thou didst interpret Pharaoh's dream and didst speak truly unto him? how then dost thou not know in thy wisdom whether my sons are spies or not?

C.2 I find this letter by Jacob to Pharaoh's right-hand man Joseph to be absolutely splendid and very wise. Jacob is stating that if Pharaoh's right-hand man could so accurately interpret Pharaoh's dreams, then he must have the gift of discernment and wisdom, and why therefore couldn't he determine if Jacob's sons were spies or true men? This action by Joseph as to not discern is deliberate. As I said before God also hid Jacob's discernment from him concerning Joseph. And in both cases mentioned it was for an important purpose.

34 Now therefore, my lord and king, behold I have sent my son before thee, as thou didst speak unto my sons; I beseech thee to put thy eyes upon him until he is returned to me in peace with his brethren.

35 For dost thou not know, or hast thou not heard that which our God did unto Pharaoh when he took my grandmother Sarah, and what he did unto Abimelech king of the Philistines on account of her, and also what our father Abraham did unto the nine kings of Elam, how he smote them all with a few men that were with him?

97

36 And also what my two sons Simeon and Levi did unto the eight cities of the Amorites, how they destroyed them on account of their sister Dinah?

37 And also on account of their brother Benjamin they consoled themselves for the loss of his brother Joseph; what will they then do for him when they see the hand of any people prevailing over them, for his sake?

38 Dost thou not know, O king of Egypt, that the power of God is with us, and that also God ever heareth our prayers and forsaketh us not all the days?

39 And when my sons told me of thy dealings with them, I called not unto the Lord on account of thee, for then thou wouldst have perished with thy men before my son Benjamin came before thee, but I thought that as Simeon my son was in thy house, perhaps thou mightest deal kindly with him, therefore I did not this thing unto thee.

40 Now therefore behold Benjamin my son cometh unto thee with my sons, take heed of him and put thy eyes upon him, and then will God place his eyes over thee and throughout thy kingdom.

41 Now I have told thee all that is in my heart, and behold my sons are coming to thee with their brother, examine the face of the whole earth for their sake and send them back in peace with their brethren.

42 And Jacob gave the record to his sons into the care of Judah to give it unto the king of Egypt.

Chapter 53

1 And the sons of Jacob rose up and took Benjamin and the whole of the presents, and they went and came to Egypt and they stood before Joseph.

GEN.43:15 And the men took that present, and they took double money in their hand and Benjamin; and rose up, and went down to Egypt, and stood before Joseph.

GEN.43:16 And when Joseph saw Benjamin with them, he said to the ruler of his house, 'Bring these men home, and slay*, and make ready; for these men shall dine with me at noon'. (* to kill animals for a feast)

2 And Joseph beheld his brother Benjamin with them, and he saluted them, and these men came to Joseph's house.

3 And Joseph commanded the superintendent of his house to give to his brethren to eat, and he did so unto them.

4 And at noon time Joseph sent for the men to come before him with Benjamin, and the men told the superintendent of Joseph's house concerning the silver that was returned in their sacks, and he said unto them, It will be well with you, fear not, and he brought their brother Simeon unto them.

5 And Simeon said unto his brethren, The lord of the Egyptians has acted very kindly unto me, he did not keep me bound, as you saw with your eyes, for when you went out from the city he let me free and dealt kindly with me in his house.

6 And Judah took Benjamin by the hand, and they came before Joseph, and they bowed down to him to the ground.

7 And the men gave the present unto Joseph and they all sat before him, and Joseph said unto them, Is it well with you, is it well with your children, is it well with your aged father? and they said, It is well, and Judah took the record which Jacob had sent and gave it into the hand of Joseph.

8 And Joseph read the letter and knew his father's writing, and he wished to weep and he went into an inner room and he wept a great weeping; and he went out.

9 And he lifted up his eyes and beheld his brother Benjamin, and he said, Is this your brother of whom you spoke unto me? And Benjamin approached Joseph, and Joseph placed his hand upon his head and he said unto him, May God be gracious unto thee my son.

10 And when Joseph saw his brother, the son of his mother, he again wished to weep, and he entered the chamber, and he wept there, and he washed his face, and went out and refrained from weeping, and he said, Prepare food.

11 And Joseph had a cup from which he drank, and it was of silver beautifully inlaid with onyx stones and bdellium, and Joseph struck the cup in the sight of his brethren whilst they were sitting to eat with him.

12 And Joseph said unto the men, I know by this cup that Reuben the first born, Simeon and Levi and Judah, Issachar and Zebulun are children from one mother, seat yourselves to eat according to your births.

13 And he also placed the others according to their births, and he said, I know that this your youngest brother has no brother, and I, like him, have no brother, he shall therefore sit down to eat with me.

14 And Benjamin went up before Joseph and sat upon the throne, and the men beheld the acts of Joseph, and they were astonished at them; and the men ate and drank at that time with Joseph, and he then gave presents unto them, and Joseph gave one gift unto Benjamin, and Manasseh and Ephraim saw the acts of their father, and they also gave presents unto him, and Osnath gave him one present, and they were five presents in the hand of Benjamin.

15 And Joseph brought them out wine to drink, and they would not drink, and they said, From the day on which Joseph was lost we have not drunk wine, nor eaten any delicacies.

16 And Joseph swore unto them, and he pressed them hard, and they drank plentifully with him on that day, and Joseph afterward turned to his brother Benjamin to speak with him, and Benjamin was still sitting upon the throne before Joseph.

17 And Joseph said unto him, Hast thou begotten any children? and he said, Thy servant has ten sons, and these are their names, Bela, Becher, Ashbal, Gera, Naaman, Achi, Rosh, Mupim, Chupim, and Ord, and I called their names after my brother whom I have not seen.

18 And he ordered them to bring before him his map of the stars, whereby Joseph knew all the times, and Joseph said unto Benjamin, I have heard that the Hebrews are acquainted with all wisdom, dost thou know anything of this?

19 And Benjamin said, Thy servant is knowing also in all the wisdom which my father taught me, and Joseph said unto Benjamin, Look now at this instrument and understand where thy brother Joseph is in Egypt, who you said went down to Egypt.

20 And Benjamin beheld that instrument with the map of the stars of heaven, and he was wise and looked therein to know where his brother was, and Benjamin divided the whole land of Egypt into four divisions, and he found that he who was sitting upon the throne before him was his brother Joseph, and Benjamin wondered greatly, and when Joseph saw that his brother Benjamin was so much astonished, he said unto Benjamin, What hast thou seen, and why art thou astonished?

21 And Benjamin said unto Joseph, I can see by this that Joseph my brother sitteth here with me upon the throne, and Joseph said unto him, I am Joseph thy brother, reveal not this thing unto thy brethren; behold I will send thee with them when they go away, and I will command them to be brought back again into the city, and I will take thee away from them.

22 And if they dare their lives and fight for thee, then shall I know that they have repented of what they did unto me, and I will make myself known to them, and if they forsake thee when I take thee, then shalt

thou remain with me, and I will wrangle with them, and they shall go away, and I will not become known to them.

23 At that time Joseph commanded his officer to fill their sacks with food, and to put each man's money into his sack, and to put the cup in the sack of Benjamin, and to give them provision for the road, and they did so unto them.

24 And on the next day the men rose up early in the morning, and they loaded their asses with their corn, and they went forth with Benjamin, and they went to the land of Canaan with their brother Benjamin.

25 They had not gone far from Egypt when Joseph commanded him that was set over his house, saying, Rise, pursue these men before they get too far from Egypt, and say unto them, Why have you stolen my master's cup?

26 And Joseph's officer rose up and he reached them, and he spoke unto them all the words of Joseph; and when they heard this thing they became exceedingly wroth, and they said, He with whom thy master's cup shall be found shall die, and we will also become slaves.

27 And they hastened and each man brought down his sack from his ass, and they looked in their bags and the cup was found in Benjamin's bag, and they all tore their garments and they returned to the city, and they smote Benjamin in the road, continually smiting him until he came into the city, and they stood before Joseph.

28 And Judah's anger was kindled, and he said, This man has only brought me back to destroy Egypt this day.

29 And the men came to Joseph's house, and they found Joseph sitting upon his throne, and all the mighty men standing at his right and left.

30 And Joseph said unto them, What is this act that you have done, that you took away my silver cup and went away? but I know that you took my cup in order to know thereby in what part of the land your brother was.

31 And Judah said, What shall we say to our lord, what shall we speak and how shall we justify ourselves, God has this day found the iniquity of all thy servants, therefore has he done this thing to us this day.

32 And Joseph rose up and caught hold of Benjamin and took him from his brethren with violence, and he came to the house and locked the door at them, and Joseph commanded him that was set over his house that he should say unto them, Thus saith the king, Go in peace to your father, behold I have taken the man in whose hand my cup was found.

Chapter 54

1 And when Judah saw the dealings of Joseph with them, Judah approached him and broke open the door, and came with his brethren before Joseph.

Comment:1: Now Judah is getting really mad! This story as to how super-naturally strong and violent the sons of Jacob were, is not fully portrayed in the Bible. Judah just didn't understand that he was dealing with his long-lost brother who was just as strong as he was, not to mention both of Joseph's sons Manesses and Ephraim who were also just as strong as Judah.

2 And Judah said unto Joseph, Let it not seem grievous in the sight of my lord, may thy servant I pray thee speak a word before thee? and Joseph said unto him, Speak.

3 And Judah spoke before Joseph, and his brethren were there standing before them; and Judah said unto Joseph, Surely when we first came to our lord to buy food, thou didst consider us as spies of the land, and we brought Benjamin before thee, and thou still makest sport of us this day.

4 Now therefore let the king hear my words, and send I pray thee our brother that he may go along with us to our father, lest thy soul perish this day with all the souls of the inhabitants of Egypt.

5 Dost thou not know what two of my brethren, Simeon and Levi, did unto the city of Shechem, and unto seven cities of the Amorites, on account of our sister Dinah, and also what they would do for the sake of their brother Benjamin?

6 And I with my strength, who am greater and mightier than both of them, come this day upon thee and thy land if thou art unwilling to send our brother.

7 Hast thou not heard what our God who made choice of us did unto Pharaoh on account of Sarah our mother, whom he took away from our father, that he smote him and his household with heavy plagues, that even unto this day the Egyptians relate this wonder to each other? so will our God do unto thee on account of Benjamin whom thou hast this day taken from his father, and on account of the evils which thou

this day heapest over us in thy land; for our God will remember his covenant with our father Abraham and bring evil upon thee, because thou hast grieved the soul of our father this day.

8 Now therefore hear my words that I have this day spoken unto thee and send our brother that he may go away lest thou and the people of thy land die by the sword, for you cannot all prevail over me.

9 And Joseph answered Judah, saying, Why hast thou opened wide thy mouth and why dost thou boast over us, saying, Strength is with thee? as Pharaoh liveth, if I command all my valiant men to fight with you, surely thou and these thy brethren would sink in the mire.

10 And Judah said unto Joseph, Surely it becometh thee and thy people to fear me; as the Lord liveth if I once draw my sword I shall not sheathe it again until I shall this day have slain all Egypt, and I will commence with thee and finish with Pharaoh thy master.

11 And Joseph answered and said unto him, Surely strength belongeth not alone to thee; I am stronger and mightier than thou, surely if thou drawest thy sword I will put it to thy neck and the necks of all thy brethren.

12 And Judah said unto him, Surely if I this day open my mouth against thee I would swallow thee up that thou be destroyed from off the earth and perish this day from thy kingdom. And Joseph said, Surely if thou openest thy mouth I have power and might to close thy mouth with a stone until thou shalt not be able to utter a word; see how many stones are before us, truly I can take a stone, and force it into thy mouth and break thy jaws.

13 And Judah said, God is witness between us, that we have not hitherto desired to battle with thee, only give us our brother and we will go from thee; and Joseph answered and said, As Pharaoh liveth, if all the kings of Canaan came together with you, you should not take him from my hand.

14 Now therefore go your way to your father, and your brother shall be unto me for a slave, for he has robbed the king's house. And Judah said,

What is it to thee or to the character of the king, surely the king sendeth forth from his house, throughout the land, silver and gold either in gifts or expenses, and thou still talkest about thy cup which thou didst place in our brother's bag and sayest that he has stolen it from thee?

15 God forbid that our brother Benjamin or any of the seed of Abraham should do this thing to steal from thee, or from anyone else, whether king, prince, or any man.

16 Now therefore cease this accusation lest the whole earth hear thy words, saying, For a little silver the king of Egypt wrangled with the men, and he accused them and took their brother for a slave.

17 And Joseph answered and said, Take unto you this cup and go from me and leave your brother for a slave, for it is the judgment of a thief to be a slave.

18 And Judah said, Why art thou not ashamed of thy words, to leave our brother and to take thy cup? Surely if thou givest us thy cup, or a thousand times as much, we will not leave our brother for the silver which is found in the hand of any man, that we will not die over him.

19 And Joseph answered, And why did you forsake your brother and sell him for twenty pieces of silver unto this day, and why then will you not do the same to this your brother?

20 And Judah said, the Lord is witness between me and thee that we desire not thy battles; now therefore give us our brother and we will go from there without quarreling.

21 And Joseph answered and said, If all the kings of the land should assemble they will not be able to take your brother from my hand; and Judah said, What shall we say unto our father, when he seeth that our brother cometh not with us, and will grieve over him?

22 And Joseph answered and said, This is the thing which you shall tell unto your father, saying, The rope has gone after the bucket.

C.2 What does Joseph mean by stating 'The rope has gone after the bucket'. What he is saying is that 'what his brothers have sowed' is now coming back down on their own heads. They didn't yet realise that this Ruler standing in front of them was in fact their long-lost brother whom they had sold into slavery when he was only 17. A very cruel act indeed, So, is it any wonder that Joseph wanted to severely 'test' his brothers to see if they had changed in character after all these 20-some years?

23 And Judah said, Surely thou art a king, and why speakest thou these things, giving a false judgment? woe unto the king who is like unto thee.

24 And Joseph answered and said, There is no false judgment in the word that I spoke on account of your brother Joseph, for all of you sold him to the Midianites for twenty pieces of silver, and you all denied it to your father and said unto him, An evil beast has devoured him, Joseph has been torn to pieces.

25 And Judah said, Behold the fire of Shem burneth in my heart, now I will burn all your land with fire; and Joseph answered and said, Surely thy sister-in-law Tamar, who killed your sons, extinguished the fire of Shechem.

26 And Judah said, If I pluck out a single hair from my flesh, I will fill all Egypt with its blood.

27 And Joseph answered and said, Such is your custom to do as you did to your brother whom you sold, and you dipped his coat in blood and brought it to your father in order that he might say an evil beast devoured him and here is his blood.

28 And when Judah heard this thing he was exceedingly wroth and his anger burned within him, and there was before him in that place a stone, the weight of which was about four hundred shekels, and Judah's anger was kindled and he took the stone in one hand and cast it to the heavens and caught it with his left hand.

29 And he placed it afterward under his legs, and he sat upon it with all his strength and the stone was turned into dust from the force of Judah.

30 And Joseph saw the act of Judah and he was very much afraid, but he commanded Manassah his son and he also did with another stone like unto the act of Judah, and Judah said unto his brethren, Let not any of you say, this man is an Egyptian, but by his doing this thing he is of our father's family.

C.3 Here we see Manassah do exactly the same thing with a stone that Judah had just done, and yet Joseph's brethren didn't even recognise that Joseph was their long-lost brother! They even stated that no one had this kind of strength as also manifested by Manassah unless he was one of the sons of Jacob – which he in fact he was. Well he was in fact Jacob's grandson.

31 And Joseph said, Not to you only is strength given, for we are also powerful men, and why will you boast over us all? and Judah said unto Joseph, Send I pray thee our brother and ruin not thy country this day.

32 And Joseph answered and said unto them, Go and tell your father, an evil beast hath devoured him as you said concerning your brother Joseph.

33 And Judah spoke to his brother Naphtali, and he said unto him, Make haste, go now and number all the streets of Egypt and come and tell me; and Simeon said unto him, Let not this thing be a trouble to thee; now I will go to the mount and take up one large stone from the mount and level it at every one in Egypt, and kill all that are in it.

34 And Joseph heard all these words that his brethren spoke before him, and they did not know that Joseph understood them, for they imagined that he knew not to speak Hebrew.

35 And Joseph was greatly afraid at the words of his brethren lest they should destroy Egypt, and he commanded his son Manasseh, saying, Go now make haste and gather unto me all the inhabitants of Egypt, and all the valiant men together, and let them come to me now upon horseback and on foot and with all sorts of musical instruments, and Manasseh went and did so.

36 And Naphtali went as Judah had commanded him, for Naphtali was light-footed as one of the swift stags, and he would go upon the ears of corn and they would not break under him.

37 And he went and numbered all the streets of Egypt, and found them to be twelve, and he came hastily and told Judah, and Judah said unto his brethren, Hasten you and put on every man his sword upon his loins and we will come over Egypt, and smite them all, and let not a remnant remain.

38 And Judah said, Behold, I will destroy three of the streets with my strength, and you shall each destroy one street; and when Judah was speaking this thing, behold the inhabitants of Egypt and all the mighty men came toward them with all sorts of musical instruments and with loud shouting.

39 And their number was five hundred cavalry and ten thousand infantry, and four hundred men who could fight without sword or spear, only with their hands and strength.

40 And all the mighty men came with great storming and shouting, and they all surrounded the sons of Jacob and terrified them, and the ground quaked at the sound of their shouting.

41 And when the sons of Jacob saw these troops they were greatly afraid of their lives, and Joseph did so in order to terrify the sons of Jacob to become tranquilized.

42 And Judah, seeing some of his brethren terrified, said unto them, Why are you afraid whilst the grace of God is with us? and when Judah saw all the people of Egypt surrounding them at the command of Joseph to terrify them, only Joseph commanded them, saying, Do not touch any of them.

43 Then Judah hastened and drew his sword, and uttered a loud and bitter scream, and he smote with his sword, and he sprang upon the ground and he still continued to shout against all the people.

44 And when he did this thing the Lord caused the terror of Judah and his brethren to fall upon the valiant men and all the people that surrounded them.

45 And they all fled at the sound of the shouting, and they were terrified and fell one upon the other, and many of them died as they fell, and they all fled from before Judah and his brethren and from before Joseph.

46 And whilst they were fleeing, Judah and his brethren pursued them unto the house of Pharaoh, and they all escaped, and Judah again sat before Joseph and roared at him like a lion, and gave a great and tremendous shriek at him.

47 And the shriek was heard at a distance, and all the inhabitants of Succoth heard it, and all Egypt quaked at the sound of the shriek, and also the walls of Egypt and of the land of Goshen fell in from the shaking of the earth, and Pharaoh also fell from his throne upon the ground, and also all the pregnant women of Egypt and Goshen miscarried when they heard the noise of the shaking, for they were terribly afraid.

48 And Pharaoh sent word, saying, What is this thing that has this day happened in the land of Egypt? and they came and told him all the things from beginning to end, and Pharaoh was alarmed and he wondered and was greatly afraid.

49 And his fright increased when he heard all these things, and he sent unto Joseph, saying, Thou hast brought unto me the Hebrews to destroy all Egypt; what wilt thou do with that thievish slave? send him away and let him go with his brethren, and let us not perish through their evil, even we, you and all Egypt.

50 And if thou desirest not to do this thing, cast off from thee all my valuable things, and go with them to their land, if thou delightest in it, for they will this day destroy my whole country and slay all my people; even all the women of Egypt have miscarried through their screams; see what they have done merely by their shouting and speaking, moreover if they fight with the sword, they will destroy the land; now therefore choose that which thou desirest, whether me or the Hebrews, whether Egypt or the land of the Hebrews.

51 And they came and told Joseph all the words of Pharaoh that he had said concerning him, and Joseph was greatly afraid at the words of

Pharaoh and Judah and his brethren were still standing before Joseph indignant and enraged, and all the sons of Jacob roared at Joseph, like the roaring of the sea and its waves.

52 And Joseph was greatly afraid of his brethren and on account of Pharaoh, and Joseph sought a pretext to make himself known unto his brethren, lest they should destroy all Egypt.

53 And Joseph commanded his son Manasseh, and Manasseh went and approached Judah, and placed his hand upon his shoulder, and the anger of Judah was stilled.

54 And Judah said unto his brethren, Let no one of you say that this is the act of an Egyptian youth for this is the work of my father's house.

55 And Joseph seeing and knowing that Judah's anger was stilled, he approached to speak unto Judah in the language of mildness.

56 And Joseph said unto Judah, Surely you speak truth and have this day verified your assertions concerning your strength, and may your God who delighteth in you, increase your welfare; but tell me truly why from amongst all thy brethren dost thou wrangle with me on account of the lad, as none of them have spoken one word to me concerning him.

57 And Judah answered Joseph, saying, Surely thou must know that I was security for the lad to his father, saying, If I brought him not unto him I should bear his blame forever.

58 Therefore have I approached thee from amongst all my brethren, for I saw that thou wast unwilling to suffer him to go from thee; now therefore may I find grace in thy sight that thou shalt send him to go with us, and behold I will remain as a substitute for him, to serve thee in whatever thou desirest, for wheresoever thou shalt send me I will go to serve thee with great energy.

59 Send me now to a mighty king who has rebelled against thee, and thou shalt know what I will do unto him and unto his land; although he may have cavalry and infantry or an exceeding mighty people, I will slay them all and bring the king's head before thee.

60 Dost thou not know or hast thou not heard that our father Abraham with his servant Eliezer smote all the kings of Elam with their hosts in one night, they left not one remaining? and ever since that day our father's strength was given unto us for an inheritance, for us and our seed forever.

61 And Joseph answered and said, You speak truth, and falsehood is not in your mouth, for it was also told unto us that the Hebrews have power and that the Lord their God delighteth much in them, and who then can stand before them?

62 However, on this condition will I send your brother, if you will bring before me his brother the son of his mother, of whom you said that he had gone from you down to Egypt; and it shall come to pass when you bring unto me his brother I will take him in his stead, because not one of you was security for him to your father, and when he shall come unto me, I will then send with you his brother for whom you have been security.

63 And Judah's anger was kindled against Joseph when he spoke this thing, and his eyes dropped blood with anger, and he said unto his brethren, How doth this man this day seek his own destruction and that of all Egypt!

64 And Simeon answered Joseph, saying, Did we not tell thee at first that we knew not the particular spot to which he went, and whether he be dead or alive, and wherefore speaketh my lord like unto these things?

65 And Joseph observing the countenance of Judah discerned that his anger began to kindle when he spoke unto him, saying, Bring unto me your other brother instead of this brother.

66 And Joseph said unto his brethren, Surely you said that your brother was either dead or lost, now if I should call him this day and he should come before you, would you give him unto me instead of his brother?

67 And Joseph began to speak and call out, Joseph, Joseph, come this day before me, and appear to thy brethren and sit before them.

68 And when Joseph spoke this thing before them, they looked each a different way to see from whence Joseph would come before them.

69 And Joseph observed all their acts, and said unto them, Why do you look here and there? I am Joseph whom you sold to Egypt, now therefore let it not grieve you that you sold me, for as a support during the famine did God send me before you.

C.4 What an incredible climax to this incredible drama. Here is the build-up and the crescendo and 'lo and behold' Joseph reveals himself finally to his brethren. Of course, as soon as they fully realized who this powerful ruler of Egypt was, then they became very afraid for their lives. All of a sudden, they felt the extreme guilt of having sold Joseph as a slave at only 17 years old, and his having suffered many things, including the separation from his own family for over 20 years! In a flash of a moment - everything that had transpired to Judah and his brothers since first coming down to Egypt, suddenly all made perfect sense and they felt like fools! So, yes, his brethren would have felt absolutely guilty and terrible at the very moment that Joseph finally and suddenly revealed himself to his brethren whom he really was, their own long-lost brother - Joseph.

70 And his brethren were terrified at him when they heard the words of Joseph, and Judah was exceedingly terrified at him.

71 And when Benjamin heard the words of Joseph he was before them in the inner part of the house, and Benjamin ran unto Joseph his brother, and embraced him and fell upon his neck, and they wept.

72 And when Joseph's brethren saw that Benjamin had fallen upon his brother's neck and wept with him, they also fell upon Joseph and embraced him, and they wept a great weeping with Joseph.

73 And the voice was heard in the house of Joseph that they were Joseph's brethren, and it pleased Pharaoh exceedingly, for he was afraid of them lest they should destroy Egypt.

74 And Pharaoh sent his servants unto Joseph to congratulate him concerning his brethren who had come to him, and all the captains of the armies and troops that were in Egypt came to rejoice with Joseph, and all Egypt rejoiced greatly about Joseph's brethren.

75 And Pharaoh sent his servants to Joseph, saying, Tell thy brethren to fetch all belonging to them and let them come unto me, and I will place them in the best part of the land of Egypt, and they did so.

76 And Joseph commanded him that was set over his house to bring out to his brethren gifts and garments, and he brought out to them many garments being robes of royalty and many gifts, and Joseph divided them amongst his brethren.

77 And he gave unto each of his brethren a change of garments of gold and silver, and three hundred pieces of silver, and Joseph commanded them all to be dressed in these garments, and to be brought before Pharaoh.

78 And Pharaoh seeing that all Joseph's brethren were valiant men, and of beautiful appearance, he greatly rejoiced.

79 And they afterward went out from the presence of Pharaoh to go to the land of Canaan, to their father, and their brother Benjamin was with them.

80 And Joseph rose up and gave unto them eleven chariots from Pharaoh, and Joseph gave unto them his chariot, upon which he rode on the day of his being crowned in Egypt, to fetch his father to Egypt; and Joseph sent to all his brothers' children, garments according to their numbers, and a hundred pieces of silver to each of them, and he also sent garments to the wives of his brethren from the garments of the king's wives, and he sent them.

81 And he gave unto each of his brethren ten men to go with them to the land of Canaan to serve them, to serve their children and all belonging to them in coming to Egypt.

82 And Joseph sent by the hand of his brother Benjamin ten suits of garments for his ten sons, a portion above the rest of the children of the sons of Jacob.

83 And he sent to each fifty pieces of silver, and ten chariots on the account of Pharaoh, and he sent to his father ten asses laden with all the luxuries of Egypt, and ten she asses laden with corn and bread and nourishment for his father, and to all that were with him as provisions for the road.

84 And he sent to his sister Dinah garments of silver and gold, and frankincense and myrrh, and aloes and women's ornaments in great plenty, and he sent the same from the wives of Pharaoh to the wives of Benjamin.

C.5 Unlike the Book of Jubilees here in the Book of Jasher it is stating that Dinah did not die upon '*hearing the news of Joseph having been killed by a wild animal story*', some 20 years earlier, as concocted by Joseph's brethren, but was still alive. Joseph, the Ruler in Egypt & her long-lost brother sent gifts to her from Egypt. This was also the time when Joseph's brothers finally told the truth concerning Joseph to their father. It must have been very awkward for them all!

C.6 Jacob would have finally realized that Joseph obviously hadn't been killed by a wild animal and all of a sudden Jacob would have fully realized what had really happened in the past to his long-lost son Joseph. He would have been very upset at his other sons I would imagine. At least until God showed him the bigger picture and that was that God had allowed it all to happen in order to save their lives from the coming great famine.

85 And he gave unto all his brethren, also to their wives, all sorts of onyx stones and bdellium, and from all the valuable things amongst the great people of Egypt, nothing of all the costly things was left but what Joseph sent to his father's household.

86 And he sent his brethren away, and they went, and he sent his brother Benjamin with them.

87 And Joseph went out with them to accompany them on the road unto the borders of Egypt, and he commanded them concerning his father and his household, to come to Egypt.

88 And he said unto them, Do not quarrel on the road, for this thing was from the Lord to keep a great people from starvation, for there will be yet five years of famine in the land.

89 And he commanded them, saying, When you come unto the land of Canaan, do not come suddenly before my father in this affair, but act in your wisdom.

90 And Joseph ceased to command them, and he turned and went back to Egypt, and the sons of Jacob went to the land of Canaan with joy and cheerfulness to their father Jacob.

91 And they came unto the borders of the land, and they said to each other, What shall we do in this matter before our father, for if we come suddenly to him and tell him the matter, he will be greatly alarmed at our words and will not believe us.

92 And they went along until they came nigh unto their houses, and they found Serach, the daughter of Asher, going forth to meet them, and the damsel was very good and subtle, and knew how to play upon the harp.

93 And they called unto her and she came before them, and she kissed them, and they took her and gave unto her a harp, saying, Go now before our father, and sit before him, and strike upon the harp, and speak these words.

94 And they commanded her to go to their house, and she took the harp and hastened before them, and she came and sat near Jacob.

95 And she played well and sang, and uttered in the sweetness of her words, Joseph my uncle is living, and he ruleth throughout the land of Egypt, and is not dead.

96 And she continued to repeat and utter these words, and Jacob heard her words and they were agreeable to him.

97 He listened whilst she repeated them twice and thrice, and joy entered the heart of Jacob at the sweetness of her words, and the spirit of God was upon him, and he knew all her words to be true.

98 And Jacob blessed Serach when she spoke these words before him, and he said unto her, My daughter, may death never prevail over thee, for thou hast revived my spirit; only speak yet before me as thou hast spoken, for thou hast gladdened me with all thy words.

99 And she continued to sing these words, and Jacob listened and it pleased him, and he rejoiced, and the spirit of God was upon him.

100 Whilst he was yet speaking with her, behold his sons came to him with horses and chariots and royal garments and servants running before them.

101 And Jacob rose up to meet them, and saw his sons dressed in royal garments and he saw all the treasures that Joseph had sent to them.

102 And they said unto him, Be informed that our brother Joseph is living, and it is he who ruleth throughout the land of Egypt, and it is he who spoke unto us as we told thee.

103 And Jacob heard all the words of his sons, and his heart palpitated at their words, for he could not believe them until he saw all that Joseph had given them and what he had sent him, and all the signs which Joseph had spoken unto them.

104 And they opened out before him, and showed him all that Joseph had sent, they gave unto each what Joseph had sent him, and he knew that they had spoken the truth, and he rejoiced exceedingly an account of his son.

105 And Jacob said, It is enough for me that my son Joseph is still living, I will go and see him before I die.

106 And his sons told him all that had befallen them, and Jacob said, I will go down to Egypt to see my son and his offspring.

107 And Jacob rose up and put on the garments which Joseph had sent him, and after he had washed, and shaved his hair, he put upon his head the turban which Joseph had sent him.

108 And all the people of Jacob's house and their wives put on the garments which Joseph had sent to them, and they greatly rejoiced at Joseph that he was still living and that he was ruling in Egypt,

109 And all the inhabitants of Canaan heard of this thing, and they came and rejoiced much with Jacob that he was still living.

110 And Jacob made a feast for them for three days, and all the kings of Canaan and nobles of the land ate and drank and rejoiced in the house of Jacob.

C.7 This story of the wisdom of Joseph in 'trying his brethren', to see if they had 'changed their ways', and God's resultant forgiveness of them through Joseph, is truly a heart-wrenching story that never fails to bring tears to my eyes. It is a unique and incredible story of FORGIVENESS when one considers all that Joseph went through for 20 years in being separated from his family. Sold as a slave at 17 years old by his own brethren. Falsely accused by Potiphar and his wife in Egypt. Thrown jail for in for years ... and yet God finally delivered him to become 2nd to Pharaoh himself and Lord over the whole land of Egypt.

Chapter 55

> 1 And it came to pass after this that Jacob said, I will go and see my son in Egypt and will then come back to the land of Canaan of which God had spoken unto Abraham, for I cannot leave the land of my birth-place.

Comment:1: God speaks directly to Jacob:

> 2 Behold the word of the Lord came unto him, saying, 'Go down to Egypt with all thy household and remain there, fear not to go down to Egypt for I will there make thee a great nation'.
>
> 3 And Jacob said within himself, I will go and see my son whether the fear of his God is yet in his heart amidst all the inhabitants of Egypt.
>
> 4 And the Lord said unto Jacob, Fear not about Joseph, for he still retaineth his integrity to serve me, as will seem good in thy sight, and Jacob rejoiced exceedingly concerning his son.

C.2 It is beautiful here to see God directly talking to Jacob and giving him important details to encourage him. I have to admit that the terrible trials that Jacob went through were indeed very extreme.

> 5 At that time Jacob commanded his sons and household to go to Egypt according to the word of the Lord unto him, and Jacob rose up with his sons and all his household, and he went out from the land of Canaan from Beersheba, with joy and gladness of heart, and they went to the land of Egypt.
>
> 6 And it came to pass when they came near Egypt, Jacob sent Judah before him to Joseph that he might show him a situation in Egypt, and Judah did according to the word of his father, and he hastened and ran and came to Joseph, and they assigned for them a place in the land of Goshen for all his household, and Judah returned and came along the road to his father.
>
> 7 And Joseph harnessed the chariot, and he assembled all his mighty men and his servants and all the officers of Egypt in order to go and meet his father Jacob, and Joseph's mandate was proclaimed in Egypt, saying, All that do not go to meet Jacob shall die.

8 And on the next day Joseph went forth with all Egypt a great and mighty host, all dressed in garments of fine linen and purple and with instruments of silver and gold and with their instruments of war with them.

9 And they all went to meet Jacob with all sorts of musical instruments, with drums and timbrels, strewing myrrh and aloes all along the road, and they all went after this fashion, and the earth shook at their shouting.

10 And all the women of Egypt went upon the roofs of Egypt and upon the walls to meet Jacob, and upon the head of Joseph was Pharaoh's regal crown, for Pharaoh had sent it unto him to put on at the time of his going to meet his father.

11 And when Joseph came within fifty cubits of his father, he alighted from the chariot and he walked toward his father, and when all the officers of Egypt and her nobles saw that Joseph had gone on foot toward his father, they also alighted and walked on foot toward Jacob.

12 And when Jacob approached the camp of Joseph, Jacob observed the camp that was coming toward him with Joseph, and it gratified him and Jacob was astonished at it.

13 And Jacob said unto Judah, Who is that man whom I see in the camp of Egypt dressed in kingly robes with a very red garment upon him and a royal crown upon his head, who has alighted from his chariot and is coming toward us? and Judah answered his father, saying, He is thy son Joseph the king; and Jacob rejoiced in seeing the glory of his son.

14 And Joseph came nigh unto his father and he bowed to his father, and all the men of the camp bowed to the ground with him before Jacob.

15 And behold Jacob ran and hastened to his son Joseph and fell upon his neck and kissed him, and they wept, and Joseph also embraced his father and kissed him, and they wept and all the people of Egypt wept with them.

16 And Jacob said unto Joseph, Now I will die cheerfully after I have seen thy face, that thou art still living and with glory.

17 And the sons of Jacob and their wives and their children and their servants, and all the household of Jacob wept exceedingly with Joseph, and they kissed him and wept greatly with him.

18 And Joseph and all his people returned afterward home to Egypt, and Jacob and his sons and all the children of his household came with Joseph to Egypt, and Joseph placed them in the best part of Egypt, in the land of Goshen.

19 And Joseph said unto his father and unto his brethren, I will go up and tell Pharaoh, saying, My brethren and my father's household and all belonging to them have come unto me, and behold they are in the land of Goshen.

20 And Joseph did so and took from his brethren Reuben, Issachar Zebulun and his brother Benjamin and he placed them before Pharaoh.

21 And Joseph spoke unto Pharaoh, saying, My brethren and my father's household and all belonging to them, together with their flocks and cattle have come unto me from the land of Canaan, to sojourn in Egypt; for the famine was sore upon them.

22 And Pharaoh said unto Joseph, Place thy father and brethren in the best part of the land, withhold not from them all that is good, and cause them to eat of the fat of the land.

23 And Joseph answered, saying, Behold I have stationed them in the land of Goshen, for they are shepherds, therefore let them remain in Goshen to feed their flocks apart from the Egyptians.

24 And Pharaoh said unto Joseph, Do with thy brethren all that they shall say unto thee; and the sons of Jacob bowed down to Pharaoh, and they went forth from him in peace, and Joseph afterward brought his father before Pharaoh.

25 And Jacob came and bowed down to Pharaoh, and Jacob blessed Pharaoh, and he then went out; and Jacob and all his sons, and all his household dwelt in the land of Goshen.

26 In the second year, that is in the hundred and thirtieth year of the life of Jacob, Joseph maintained his father and his brethren, and all his father's household, with bread according to their little ones, all the days of the famine; they lacked nothing.

27 And Joseph gave unto them the best part of the whole land; the best of Egypt had they all the days of Joseph; and Joseph also gave unto them and unto the whole of his father's household, clothes and garments year by year; and the sons of Jacob remained securely in Egypt all the days of their brother.

C.3 The final 'togetherness' of Jacob and all of his sons after more than 20 years leave of absence.

28 And Jacob always ate at Joseph's table, Jacob and his sons did not leave Joseph's table day or night, besides what Jacob's children consumed in their houses.

29 And all Egypt ate bread during the days of the famine from the house of Joseph, for all the Egyptians sold all belonging to them on account of the famine.

30 And Joseph purchased all the lands and fields of Egypt for bread on the account of Pharaoh, and Joseph supplied all Egypt with bread all the days of the famine, and Joseph collected all the silver and gold that came unto him for the corn which they bought throughout the land, and he accumulated much gold and silver, besides an immense quantity of onyx stones, bdellium and valuable garments which they brought unto Joseph from every part of the land when their money was spent.

31 And Joseph took all the silver and gold that came into his hand, about seventy two talents of gold and silver, and also onyx stones and bdellium in great abundance, and Joseph went and concealed them in four parts, and he concealed one part in the wilderness near the Red sea, and one part by the river Perath, and the third and fourth part he concealed in the desert opposite to the wilderness of Persia and Media.

32 And he took part of the gold and silver that was left, and gave it unto all his brothers and unto all his father's household, and unto all the women of his father's household, and the rest he brought to the house of Pharaoh, about twenty talents of gold and silver.

33 And Joseph gave all the gold and silver that was left unto Pharaoh, and Pharaoh placed it in the treasury, and the days of the famine ceased after that in the land, and they sowed and reaped in the whole land, and they obtained their usual quantity year by year; they lacked nothing.

34 And Joseph dwelt securely in Egypt, and the whole land was under his advice, and his father and all his brethren dwelt in the land of Goshen and took possession of it.

35 And Joseph was very aged, advanced in days, and his two sons, Ephraim and Manasseh, remained constantly in the house of Jacob, together with the children of the sons of Jacob their brethren, to learn the ways of the Lord and his law.

36 And Jacob and his sons dwelt in the land of Egypt in the land of Goshen, and they took possession in it, and they were fruitful and multiplied in it.

C.4 Jacob was separated from his family (mother and father) for 21, years whilst escaping from his corrupt brother Esau who wanted to kill him.

C.5 Jacob was tricked into having extra wives by his crooked uncle Laban, when he only wanted Rachel. He ended with her sister Leah as well. That was just the start of his being a husband, as Rachel gave Jacob an extra wife in her handmaiden, as she could not bare any children.

C.6 Later on, when Leah had paused in child-bearing, Leah then gave her hand-maiden to Jacob to wife, and thus he ended up with 4 wives which must have been quite a challenge; as one women wants all of a man's time - never mind four. If they all ganged up against him then his boat was sunk for sure!

C.7 Sadly, Jacob lost Rachel when she was only 46 years old. He also lost Leah when she was only 51 whilst Jacob was over 100 and ended up living until he was 147 years old. Rachel's handmaiden also died shortly after Rachel so that Jacob was left with only the handmaiden of Leah, as his wife. Then seemingly his son Joseph had been 'killed'. Jacob became so full of sorrow that he was inconsolable.

C.8 Jacob suffered a lot of pain and sorrow in his life, as well as extreme danger from enemies. However, all was part of God's greater plan to make him into the very great Patriarch of Jacob as we know him to be today, and whom many races trace their ancestry all the way back to his grand-father Abraham.

C.9 Thus, was it indeed fulfilled that Abraham would become the father of many nations in both his own sons through three wives and 2 concubines, but even more so through his grandson Jacob and his 4 wives.

Chapter 56

1 And Jacob lived in the land of Egypt seventeen years, and the days of Jacob, and the years of his life were a hundred and forty seven years.

2 At that time Jacob was attacked with that illness of which he died and he sent and called for his son Joseph from Egypt, and Joseph his son came from Egypt and Joseph came unto his father.

3 And Jacob said unto Joseph and unto his sons, Behold I die, and the God of your ancestors will visit you, and bring you back to the land, which the Lord sware to give unto you and unto your children after you, now therefore when I am dead, bury me in the cave which is in Machpelah in Hebron in the land of Canaan, near my ancestors.

4 And Jacob made his sons swear to bury him in Machpelah, in Hebron, and his sons swore unto him concerning this thing.

Comment:1: Machpelah was the double cave that Abraham had originally purchased in order to bury his wife Sarah. There is a great mystery behind this cave according to Jewish legend. According to the Jewish mystic book called the Zohar this double cave of Machpelah led down deep into the surface of the earth and ended up on the inside on the underside of a hollow earth where the Garden of Eden is supposed to be to this day. It would appear that the learned Jews have tried to keep the 'hidden secrets' from the Goyim as they call all none Jewish people. Fortunately, there are many friendly Jews willing to explain some of the mystical long-lost secrets of the Kabbalah and no more so than the mystical book of the Zohar.

C.2 As in regard to that which is supposed 'Hidden' knowledge:

LUK.12:3 Therefore whatsoever ye have spoken in darkness shall be heard in the light; and that which ye have spoken in the ear in closets shall be proclaimed upon the housetops.

5 And he commanded them, saying, Serve the Lord your God, for he who delivered your fathers will also deliver you from all trouble.

6 And Jacob said, Call all your children unto me, and all the children of Jacob's sons came and sat before him, and Jacob blessed them, and he said unto them, The Lord God of your fathers shall grant you a thousand times as much and bless you, and may he give you the blessing of

your father Abraham; and all the children of Jacob's sons went forth on that day after he had blessed them.

7 And on the next day Jacob again called for his sons, and they all assembled and came to him and sat before him, and Jacob on that day blessed his sons before his death, each man did he bless according to his blessing; behold it is written in the book of the law of the Lord appertaining to Israel.

8 And Jacob said unto Judah, I know my son that thou art a mighty man for thy brethren; reign over them, and thy sons shall reign over their sons forever.

C.3 Is it not amazing that although Judah was not the eldest of 11 brothers, he inherited the mantle of leadership of his entire family and his Tribe of Judah inherited the symbol of the Lion as Judah himself was indeed lion-hearted and was endowed with even more supernatural strength than his brothers Simeon and Levi. Eventually the Messiah Himself was the Lion to descend from the Tribe of Judah which was the Tribe of the Kings. So, God truly knew what He was doing when he made Judah the Tribe of the Kings.

9 Only teach thy sons the bow and all the weapons of war, in order that they may fight the battles of their brother who will rule over his enemies.

10 And Jacob again commanded his sons on that day, saying, Behold I shall be this day gathered unto my people; carry me up from Egypt, and bury me in the cave of Machpelah as I have commanded you.

11 Howbeit take heed I pray you that none of your sons carry me, only yourselves, and this is the manner you shall do unto me, when you carry my body to go with it to the land of Canaan to bury me,

12 Judah, Issachar and Zebulun shall carry my bier at the eastern side; Reuben, Simeon and Gad at the south, Ephraim, Manasseh and Benjamin at the west, Dan, Asher and Naphtali at the north.

C.4 Joseph and Levi are noticeably missing of the sons of Jacob. Why is that? Joseph was practically Pharaoh in Egypt and couldn't leave his post. Levi was given the special position of being the High Priest as his job was to carry the Ark of the covenant. As Joseph was unable to attend then he sent his two sons Ephraim and Manasseh to represents him in carrying his father's bier or coffin to the pre-arranged funeral place.

13 Let not Levi carry with you, for he and his sons will carry the ark of the covenant of the Lord with the Israelites in the camp, neither let Joseph my son carry, for as a king so let his glory be; howbeit, Ephraim and Manasseh shall be in their stead.

14 Thus shall you do unto me when you carry me away; do not neglect any thing of all that I command you; and it shall come to pass when you do this unto me, that the Lord will remember you favourably and your children after you forever.

15 And you my sons, honor each his brother and his relative, and command your children and your children's children after you to serve the Lord God of your ancestors all the days.

16 In order that you may prolong your days in the land, you and your children and your children's children for ever, when you do what is good and upright in the sight of the Lord your God, to go in all his ways.

17 And thou, Joseph my son, forgive I pray thee the prongs of thy brethren and all their misdeeds in the injury that they heaped upon thee, for God intended it for thine and thy children's benefit.

C.5 Joseph *was apparently present* at the funeral of his father but in a more official position and thus he sent his sons to actually physically carry the coffin of his beloved father. Jacob was imploring his son Joseph to forgive his brothers for having sold him into slavery when he was but 17 years old, as God Himself had intended it for their overall good.

18 And O my son leave not thy brethren to the inhabitants of Egypt, neither hurt their feelings, for behold I consign them to the hand of God and in thy hand to guard them from the Egyptians; and the sons of Jacob answered their father saying, O, our father, all that thou hast commanded us, so will we do; may God only be with us.

19 And Jacob said unto his sons, So may God be with you when you keep all his ways; turn not from his ways either to the right or the left in performing what is good and upright in his sight.

127

C.6 Prophecy by Jacob about the future bondage of the 'Children of Israel' in Egypt

20 For I know that many and grievous troubles will befall you in the latter days in the land, yea your children and children's children, only serve the Lord and he will save you from all trouble.

21 And it shall come to pass when you shall go after God to serve him and will teach your children after you, and your children's children, to know the Lord, then will the Lord raise up unto you and your children a servant from amongst your children, and the Lord will deliver you through his hand from all affliction, and bring you out of Egypt and bring you back to the land of your fathers to inherit it securely.

C.7 Jacob is prophesying right before his death that his son's descendants as Israel will go into bondage in Egypt. He also predicts that if they turn to the Lord then he will both save them and send them a deliverer.

22 And Jacob ceased commanding his sons, and he drew his feet into the bed, he died and was gathered to his people.

23 And Joseph fell upon his father and he cried out and wept over him and he kissed him, and he called out in a bitter voice, and he said, O my father, my father.

24 And his son's wives and all his household came and fell upon Jacob, and they wept over him, and cried in a very loud voice concerning Jacob.

25 And all the sons of Jacob rose up together, and they tore their garments, and they all put sackcloth upon their loins, and they fell upon their faces, and they cast dust upon their heads toward the heavens.

26 And the thing was told unto Osnath Joseph's wife, and she rose up and put on a sack and she with all the Egyptian women with her came and mourned and wept for Jacob.

27 And also all the people of Egypt who knew Jacob came all on that day when they heard this thing, and all Egypt wept for many days.

28 And also from the land of Canaan did the women come unto Egypt when they heard that Jacob was dead, and they wept for him in Egypt for seventy days.

29 And it came to pass after this that Joseph commanded his servants the doctors to embalm his father with myrrh and frankincense and all manner of incense and perfume, and the doctors embalmed Jacob as Joseph had commanded them.

30 And all the people of Egypt and the elders and all the inhabitants of the land of Goshen wept and mourned over Jacob, and all his sons and the children of his household lamented and mourned over their father Jacob many days.

31 And after the days of his weeping had passed away, at the end of seventy days, Joseph said unto Pharaoh, I will go up and bury my father in the land of Canaan as he made me swear, and then I will return.

32 And Pharaoh sent Joseph, saying, Go up and bury thy father as he said, and as he made thee swear; and Joseph rose up with all his brethren to go to the land of Canaan to bury their father Jacob as he had commanded them.

33 And Pharaoh commanded that it should be proclaimed throughout Egypt, saying, Whoever goeth not up with Joseph and his brethren to the land of Canaan to bury Jacob, shall die.

34 And all Egypt heard of Pharaoh's proclamation, and they all rose up together, and all the servants of Pharaoh, and the elders of his house, and all the elders of the land of Egypt went up with Joseph, and all the officers and nobles of Pharaoh went up as the servants of Joseph, and they went to bury Jacob in the land of Canaan.

35 And the sons of Jacob carried the bier upon which he lay; according to all that their father commanded them, so did his sons unto him.

36 And the bier was of pure gold, and it was inlaid roundabout with onyx stones and bdellium; and the covering of the bier was gold woven

work, joined with threads, and over them were hooks of onyx stones and bdellium.

37 And Joseph placed upon the head of his father Jacob a large golden crown, and he put a golden sceptre in his hand, and they surrounded the bier as was the custom of kings during their lives.

38 And all the troops of Egypt went before him in this array, at first all the mighty men of Pharaoh, and the mighty men of Joseph, and after them the rest of the inhabitants of Egypt, and they were all girded with swords and equipped with coats of mail, and the trappings of war were upon them.

39 And all the weepers and mourners went at a distance opposite to the bier, going and weeping and lamenting, and the rest of the people went after the bier.

40 And Joseph and his household went together near the bier barefooted and weeping, and the rest of Joseph's servants went around him; each man had his ornaments upon him, and they were all armed with their weapons of war.

41 And fifty of Jacob's servants went in front of the bier, and they strewed along the road myrrh and aloes, and all manner of perfume, and all the sons of Jacob that carried the bier walked upon the perfumery, and the servants of Jacob went before them strewing the perfume along the road.

42 And Joseph went up with a heavy camp, and they did after this manner every day until they reached the land of Canaan, and they came to the threshing floor of Atad, which was on the other side of Jordan, and they mourned an exceeding great and heavy mourning in that place.

43 And all the kings of Canaan heard of this thing and they all went forth, each man from his house, thirty-one kings of Canaan, and they all came with their men to mourn and weep over Jacob.

44 And all these kings beheld Jacob's bier, and behold Joseph's crown was upon it, and they also put their crowns upon the bier, and encircled it with crowns.

45 And all these kings made in that place a great and heavy mourning with the sons of Jacob and Egypt over Jacob, for all the kings of Canaan knew the valour of Jacob and his sons.

46 And the report reached Esau, saying, Jacob died in Egypt, and his sons and all Egypt are conveying him to the land of Canaan to bury him.

47 And Esau heard this thing, and he was dwelling in mount Seir, and he rose up with his sons and all his people and all his household, a people exceedingly great, and they came to mourn and weep over Jacob.

48 And it came to pass, when Esau came he mourned for his brother Jacob, and all Egypt and all Canaan again rose up and mourned a great mourning with Esau over Jacob in that place.

C.8 This Book of Jasher tells a different story than the Book of Jubilees. In the book of Jubilees, it states that Jacob had killed Esau his brother many years before Jacob died. What does the Bible say?

GEN.36:6 And Esau took his wives, and his sons, and his daughters, and all the persons of his house, and his cattle, and all his beasts, and all his substance, which he had got in the land of Canaan; and went into the country from the face of his brother Jacob.

GEN.36:7 For their riches were more than that they might dwell together; and the land wherein they were strangers could not bear them because of their cattle.

GEN.36:8 Thus dwelt Esau in mount Seir.

C.9 DIFFERENCES: In the Bible there is no indication that Jacob killed his brother Esau as mentioned in the Book of Jubilees or that Esau attended Jacob's funeral as in this book of Jasher. Which of these three books is correct as to the exact details? Well, it would appear that the Bible tends to give the overall story generally speaking. The book of Jasher, in particular, gives a lot more details, as does the book of Jubilees upon occasion. What to do, when one story clashes in content? Well, in my opinion, often it doesn't really matter which one is correct, as the general or main story remains the same.

GEN.49:33 And when Jacob had made an end of commanding his sons, he gathered up his feet into the bed, and yielded up the ghost, and was gathered unto his people.

49 And Joseph and his brethren brought their father Jacob from that place, and they went to Hebron to bury Jacob in the cave by his fathers.

50 And they came unto Kireath-arba, to the cave, and as they came Esau stood with his sons against Joseph and his brethren as a hindrance in the cave, saying, Jacob shall not be buried therein, for it belongeth to us and to our father.

51 And Joseph and his brethren heard the words of Esau's sons, and they were exceedingly wroth, and Joseph approached unto Esau, saying, What is this thing which they have spoken? surely my father Jacob bought it from thee for great riches after the death of Isaac, now five and twenty years ago, and also all the land of Canaan he bought from thee and from thy sons, and thy seed after thee.

52 And Jacob bought it for his sons and his seed after him for an inheritance for ever, and why speakest thou these things this day?

53 And Esau answered, saying, Thou speakest falsely and utterest lies, for I sold not anything belonging to me in all this land, as thou sayest, neither did my brother Jacob buy aught belonging to me in this land.

54 And Esau spoke these things in order to deceive Joseph with his words, for Esau knew that Joseph was not present in those days when Esau sold all belonging to him in the land of Canaan to Jacob.

55 And Joseph said unto Esau, Surely my father inserted these things with thee in the record of purchase, and testified the record with witnesses, and behold it is with us in Egypt.

56 And Esau answered, saying unto him, Bring the record, all that thou wilt find in the record, so will we do.

57 And Joseph called unto Naphtali his brother, and he said, Hasten quickly, stay not, and run I pray thee to Egypt and bring all the records; the record of the purchase, the sealed record and the open record, and also all the first records in which all the transactions of the birth-right are written, fetch thou.

58 And thou shalt bring them unto us hither, that we may know from them all the words of Esau and his sons which they spoke this day.

59 And Naphtali hearkened to the voice of Joseph and he hastened and ran to go down to Egypt, and Naphtali was lighter on foot than any of the stags that were upon the wilderness, for he would go upon ears of corn without crushing them.

60 And when Esau saw that Naphtali had gone to fetch the records, he and his sons increased their resistance against the cave, and Esau and all his people rose up against Joseph and his brethren to battle.

61 And all the sons of Jacob and the people of Egypt fought with Esau and his men, and the sons of Esau and his people were smitten before the sons of Jacob, and the sons of Jacob slew of Esau's people forty men.

62 And Chushim the son of Dan, the son of Jacob, was at that time with Jacob's sons, but he was about a hundred cubits distant from the place of battle, for he remained with the children of Jacob's sons by Jacob's bier to guard it.

63 And Chushim was dumb and deaf, still he understood the voice of consternation amongst men.

64 And he asked, saying, Why do you not bury the dead, and what is this great consternation? and they answered him the words of Esau and his sons; and he ran to Esau in the midst of the battle, and he slew Esau with a sword, and he cut off his head, and it sprang to a distance, and Esau fell amongst the people of the battle.

C.10 DIFFERENCES II This story of Esau being killed by Chushim is not mentioned in the Bible. In fact, the Bible simply does not mention Esau being killed at all. In the book of Jubilees, it states that Jacob killed his brother Esau by firing arrows at him from the city wall. Which story is right? Now that is a very good question. We know that Esau was a very violent and evil man - so the stories about his being killed by either Jacob himself or one of his sons are indeed very possible and even likely.

65 And when Chushim did this thing the sons of Jacob prevailed over the sons of Esau, and the sons of Jacob buried their father Jacob by force in the cave, and the sons of Esau beheld it.

66 And Jacob was buried in Hebron, in the cave of Machpelah which Abraham had bought from the sons of Heth for the possession of a burial place, and he was buried in very costly garments.

67 And no king had such honor paid him as Joseph paid unto his father at his death, for he buried him with great honor like unto the burial of kings.

68 And Joseph and his brethren made a mourning of seven days for their father.

Chapter 57

1 And it was after this that the sons of Esau waged war with the sons of Jacob, and the sons of Esau fought with the sons of Jacob in Hebron, and Esau was still lying dead, and not buried.

2 And the battle was heavy between them, and the sons of Esau were smitten before the sons of Jacob, and the sons of Jacob slew of the sons of Esau eighty men, and not one died of the people of the sons of Jacob; and the hand of Joseph prevailed over all the people of the sons of Esau, and he took Zepho, the son of Eliphaz, the son of Esau, and fifty of his men captive, and he bound them with chains of iron, and gave them into the hand of his servants to bring them to Egypt.

C.1 Notice how that Joseph took Zepho the grandson of Esau as a captive down to Egypt as he and his 50 well-trained warriors, were the ringleaders causing great trouble against Jacob's sons. Zepho eventually escaped his bondage in Egypt and became a famous warrior and a king in his own right.

3 And it came to pass when the sons of Jacob had taken Zepho and his people captive, all those that remained were greatly afraid of their lives from the house of Esau, lest they should also be taken captive, and they all fled with Eliphaz the son of Esau and his people, with Esau's body, and they went on their road to Mount Seir.

4 And they came unto Mount Seir and they buried Esau in Seir, but they had not brought his head with them to Seir, for it was buried in that place where the battle had been in Hebron.

5 And it came to pass when the sons of Esau had fled from before the sons of Jacob, the sons of Jacob pursued them unto the borders of Seir, but they did not slay a single man from amongst them when they pursued them, for Esau's body which they carried with them excited their confusion, so they fled and the sons of Jacob turned back from them and came up to the place where their brethren were in Hebron, and they remained there on that day, and on the next day until they rested from the battle.

6 And it came to pass on the third day they assembled all the sons of Seir the Horite, and they assembled all the children of the east, a multitude of people like the sand of the sea, and they went and came down to Egypt to fight with Joseph and his brethren, in order to deliver their brethren.

7 And Joseph and all the sons of Jacob heard that the sons of Esau and the children of the east had come upon them to battle in order to deliver their brethren.

8 And Joseph and his brethren and the strong men of Egypt went forth and fought in the city of Rameses, and Joseph and his brethren dealt out a tremendous blow amongst the sons of Esau and the children of the east.

9 And they slew of them six hundred thousand men, and they slew amongst them all the mighty men of the children of Seir the Horite; there were only a few of them left, and they slew also a great many of the children of the east, and of the children of Esau; and Eliphaz the son of Esau, and the children of the east all fled before Joseph and his brethren.

10 And Joseph and his brethren pursued them until they came unto Succoth, and they yet slew of them in Succoth thirty men, and the rest escaped, and they fled each to his city.

11 And Joseph and his brethren and the mighty men of Egypt turned back from them with joy and cheerfulness of heart, for they had smitten all their enemies.

12 And Zepho the son of Eliphaz and his men were still slaves in Egypt to the sons of Jacob, and their pains increased.

13 And when the sons of Esau and the sons of Seir returned to their land, the sons of Seir saw that they had all fallen into the hands of the sons of Jacob, and the people of Egypt, on account of the battle of the sons of Esau.

14 And the sons of Seir said unto the sons of Esau, You have seen and therefore you know that this camp was on your account, and not one mighty man or an adept in war remaineth.

15 Now therefore go forth from our land, go from us to the land of Canaan to the land of the dwelling of your fathers; wherefore shall your children inherit the effects of our children in latter days?

16 And the children of Esau would not listen to the children of Seir, and the children of Seir considered to make war with them.

17 And the children of Esau sent secretly to Angeas king of Africa, the same is Dinhabah, saying,

18 Send unto us some of thy men and let them come unto us, and we will fight together with the children of Seir the Horite, for they have resolved to fight with us to drive us away from the land.

19 And Angeas king of Dinhabah did so, for he was in those days friendly to the children of Esau, and Angeas sent five hundred valiant infantry to the children of Esau, and eight hundred cavalry.

20 And the children of Seir sent unto the children of the east and unto the children of Midian, saying, You have seen what the children of Esau have done unto us, upon whose account we are almost all destroyed, in their battle with the sons of Jacob.

21 Now therefore come unto us and assist us, and we will fight them together, and we will drive them from the land and be avenged of the cause of our brethren who died for their sakes in their battle with their brethren the sons of Jacob.

22 And all the children of the east listened to the children of Seir, and they came unto them about eight hundred men with drawn swords, and the children of Esau fought with the children of Seir at that time in the wilderness of Paran.

23 And the children of Seir prevailed then over the sons of Esau, and the

children of Seir slew on that day of the children of Esau in that battle about two hundred men of the people of Angeas king of Dinhabah.

24 And on the second day the children of Esau came again to fight a second time with the children of Seir, and the battle was sore upon the children of Esau this second time, and it troubled them greatly on account of the children of Seir.

25 And when the children of Esau saw that the children of Seir were more powerful than they were, some men of the children of Esau turned and assisted the children of Seir their enemies.

26 And there fell yet of the people of the children of Esau in the second battle fifty-eight men of the people at Angeas king of Dinhabah.

27 And on the third day the children of Esau heard that some of their brethren had turned from them to fight against them in the second battle; and the children of Esau mourned when they heard this thing.

28 And they said, What shall we do unto our brethren who turned from us to assist the children of Seir our enemies? and the children of Esau again sent to Angeas king of Dinhabah, saying,

29 Send unto us again other men that with them we may fight with the children of Seir, for they have already twice been heavier than we were.

30 And Angeas again sent to the children of Esau about six hundred valiant men, and they came to assist the children of Esau.

31 And in ten days' time the children of Esau again waged war with the children of Seir in the wilderness of Paran, and the battle was very severe upon the children of Seir, and the children of Esau prevailed at this time over the children of Seir, and the children of Seir were smitten before the children of Esau, and the children of Esau slew from them about two thousand men.

32 And all the mighty men of the children of Seir died in this battle, and there only remained their young children that were left in their cities.

33 And all Midian and the children of the east betook themselves to flight from the battle, and they left the children of Seir and fled when they saw that the battle was severe upon them, and the children of Esau pursued all the children of the east until they reached their land.

34 And the children of Esau slew yet of them about two hundred and fifty men and from the people of the children of Esau there fell in that battle about thirty men, but this evil came upon them through their brethren turning from them to assist the children of Seir the Horite, and the children of Esau again heard of the evil doings of their brethren, and they again mourned on account of this thing.

35 And it came to pass after the battle, the children of Esau turned back and came home unto Seir, and the children of Esau slew those who had remained in the land of the children of Seir; they slew also their wives and little ones, they left not a soul alive except fifty young lads and damsels whom they suffered to live, and the children of Esau did not put them to death, and the lads became their slaves, and the damsels they took for wives.

36 And the children of Esau dwelt in Seir in the place of the children of Seir, and they inherited their land and took possession of it.

37 And the children of Esau took all belonging in the land to the children of Seir, also their flocks, their bullocks and their goods, and all belonging to the children of Seir, did the children of Esau take, and the children of Esau dwelt in Seir in the place of the children of Seir unto this day, and the children of Esau divided the land into divisions to the five sons of Esau, according to their families.

38 And it came to pass in those days, that the children of Esau resolved to crown a king over them in the land of which they became possessed. And they said to each other, Not so, for he shall reign over us in our land, and we shall be under his counsel and he shall fight our battles, against our enemies, and they did so.

39 And all the children of Esau swore, saying, That none of their brethren should ever reign over them, but a strange man who is not of their

brethren, for the souls of all the children of Esau were embittered every man against his son, brother and friend, on account of the evil they sustained from their brethren when they fought with the children of Seir.

40 Therefore the sons of Esau swore, saying, From that day forward they would not choose a king from their brethren, but one from a strange land unto this day.

41 And there was a man there from the people of Angeas king of Dinhabah; his name was Bela the son of Beor, who was a very valiant man, beautiful and comely and wise in all wisdom, and a man of sense and counsel; and there was none of the people of Angeas like unto him.

42 And all the children of Esau took him and anointed him and they crowned him for a king, and they bowed down to him, and they said unto him, May the king live, may the king live.

43 And they spread out the sheet, and they brought him each man earrings of gold and silver or rings or bracelets, and they made him very rich in silver and in gold, in onyx stones and bdellium, and they made him a royal throne, and they placed a regal crown upon his head, and they built a palace for him and he dwelt therein, and he became king over all the children of Esau.

44 And the people of Angeas took their hire for their battle from the children of Esau, and they went and returned at that time to their master in Dinhabah.

45 And Bela reigned over the children of Esau thirty years, and the children of Esau dwelt in the land instead of the children of Seir, and they dwelt securely in their stead unto this day.

Chapter 58

1 And it came to pass in the thirty-second year of the Israelites going down to Egypt, that is in the seventy-first year of the life of Joseph, in that year died Pharaoh king of Egypt, and Magron his son reigned in his stead.

2 And Pharaoh commanded Joseph before his death to be a father to his son, Magron, and that Magron should be under the care of Joseph and under his counsel.

3 And all Egypt consented to this thing that Joseph should be king over them, for all the Egyptians loved Joseph as of heretofore, only Magron the son of Pharaoh sat upon, his father's throne, and he became king in those days in his father's stead.

4 Magron was forty-one years old when he began to reign, and forty years he reigned in Egypt, and all Egypt called his name Pharaoh after the name of his father, as it was their custom to do in Egypt to every king that reigned over them.

5 And it came to pass when Pharaoh reigned in his father's stead, he placed the laws of Egypt and all the affairs of government in the hand of Joseph, as his father had commanded him.

6 And Joseph became king over Egypt, for he superintended over all Egypt, and all Egypt was under his care and under his counsel, for all Egypt inclined to Joseph after the death of Pharaoh, and they loved him exceedingly to reign over them.

7 But there were some people amongst them, who did not like him, saying, No stranger shall reign over us; still the whole government of Egypt devolved in those days upon Joseph, after the death of Pharaoh, he being the regulator, doing as he liked throughout the land without any one interfering.

8 And all Egypt was under the care of Joseph, and Joseph made war with all his surrounding enemies, and he subdued them; also all the

land and all the Philistines, unto the borders of Canaan, did Joseph subdue, and they were all under his power and they gave a yearly tax unto Joseph.

9 And Pharaoh king of Egypt sat upon his throne in his father's stead, but he was under the control and counsel of Joseph, as he was at first under the control of his father.

10 Neither did he reign but in the land of Egypt only, under the counsel of Joseph, but Joseph reigned over the whole country at that time, from Egypt unto the great river Perath.

11 And Joseph was successful in all his ways, and the Lord was with him, and the Lord gave Joseph additional wisdom, and honor, and glory, and love toward him in the hearts of the Egyptians and throughout the land, and Joseph reigned over the whole country forty years.

12 And all the countries of the Philistines and Canaan and Zidon, and on the other side of Jordan, brought presents unto Joseph all his days, and the whole country was in the hand of Joseph, and they brought unto him a yearly tribute as it was regulated, for Joseph had fought against all his surrounding enemies and subdued them, and the whole country was in the hand of Joseph, and Joseph sat securely upon his throne in Egypt.

13 And also all his brethren the sons of Jacob dwelt securely in the land, all the days of Joseph, and they were fruitful and multiplied exceedingly in the land, and they served the Lord all their days, as their father Jacob had commanded them.

14 And it came to pass at the end of many days and years, when the children of Esau were dwelling quietly in their land with Bela their king, that the children of Esau were fruitful and multiplied in the land, and they resolved to go and fight with the sons of Jacob and all Egypt, and to deliver their brother Zepho, the son of Eliphaz, and his men, for they were yet in those days slaves to Joseph.

15 And the children of Esau sent unto all the children of the east, and they made peace with them, and all the children of the east came unto them to go with the children of Esau to Egypt to battle.

16 And there came also unto them of the people of Angeas, king of Dinhabah, and they also sent unto the children of Ishmael and they also came unto them.

17 And all this people assembled and came unto Seir to assist the children of Esau in their battle, and this camp was very large and heavy with people, numerous as the sand of the sea, about eight hundred thousand men, infantry and cavalry, and all these troops went down to Egypt to fight with the sons of Jacob, and they encamped by Rameses.

18 And Joseph went forth with his brethren with the mighty men of Egypt, about six hundred men, and they fought with them in the land of Rameses; and the sons of Jacob at that time again fought with the children of Esau, in the fiftieth year of the sons of Jacob going down to Egypt, that is the thirtieth year of the reign of Bela over the children of Esau in Seir.

Comment:1: It would appear that the numbers here must be wrong either unintentionally or deliberately but why? It is not normal to send only 600 warriors to fight against 800,000 soldiers. One is likely to get slaughtered. I think knowing that Egypt was all under the command of Joseph and that Egypt had a very mighty army, then the number should read 60,000 Egyptians. If Joseph defeated his enemies' army of 800,000 with only 60,000, then he had a very well-trained army indeed. I think it very unlikely that he had only 600 men, although I could be wrong.

C.2 We all know the story of Gideon in the Old Testament where Gideon with only 300 men totally routed the whole Midianite army, which was numbered as the 'sand on the seashore' or hundreds of thousands. So, in the case of God's hand doing a great miracle as He often did in Bible times, then I suppose Joseph could have defeated 800,000 troops of his enemies with only 600 men especially if God Himself was fighting for Israel?

JDG.7:7 And the LORD said unto Gideon, By the three hundred men that lapped will I save you and deliver the Midianites into thine hand: and let all the other people go every man unto his place.

JDG.7:12 And the Midianites and the Amalekites and all the children of the east lay along in the valley like grasshoppers for multitude; and their camels were without number, as the sand by the seaside for multitude.

C.3 In reading this book of Jasher, which I find amazingly interesting for many reasons, one notices that the numbers and dates are sometimes seemingly a bit 'off target' in some way when comparing with the Bible or even the book of Jubilees. Why is that? This is the reason I think that an otherwise 'excellent book' is not included as part of the modern canon, although it was considered part of the canon by the Jews themselves, and is seen as a dramatic history book of the Jews ancestors.

C.4 One thought I have on this is that some Jewish books were meant for the general public and some were supposed to be kept for only the 'initiated'. I wonder if originally, this 'Book of Jasher' was only supposed to be read by the initiated, and therefore someone important deliberately altered some of the 'dates and times' in this book knowing that it would therefore not become part of a recognized canon of scriptures. In spite of all that, I personally highly recommend this Book of Jasher as it does indeed reveal so much more information and adds many details to many of the Bible stories and thus making them sometimes even more miraculous and portrays God's people as being supernaturally protected by God Himself, which I think was indeed true.

---

19 And the Lord gave all the mighty men of Esau and the children of the east into the hand of Joseph and his brethren, and the people of the children of Esau and the children of the east were smitten before Joseph.

20 And of the people of Esau and the children of the east that were slain, there fell before the sons of Jacob about two hundred thousand men, and their king Bela the son of Beor fell with them in the battle, and when the children of Esau saw that their king had fallen in battle and was dead, their hands became weak in the combat.

21 And Joseph and his brethren and all Egypt were still smiting the people of the house of Esau, and all Esau's people were afraid of the sons of Jacob and fled from before them.

22 And Joseph and his brethren and all Egypt pursued them a day's journey, and they slew yet from them about three hundred men, continuing to smite them in the road; and they afterward turned back from them.

23 And Joseph and all his brethren returned to Egypt, not one man was missing from them, but of the Egyptians there fell twelve men.

---

24 And when Joseph returned to Egypt he ordered Zepho and his men to be additionally bound, and they bound them in irons and they increased their grief.

25 And all the people of the children of Esau, and the children of the east, returned in shame each unto his city, for all the mighty men that were with them had fallen in battle.

26 And when the children of Esau saw that their king had died in battle they hastened and took a man from the people of the children of the east; his name was Jobab the son of Zarach, from the land of Botzrah, and they caused him to reign over them instead of Bela their king.

27 And Jobab sat upon the throne of Bela as king in his stead, and Jobab reigned in Edom over all the children of Esau ten years, and the children of Esau went no more to fight with the sons of Jacob from that day forward, for the sons of Esau knew the valour of the sons of Jacob, and they were greatly afraid of them.

28 But from that day forward the children of Esau hated the sons of Jacob, and the hatred and enmity were very strong between them all the days, unto this day.

29 And it came to pass after this, at the end of ten years, Jobab, the son of Zarach, from Botzrah, died, and the children of Esau took a man whose name was Chusham, from the land of Teman, and they made him king over them instead of Jobab, and Chusham reigned in Edom over all the children of Esau for twenty years.

30 And Joseph, king of Egypt, and his brethren, and all the children of Israel dwelt securely in Egypt in those days, together with all the children of Joseph and his brethren, having no hindrance or evil accident and the land of Egypt was at that time at rest from war in the days of Joseph and his brethren.

Chapter 59

1 And these are the names of the sons of Israel who dwelt in Egypt, who had come with Jacob, all the sons of Jacob came unto Egypt, every man with his household.

2 The children of Leah were Reuben, Simeon, Levi, Judah, Issachar and Zebulun, and their sister Dinah.

3 And the sons of Rachel were Joseph and Benjamin.

4 And the sons of Zilpah, the handmaid of Leah, were Gad and Asher.

5 And the sons of Bilhah, the handmaid of Rachel, were Dan and Naphtali.

6 And these were their offspring that were born unto them in the land of Canaan, before they came unto Egypt with their father Jacob.

7 The sons of Reuben were Chanoch, Pallu, Chetzron and Carmi.

8 And the sons of Simeon were Jemuel, Jamin, Ohad, Jachin, Zochar and Saul, the son of the Canaanitish woman.

9 And the children of Levi were Gershon, Kehath and Merari, and their sister Jochebed, who was born unto them in their going down to Egypt.

10 And the sons of Judah were Er, Onan, Shelah, Perez and Zarach.

11 And Er and Onan died in the land of Canaan; and the sons of Perez were Chezron and Chamul.

12 And the sons of Issachar were Tola, Puvah, Job and Shomron.

13 And the sons of Zebulun were Sered, Elon and Jachleel, and the son of Dan was Chushim.

14 And the sons of Naphtali were Jachzeel, Guni, Jetzer and Shilam.

15 And the sons of Gad were Ziphion, Chaggi, Shuni, Ezbon, Eri, Arodi and Areli.

16 And the children of Asher were Jimnah, Jishvah, Jishvi, Beriah and their sister Serach; and the sons of Beriah were Cheber and Malchiel.

17 And the sons of Benjamin were Bela, Becher, Ashbel, Gera, Naaman, Achi, Rosh, Mupim, Chupim and Ord.

18 And the sons of Joseph, that were born unto him in Egypt, were Manasseh and Ephraim.

19 And all the souls that went forth from the loins of Jacob, were seventy souls; these are they who came with Jacob their father unto Egypt to dwell there: and Joseph and all his brethren dwelt securely in Egypt, and they ate of the best of Egypt all the days of the life of Joseph.

20 And Joseph lived in the land of Egypt ninety-three years, and Joseph reigned over all Egypt eighty years.

21 And when the days of Joseph drew nigh that he should die, he sent and called for his brethren and all his father's household, and they all came together and sat before him.

22 And Joseph said unto his brethren and unto the whole of his father's household, Behold I die, and God will surely visit you and bring you up from this land to the land which he swore to your fathers to give unto them.

23 And it shall be when God shall visit you to bring you up from here to the land of your fathers, then bring up my bones with you from here.

24 And Joseph made the sons of Israel to swear for their seed after them, saying, God will surely visit you and you shall bring up my bones with you from here.

GEN.50:25 And Joseph took an oath of the children of Israel, saying, God will surely visit you, and ye shall carry up my bones from hence.

---

25 And it came to pass after this that Joseph died in that year, the seventy-first year of the Israelites going down to Egypt.

26 And Joseph was one hundred and ten years old when he died in the land of Egypt, and all his brethren and all his servants rose up and they embalmed Joseph, as was their custom, and his brethren and all Egypt mourned over him for seventy days.

GEN.50:26 So Joseph died, being an hundred and ten years old: and they embalmed him, and he was put in a coffin in Egypt.

Comment:1: Joseph died at 110 years old. His brothers died from 114-138 years old. This fulfilled God's original promise before the Great Flood that He would begin to cut short the lifespan of mankind which used to be 900+. Joseph live circa 500 years after the Great Flood. About 800 years later King David died at 70 years old. Since King David's time around 1000 B.C.E mankind's average lifespan has been circa 70.

PSA.90:10 The days of our years are threescore years and ten; and if by reason of strength they be fourscore years, yet is their strength labour and sorrow; for it is soon cut off, and we fly away.

C.2 Joseph died at 110 years old. This was when the Children of Israel had been 71 years down in Egypt. It is important to take note of this as we will find that the total time that Israel was in Captivity was 430 years but that it did not start when Jacob went down to Egypt but 215 years before that when God made the promise to Abraham Jacob's grandfather. (**See APPENDIX**)

---

27 And they put Joseph in a coffin filled with spices and all sorts of perfume, and they buried him by the side of the river, that is Sihor, and his sons and all his brethren, and the whole of his father's household made a seven day's mourning for him.

28 And it came to pass after the death of Joseph, all the Egyptians began in those days to rule over the children of Israel, and Pharaoh, king of Egypt, who reigned in his father's stead, took all the laws of Egypt and conducted the whole government of Egypt under his counsel, and he reigned securely over his people.

Chapter 60

1 And when the year came round, being the seventy-second year from the Israelites going down to Egypt, after the death of Joseph, Zepho, the son of Eliphaz, the son of Esau, fled from Egypt, he and his men, and they went away.

2 And he came to Africa, which is Dinhabah, to Angeas king of Africa, and Angeas received them with great honor, and he made Zepho the captain of his host.

3 And Zepho found favour in the sight of Angeas and in the sight of his people, and Zepho was captain of the host to Angeas king of Africa for many days.

4 And Zepho enticed Angeas king of Africa to collect all his army to go and fight with the Egyptians, and with the sons of Jacob, and to avenge of them the cause of his brethren.

5 But Angeas would not listen to Zepho to do this thing, for Angeas knew the strength of the sons of Jacob, and what they had done to his army in their warfare with the children of Esau.

6 And Zepho was in those days very great in the sight of Angeas and in the sight of all his people, and he continually enticed them to make war against Egypt, but they would not.

7 And it came to pass in those days there was in the land of Chittim a man in the city of Puzimna, whose name was Uzu, and he became degenerately deified by the children of Chittim, and the man died and had no son, only one daughter whose name was Jania.

8 And the damsel was exceedingly beautiful, comely and intelligent, there was none seen like unto her for beauty and wisdom throughout the land.

9 And the people of Angeas king of Africa saw her and they came and praised her unto him, and Angeas sent to the children of Chittim, and

he requested to take her unto himself for a wife, and the people of Chittim consented to give her unto him for a wife.

10 And when the messengers of Angeas were going forth from the land of Chittim to take their journey, behold the messengers of Turnus king of Bibentu came unto Chittim, for Turnus king of Bibentu also sent his messengers to request Jania for him, to take unto himself for a wife, for all his men had also praised her to him, therefore he sent all his servants unto her.

11 And the servants of Turnus came to Chittim, and they asked for Jania, to be taken unto Turnus their king for a wife.

12 And the people of Chittim said unto them, We cannot give her, because Angeas king of Africa desired her to take her unto him for a wife before you came, and that we should give her unto him, and now therefore we cannot do this thing to deprive Angeas of the damsel in order to give her unto Turnus.

13 For we are greatly afraid of Angeas lest he come in battle against us and destroy us, and Turnus your master will not be able to deliver us from his hand.

14 And when the messengers of Turnus heard all the words of the children of Chittim, they turned back to their master and told him all the words of the children of Chittim.

15 And the children of Chittim sent a memorial to Angeas, saying, Behold Turnus has sent for Jania to take her unto him for a wife, and thus have we answered him; and we heard that he has collected his whole army to go to war against thee, and he intends to pass by the road of Sardunia to fight against thy brother Lucus, and after that he will come to fight against thee.

16 And Angeas heard the words of the children of Chittim which they sent to him in the record, and his anger was kindled and he rose up and assembled his whole army and came through the islands of the sea, the road to Sardunia, unto his brother Lucus king of Sardunia.

17 And Niblos, the son of Lucus, heard that his uncle Angeas was coming, and he went out to meet him with a heavy army, and he kissed him and embraced him, and Niblos said unto Angeas, When thou askest my father after his welfare, when I shall go with thee to fight with Turnus, ask of him to make me captain of his host, and Angeas did so, and he came unto his brother and his brother came to meet him, and he asked him after his welfare.

18 And Angeas asked his brother Lucus after his welfare, and to make his son Niblos captain of his host, and Lucus did so, and Angeas and his brother Lucus rose up and they went toward Turnus to battle, and there was with them a great army and a heavy people.

19 And he came in ships, and they came into the province of Ashtorash, and behold Turnus came toward them, for he went forth to Sardunia, and intended to destroy it and afterward to pass on from there to Angeas to fight with him.

20 And Angeas and Lucus his brother met Turnus in the valley of Canopia, and the battle was strong and mighty between them in that place.

21 And the battle was severe upon Lucus king of Sardunia, and all his army fell, and Niblos his son fell also in that battle.

22 And his uncle Angeas commanded his servants and they made a golden coffin for Niblos and they put him into it, and Angeas again waged battle toward Turnus, and Angeas was stronger than he, and he slew him, and he smote all his people with the edge of the sword, and Angeas avenged the cause of Niblos his brother's son and the cause of the army of his brother Lucus.

23 And when Turnus died, the hands of those that survived the battle became weak, and they fled from before Angeas and Lucus his brother.

24 And Angeas and his brother Lucus pursued them unto the highroad, which is between Alphanu and Romah, and they slew the whole army of Turnus with the edge of the sword.

151

25 And Lucus king of Sardunia commanded his servants that they should make a coffin of brass, and that they should place therein the body of his son Niblos, and they buried him in that place.

26 And they built upon it a high tower there upon the highroad, and they called its name after the name of Niblos unto this day, and they also buried Turnus king of Bibentu there in that place with Niblos.

27 And behold upon the highroad between Alphanu and Romah the grave of Niblos is on one side and the grave of Turnus on the other, and a pavement between them unto this day.

28 And when Niblos was buried, Lucus his father returned with his army to his land Sardunia, and Angeas his brother king of Africa went with his people unto the city of Bibentu, that is the city of Turnus.

29 And the inhabitants of Bibentu heard of his fame and they were greatly afraid of him, and they went forth to meet him with weeping and supplication, and the inhabitants of Bibentu entreated of Angeas not to slay them nor destroy their city; and he did so, for Bibentu was in those days reckoned as one of the cities of the children of Chittim; therefore he did not destroy the city.

30 But from that day forward the troops of the king of Africa would go to Chittim to spoil and plunder it, and whenever they went, Zepho the captain of the host of Angeas would go with them.

31 And it was after this that Angeas turned with his army and they came to the city of Puzimna, and Angeas took thence Jania the daughter of Uzu for a wife and brought her unto his city unto Africa.

Chapter 61

1 And it came to pass at that time Pharaoh king of Egypt commanded all his people to make for him a strong palace in Egypt.

2 And he also commanded the sons of Jacob to assist the Egyptians in the building, and the Egyptians made a beautiful and elegant palace for a royal habitation, and he dwelt therein and he renewed his government and he reigned securely.

3 And Zebulun the son of Jacob died in that year, that is the seventy-second year of the going down of the Israelites to Egypt, and Zebulun died a hundred and fourteen years old, and was put into a coffin and given into the hands of his children.

Comment:1: Here we finally see the sons of Jacob start dying off one after the other. First it was Joseph who died at the ripe old age of 110, which was much younger than his father Jacob at 147, & his grandfather Isaac at 180 and his great-grandfather Terah at 205.

C.2 Why the sudden drastic drop in lifespan? God had promised at the time of the Great Flood that He would heavily reduce the lifespan of mankind from what used to be over 900 years old down to 120 years old.

C.3 All this started to be finally fulfilled at this particular time at the death of the sons of Jacob or to be more exact around 500 years after the Great Flood. Why did this happen at this particular time? According to Creation scientists up until the Great Flood there used to be a protective canopy of water around the whole earth which shielded the earth from the bombardment of all kinds of particles from the sun and from space. In particular, the shielding protected humans from the radiation which caused us to age. Around 500 years after the Great Flood the full effects of not having the 'protective dome' over the heads of humanity so to speak had very serious impact on mankind's lifespan. http://www.6000years.org/frame. php?page=preflood_world

C.4 When Jacob was first born, Shem, the son of Noah was still alive and lived to be 600 years old. Arphaxad son of Shem, his son Selah and grandson Eber all lived to be between 400-500 years old. There was then another big jump down to 239 in Eber son Peleg as well as his son Reu 239 and grandson Serug 230. Serug's son Nahor was only 148, and his son Terah was 205. Finally, his son was Abraham who lived to be 175 years old. When Abraham was born Noah was still alive and lived to the amazing age of 950 years old. So, in summary we see that in the time of Abraham and his immediate descendants' mankind was reduced in lifespan from 950 years before the

Great Flood to around 110 years old between the time of Abraham and his grandson Jacob.

4 And in the seventy-fifth year died his brother Simeon, he was a hundred and twenty years old at his death, and he was also put into a coffin and given into the hands of his children.

5 And Zepho the son of Eliphaz the son of Esau, captain of the host to Angeas king of Dinhabah, was still daily enticing Angeas to prepare for battle to fight with the sons of Jacob in Egypt, and Angeas was unwilling to do this thing, for his servants had related to him all the might of the sons of Jacob, what they had done unto them in their battle with the children of Esau.

6 And Zepho was in those days daily enticing Angeas to fight with the sons of Jacob in those days.

7 And after some time Angeas hearkened to the words of Zepho and consented to him to fight with the sons of Jacob in Egypt, and Angeas got all his people in order, a people numerous as the sand which is upon the sea shore, and he formed his resolution to go to Egypt to battle.

8 And amongst the servants of Angeas was a youth fifteen years old, Balaam the son of Beor was his name and the youth was very wise and understood the art of witchcraft.

C.5 This character Balaam shows up many times in this book and he also appears several times in the Bible. Balaam was an 'Evil Sorcerer' and he often advised kings of nations for a price, including Angeas and the Pharaoh of Egypt. He was originally from Mesopotamia and was capable of doing many dark arts and magical spells and was one of the magicians who eventually withstood Moses in the presence of Pharaoh. That was right before God destroyed Egypt by the hand of Moses.

9 And Angeas said unto Balaam, 'Conjure for us, I pray thee, with the witchcraft, that we may know who will prevail in this battle to which we are now proceeding'.

10 And Balaam ordered that they should bring him wax, and he made thereof the likeness of chariots and horsemen representing the army of Angeas and the army of Egypt, and he put them in the cunningly

prepared waters that he had for that purpose, and he took in his hand the boughs of myrtle trees, and he exercised his cunning, and he joined them over the water, and there appeared unto him in the water the resembling images of the hosts of Angeas falling before the resembling images of the Egyptians and the sons of Jacob.

11 And Balaam told this thing to Angeas, and Angeas despaired and did not arm himself to go down to Egypt to battle, and he remained in his city.

12 And when Zepho the son of Eliphaz saw that Angeas despaired of going forth to battle with the Egyptians, Zepho fled from Angeas from Africa, and he went and came unto Chittim.

13 And all the people of Chittim received him with great honor, and they hired him to fight their battles all the days, and Zepho became exceedingly rich in those days, and the troops of the king of Africa still spread themselves in those days, and the children of Chittim assembled and went to Mount Cuptizia on account of the troops of Angeas king of Africa, who were advancing upon them.

14 And it was one day that Zepho lost a young heifer, and he went to seek it, and he heard it lowing round about the mountain.

15 And Zepho went and he saw and behold there was a large cave at the bottom of the mountain, and there was a great stone there at the entrance of the cave, and Zepho split the stone and he came into the cave and he looked and behold, a large animal was devouring the ox; from the middle upward it resembled a man, and from the middle downward it resembled an animal, and Zepho rose up against the animal and slew it with his swords.

C.6 Here we have another story about hybrids or half-human animal hybrids. Quite an amazing story. We also read about other human-animal chimeras earlier in this book. How did they come into being after the Great Flood? We know that they had existed in Pre-flood times, but how did they come into existence after the Great Flood? It is not the first time that I have heard about that these types of creatures hiding in caves. There was a giant some 30 feet high found alive in a cave in Afghanistan by the USA special forces. He was very big and devoured some of the American soldiers before finally being killed. This was only a few years ago. Somehow or other both giants and hybrid chimeras do still exist and have been seen by many people upon occasion. (**SOURCE:** https://www.genesis6giants.com/)

C.7 The first chimera story happened in this Book of Jasher in chapter 37. Here are the relevant verses:

JASHER 37.31 *And afterward about one hundred and twenty great and terrible animals came out from the wilderness at the other side of the sea, and they all came to the place where the asses were, and they placed themselves there.*

JASHER 37.32 *And those animals, from their middle downward, were in the shape of the children of men, and from their middle upward, some had the likeness of bears, and some the likeness of the keephas, with tails behind them from between their shoulders reaching down to the earth, like the tails of the ducheephath, and these animals came and mounted and rode upon these asses, and led them away, and they went away unto this day.*

C.8 COMPARISON: In the above-mentioned two examples of human-animal hybrids they were both very different from each other in form. The first type are Human-Animal Hybrids & the 2nd type were animal-human hybrids. Very odd descriptions of mythological creatures. Some had heads and the top half of the creature as an animal and the bottom half as a human whilst the other type had the top half as a human and the bottom half as a beast.

C.9 HYBRIDS is a very big topic which I covered in detail in my book **'ENOCH INSIGHTS'**.

C.10 TRANSHUMANISM: There is quite a contrast between why hybrids of all sorts came into being in Pre-Flood times as opposed to why would scientists today would want to tinker around with genetic engineering? **TRANSHUMANISM:** https://youtu.be/LWHNWBN2gwU?t=613

C.11 Anyone who has watched any kind of super-heroes such as X-Men or Superman or Batman or Spiderman, will get the idea that man wants to make himself greater than has been created by God. Why? How to do it?

> 16 And the inhabitants of Chittim heard of this thing, and they rejoiced exceedingly, and they said, What shall we do unto this man who has slain this animal that devoured our cattle?

C.12 This hybrid had been a big nuisance and had been devouring the cattle of the local people. So, hybrids have a bad reputation for being extremely dangerous and destructive.

> 17 And they all assembled to consecrate one day in the year to him, and they called the name thereof Zepho after his name, and they brought unto him drink offerings year after year on that day, and they brought unto him gifts.

18 At that time Jania the daughter of Uzu wife of king Angeas became ill, and her illness was heavily felt by Angeas and his officers, and Angeas said unto his wise men, What shall I do to Jania and how shall I heal her from her illness? And his wise men said unto him, Because the air of our country is not like the air of the land of Chittim, and our water is not like their water, therefore from this has the queen become ill.

19 For through the change of air and water she became ill, and also because in her country she drank only the water which came from Purmah, which her ancestors had brought up with bridges.

20 And Angeas commanded his servants, and they brought unto him in vessels of the waters of Purmah belonging to Chittim, and they weighed those waters with all the waters of the land of Africa, and they found those waters lighter than the waters of Africa.

21 And Angeas saw this thing, and he commanded all his officers to assemble the hewers of stone in thousands and tens of thousands, and they hewed stone without number, and the builders came and they built an exceedingly strong bridge, and they conveyed the spring of water from the land of Chittim unto Africa, and those waters were for Jania the queen and for all her concerns, to drink from and to bake, wash and bathe therewith, and also to water therewith all seed from which food can be obtained, and all fruit of the ground.

22 And the king commanded that they should bring of the soil of Chittim in large ships, and they also brought stones to build therewith, and the builders built palaces for Jania the queen, and the queen became healed of her illness.

23 And at the revolution of the year the troops of Africa continued coming to the land of Chittim to plunder as usual, and Zepho son of Eliphaz heard their report, and he gave orders concerning them and he fought with them, and they fled before him, and he delivered the land of Chittim from them.

24 And the children of Chittim saw the valour of Zepho, and the children of Chittim resolved and they made Zepho king over them, and he

became king over them, and whilst he reigned, they went to subdue the children of Tubal, and all the surrounding islands.

25 And their king Zepho went at their head and they made war with Tubal and the islands, and they subdued them, and when they returned from the battle they renewed his government for him, and they built for him a very large palace for his royal habitation and seat, and they made a large throne for him, and Zepho reigned over the whole land of Chittim and over the land of Italia fifty years.

Chapter 62

1 In that year, being the seventy-ninth year of the Israelites going down to Egypt, died Reuben the son of Jacob, in the land of Egypt; Reuben was a hundred and twenty-five years old when he died, and they put him into a coffin, and he was given into the hands of his children.

Comment:1: Reuben of Jacob's 12 sons died at 125, and his brother Dan at 120 years old. His brother Issachar at 122, Asher at 123 and Gad at 125 years old respectively. All died around the age of 120 or the exact age God said that He had now allotted to mankind after the Great Flood.

2 And in the eightieth year died his brother Dan; he was a hundred and twenty years at his death, and he was also put into a coffin and given into the hands of his children.

3 And in that year died Chusham king of Edom, and after him reigned Hadad the son of Bedad, for thirty-five years; and in the eighty-first year died Issachar the son of Jacob, in Egypt, and Issachar was a hundred and twenty-two years old at his death, and he was put into a coffin in Egypt, and given into the hands of his children.

4 And in the eighty-second year died Asher his brother, he was a hundred and twenty-three years old at his death, and he was placed in a coffin in Egypt, and given into the hands of his children.

5 And in the eighty-third year died Gad, he was a hundred and twenty-five years old at his death, and he was put into a coffin in Egypt, and given into the hands of his children.

6 And it came to pass in the eighty-fourth year, that is the fiftieth year of the reign of Hadad, son of Bedad, king of Edom, that Hadad assembled all the children of Esau, and he got his whole army in readiness, about four hundred thousand men, and he directed his way to the land of Moab, and he went to fight with Moab and to make them tributary to him.

7 And the children of Moab heard this thing, and they were very much afraid, and they sent to the children of Midian to assist them in fighting with Hadad, son of Bedad, king of Edom.

8 And Hadad came unto the land of Moab, and Moab and the children of Midian went out to meet him, and they placed themselves in battle array against him in the field of Moab.

9 And Hadad fought with Moab, and there fell of the children of Moab and the children of Midian many slain ones, about two hundred thousand men.

10 And the battle was very severe upon Moab, and when the children of Moab saw that the battle was sore upon them, they weakened their hands and turned their backs, and left the children of Midian to carry on the battle.

11 And the children of Midian knew not the intentions of Moab, but they strengthened themselves in battle and fought with Hadad and all his host, and all Midian fell before him.

12 And Hadad smote all Midian with a heavy smiting, and he slew them with the edge of the sword, he left none remaining of those who came to assist Moab.

13 And when all the children of Midian had perished in battle, and the children at Moab had escaped, Hadad made all Moab at that time tributary to him, and they became under his hand, and they gave a yearly tax as it was ordered, and Hadad turned and went back to his land.

14 And at the revolution of the year, when the rest of the people of Midian that were in the land heard that all their brethren had fallen in battle with Hadad for the sake of Moab, because the children of Moab had turned their backs in battle and left Midian to fight, then five of the princes of Midian resolved with the rest of their brethren who remained in their land, to fight with Moab to avenge the cause of their brethren.

15 And the children of Midian sent to all their brethren the children of the east, and all their brethren, all the children of Keturah came to assist Midian to fight with Moab.

16 And the children of Moab heard this thing, and they were greatly afraid that all the children of the east had assembled together against them for battle, and they the children of Moab sent a memorial to the land of Edom to Hadad the son of Bedad, saying,

17 Come now unto us and assist us and we will smite Midian, for they all assembled together and have come against us with all their brethren the children of the east to battle, to avenge the cause of Midian that fell in battle.

18 And Hadad, son of Bedad, king of Edom, went forth with his whole army and went to the land of Moab to fight with Midian, and Midian and the children of the east fought with Moab in the field of Moab, and the battle was very fierce between them.

19 And Hadad smote all the children of Midian and the children of the east with the edge of the sword, and Hadad at that time delivered Moab from the hand of Midian, and those that remained of Midian and of the children of the east fled before Hadad and his army, and Hadad pursued them to their land, and smote them with a very heavy slaughter, and the slain fell in the road.

20 And Hadad delivered Moab from the hand of Midian, for all the children of Midian had fallen by the edge of the sword, and Hadad turned and went back to his land.

21 And from that day forth, the children of Midian hated the children of Moab, because they had fallen in battle for their sake, and there was a great and mighty enmity between them all the days.

22 And all that were found of Midian in the road of the land of Moab perished by the sword of Moab, and all that were found of Moab in the road of the land of Midian, perished by the sword of Midian; thus did Midian unto Moab and Moab unto Midian for many days.

23 And it came to pass at that time that Judah the son of Jacob died in Egypt, in the eighty-sixth year of Jacob's going down to Egypt, and Judah was a hundred and twenty-nine years old at his death, and they

embalmed him and put him into a coffin, and he was given into the hands of his children.

C.2 Here we see most of the remaining sons of Jacob dying off: Judah at 129 and Naphali at 132 years old.

24 And in the eighty-ninth, year died Naphtali, he was a hundred and thirty-two years old, and he was put into a coffin and given into the hands of his children.

25 And it came to pass in the ninety-first year of the Israelites going down to Egypt, that is in the thirtieth year of the reign of Zepho the son of Eliphaz, the son of Esau, over the children of Chittim, the children of Africa came upon the children of Chittim to plunder them as usual, but they had not come upon them for these thirteen years.

26 And they came to them in that year, and Zepho the son of Eliphaz went out to them with some of his men and smote them desperately, and the troops of Africa fled from before Zepho and the slain fell before him, and Zepho and his men pursued them, going on and smiting them until they were near unto Africa.

27 And Angeas king of Africa heard the thing which Zepho had done, and it vexed him exceedingly, and Angeas was afraid of Zepho all the days.

Chapter 63

> 1 And in the ninety-third year died Levi, the son of Jacob, in Egypt, and Levi was a hundred and thirty-seven years old when he died, and they put him into a coffin, and he was given into the hands of his children.

Comment:1: Finally, we see the last of Jacob's sons Levi dying at the ripe old age of 137 years old.

> 2 And it came to pass after the death of Levi, when all Egypt saw that the sons of Jacob the brethren of Joseph were dead, all the Egyptians began to afflict the children of Jacob, and to embitter their lives from that day unto the day of their going forth from Egypt, and they took from their hands all the vineyards and fields which Joseph had given unto them, and all the elegant houses in which the people of Israel lived, and all the fat of Egypt, the Egyptians took all from the sons of Jacob in those days.

C.2 So, a new Pharaoh arose who 'knew not Joseph'. So much for being thankful unto the sons of Jacob for having faithfully fought for Egypt all of their lives. As soon as they were dead, the Egyptians took away all of the wealth and riches of their descendants, that they had gotten from Egypt, and started to afflict them and cause them to become mere slaves, forcing them to build the big stone monuments as well as the big cities of Egypt of Pithom and Raamses.

EXO.1:8 Now there arose up a new king over Egypt, which knew not Joseph.

EXO.1:9 And he said unto his people, Behold, the people of the children of Israel are more and mightier than we:

EXO.1:10 Come on, let us deal wisely with them; lest they multiply, and it come to pass, that, when there falls out any war, they join also unto our enemies, and fight against us, and so get them up out of the land.

EXO.1:11 Therefore they did set over them taskmasters to afflict them with their burdens. And they built for Pharaoh treasure cities, Pithom and Raamses.

> 3 And the hand of all Egypt became more grievous in those days against the children of Israel, and the Egyptians injured the Israelites until the children of Israel were wearied of their lives on account of the Egyptians.

4 And it came to pass in those days, in the hundred and second year of Israel's going down to Egypt, that Pharaoh king of Egypt died, and Melol his son reigned in his stead, and all the mighty men of Egypt and all that generation which knew Joseph and his brethren died in those days.

C.3 This gives some interesting time details, as it shows that the Children of Israel had only been down in Egypt around 100 years when the new Pharaoh started to afflict them, making them into slaves. Understanding these dates is very important. See the APPENDIX concerning the 400 years of Captivity of the Jews, as to when it started and when it ended. This is also very important information, as from it we can together with biblical time charts, discover exactly how old the earth is and know exactly what the real date is today since creation. I recently discovered that the earth according to revised biblical time charts is 5993 years old, in this year of 2018 and not 6178 years old as previously reported by certain biblical time charts.

5 And another generation rose up in their stead, which had not known the sons of Jacob and all the good which they had done to them, and all their might in Egypt.

6 Therefore all Egypt began from that day forth to embitter the lives of the sons of Jacob, and to afflict them with all manner of hard labour, because they had not known their ancestors who had delivered them in the days of the famine.

7 And this was also from the Lord, for the children of Israel, to benefit them in their latter days, in order that all the children of Israel might know the Lord their God.

8 And in order to know the signs and mighty wonders which the Lord would do in Egypt on account of his people Israel, in order that the children of Israel might fear the Lord God of their ancestors, and walk in all his ways, they and their seed after them all the days.

9 Melol was twenty years old when he began to reign, and he reigned ninety-four years, and all Egypt called his name Pharaoh after the name of his father, as it was their custom to do to every king who reigned over them in Egypt.

10 At that time all the troops of Angeas king of Africa went forth to spread along the land of Chittim as usual for plunder.

11 And Zepho the son of Eliphaz the son of Esau heard their report, and he went forth to meet them with his army, and he fought them there in the road.

12 And Zepho smote the troops of the king of Africa with the edge of the sword, and left none remaining of them, and not even one returned to his master in Africa.

13 And Angeas heard of this which Zepho the son of Eliphaz had done to all his troops, that he had destroyed them, and Angeas assembled all his troops, all the men of the land of Africa, a people numerous like the sand by the seashore.

14 And Angeas sent to Lucus his brother, saying, Come to me with all thy men and help me to smite Zepho and all the children of Chittim who have destroyed my men, and Lucus came with his whole army, a very great force, to assist Angeas his brother to fight with Zepho and the children of Chittim.

15 And Zepho and the children of Chittim heard this thing, and they were greatly afraid and a great terror fell upon their hearts.

16 And Zepho also sent a letter to the land of Edom to Hadad the son of Bedad king of Edom and to all the children of Esau, saying,

17 I have heard that Angeas king of Africa is coming to us with his brother for battle against us, and we are greatly afraid of him, for his army is very great, particularly as he comes against us with his brother and his army likewise.

18 Now therefore come you also up with me and help me, and we will fight together against Angeas and his brother Lucus, and you will save us out of their hands, but if not, know ye that we shall all die.

19 And the children of Esau sent a letter to the children of Chittim and to Zepho their king, saying, We cannot fight against Angeas and his

people for a covenant of peace has been between us these many years, from the days of Bela the first king, and from the days of Joseph the son of Jacob king of Egypt, with whom we fought on the other side of Jordan when he buried his father.

20 And when Zepho heard the words of his brethren the children of Esau he refrained from them, and Zepho was greatly afraid of Angeas.

21 And Angeas and Lucus his brother arrayed all their forces, about eight hundred thousand men, against the children of Chittim.

22 And all the children of Chittim said unto Zepho, Pray for us to the God of thy ancestors, peradventure he may deliver us from the hand of Angeas and his army, for we have heard that he is a great God and that he delivers all who trust in him.

C.4 This is very interesting, that the people of Chittim realized that Zepho himself was a descendant of Abraham and that if he prayed to Abraham's God that God Himself might assist Zepho in his war against Angeas the king of Africa who used to be Zepho's overlord when Zepho used to be the commander of Angeas army in Africa some years before.

23 And Zepho heard their words, and Zepho sought the Lord and he said,

24 0 Lord God of Abraham and Isaac my ancestors, this day I know that thou art a true God, and all the gods of the nations are vain and useless.

25 Remember now this day unto me thy covenant with Abraham our father, which our ancestors related unto us, and do graciously with me this day for the sake of Abraham and Isaac our fathers, and save me and the children of Chittim from the hand of the king of Africa who comes against us for battle.

C.5 Because Zepho the grandson of Esau Jacob's brother sought the Lord in prayer God heard his prayer and delivered him from his enemies. So much so that Zepho ended up being king of Chittim for 40 years without being defeated in war. He only gets defeated when trying incessantly to fight against the descendants of Jacob at one battle or the other, but he never succeeds against them, but he does defeat all of his other enemies.

26 And the Lord hearkened to the voice of Zepho, and he had regard for him on account of Abraham and Isaac, and the Lord delivered Zepho and the children of Chittim from the hand of Angeas and his people.

27 And Zepho fought Angeas king of Africa and all his people on that day, and the Lord gave all the people of Angeas into the hands of the children of Chittim.

28 And the battle was severe upon Angeas, and Zepho smote all the men of Angeas and Lucus his brother, with the edge of the sword, and there fell from them unto the evening of that day about four hundred thousand men.

C.6 That is a lot of soldiers to die: 400,000 in one day. It sounds unusually high and could be an embellished number.

29 And when Angeas saw that all his men perished, he sent a letter to all the inhabitants of Africa to come to him, to assist him in the battle, and he wrote in the letter, saying, All who are found in Africa let them come unto me from ten years old and upward; let them all come unto me, and behold if he comes not he shall die, and all that he has, with his whole household, the king will take.

C.7 Think how cruel that is to demand that every male over the age of 10 years old must come to the battle and fight for the African king. Utter madness!

30 And all the rest of the inhabitants of Africa were terrified at the words of Angeas, and there went out of the city about three hundred thousand men and boys, from ten years upward, and they came to Angeas.

31 And at the end of ten days Angeas renewed the battle against Zepho and the children of Chittim, and the battle was very great and strong between them.

32 And from the army of Angeas and Lucus, Zepho sent many of the wounded unto his hand, about two thousand men, and Sosiphtar the captain of the host of Angeas fell in that battle.

33 And when Sosiphtar had fallen, the African troops turned their backs to flee, and they fled, and Angeas and Lucus his brother were with them.

34 And Zepho and the children of Chittim pursued them, and they smote them still heavily on the road, about two hundred men, and they pursued Azdrubal the son of Angeas who had fled with his father, and they smote twenty of his men in the road, and Azdrubal escaped from the children of Chittim, and they did not slay him.

35 And Angeas and Lucus his brother fled with the rest of their men, and they escaped and came into Africa with terror and consternation, and Angeas feared all the days lest Zepho the son of Eliphaz should go to war with him.

Chapter 64

1 And Balaam the son of Beor was at that time with Angeas in the battle, and when he saw that Zepho prevailed over Angeas, he fled from there and came to Chittim.

C.1 What a two-faced rogue this Balaam 'Sorcerer' character was. He basically wanted to be in the kingdom that was the triumphant one. He first lived in Mesopotamia then Africa, then Chittim and finally Egypt in the time of Moses. No sense of conviction as to what is right and wrong and no loyalty to any particular nation – just hiring one's talents of witchcraft out to the highest bidder. This Balaam sounds a lot like the modern 'Merchants of the Earth', who are not loyal to any given country, but to those who give them the most wealth and power and control and influence. I will write more about this particular nasty character Balaam in succeeding chapters as he is also mentioned quite a bit in the Bible.

REV.18:23 And the light of a candle shall shine no more at all in thee; and the voice of the bridegroom and of the bride shall be heard no more at all in thee: for thy merchants were the great men of the earth; for by thy sorceries were all nations deceived.

2 And Zepho and the children of Chittim received him with great honor, for Zepho knew Balaam's wisdom, and Zepho gave unto Balaam many gifts and he remained with him.

3 And when Zepho had returned from the war, he commanded all the children of Chittim to be numbered who had gone into battle with him and behold not one was missed.

4 And Zepho rejoiced at this thing, and he renewed his kingdom, and he made a feast to all his subjects.

5 But Zepho remembered not the Lord and considered not that the Lord had helped him in battle, and that he had delivered him and his people from the hand of the king of Africa, but still walked in the ways of the children of Chittim and the wicked children of Esau, to serve other gods which his brethren the children of Esau had taught him; it is therefore said, From the wicked goes forth wickedness.

C.2 This the exact same expression used earlier in this very book to describe both Nimrod and his son Mardon 'From the wicked goes forth wickedness.'

6 And Zepho reigned over all the children of Chittim securely, but knew not the Lord who had delivered him and all his people from the hand of the king of Africa; and the troops of Africa came no more to Chittim to plunder as usual, for they knew of the power of Zepho who had smitten them all at the edge of the sword, so Angeas was afraid of Zepho the son of Eliphaz, and of the children of Chittim all the days.

7 At that time when Zepho had returned from the war, and when Zepho had seen how he prevailed over all the people of Africa and had smitten them in battle at the edge of the sword, then Zepho advised with the children of Chittim, to go to Egypt to fight with the sons of Jacob and with Pharaoh king of Egypt.

8 For Zepho heard that the mighty men of Egypt were dead and that Joseph and his brethren the sons at Jacob were dead, and that all their children the children of Israel remained in Egypt.

9 And Zepho considered to go to fight against them and all Egypt, to avenge the cause of his brethren the children of Esau, whom Joseph with his brethren and all Egypt had smitten in the land of Canaan, when they went up to bury Jacob in Hebron.

10 And Zepho sent messengers to Hadad, son of Bedad, king of Edom, and to all his brethren the children of Esau, saying,

11 Did you not say that you would not fight against the king of Africa for he is a member of your covenant? behold I fought with him and smote him and all his people.

12 Now therefore I have resolved to fight against Egypt and the children of Jacob who are there, and I will be revenged of them for what Joseph, his brethren and ancestors did to us in the land of Canaan when they went up to bury their father in Hebron.

13 Now then if you are willing to come to me to assist me in fighting against them and Egypt, then shall we avenge the cause of our brethren.

14 And the children of Esau hearkened to the words of Zepho, and the children of Esau gathered themselves together, a very great people, and they went to assist Zepho and the children of Chittim in battle.

15 And Zepho sent to all the children of the east and to all the children of Ishmael with words like unto these, and they gathered themselves and came to the assistance of Zepho and the children of Chittim in the war upon Egypt.

16 And all these kings, the king of Edom and the children of the east, and all the children of Ishmael, and Zepho the king of Chittim went forth and arrayed all their hosts in Hebron.

17 And the camp was very heavy, extending in length a distance of three days' journey, a people numerous as the sand upon the seashore which cannot be counted.

18 And all these kings and their hosts went down and came against all Egypt in battle and encamped together in the valley of Pathros.

19 And all Egypt heard their report, and they also gathered themselves together, all the people of the land of Egypt, and of all the cities belonging to Egypt, about three hundred thousand men.

20 And the men of Egypt sent also to the children of Israel who were in those days in the land of Goshen, to come to them in order to go and fight with these kings.

21 And the men of Israel assembled and were about one hundred and fifty men, and they went into battle to assist the Egyptians.

22 And the men of Israel and of Egypt went forth, about three hundred thousand men and one hundred and fifty men, and they went toward these kings to battle, and they placed themselves from without the land of Goshen opposite Pathros.

23 And the Egyptians believed not in Israel to go with them in their camps together for battle, for all the Egyptians said, Perhaps the chil-

dren of Israel will deliver us into the hand of the children of Esau and Ishmael, for they are their brethren.

24 And all the Egyptians said unto the children of Israel, Remain you here together in your stand and we will go and fight against the children of Esau and Ishmael, and if these kings should prevail over us, then come you altogether upon them and assist us, and the children of Israel did so.

25 And Zepho the son of Eliphaz the son of Esau king of Chittim, and Hadad the son of Bedad king of Edom, and all their camps, and all the children of the east, and children of Ishmael, a people numerous as sand, encamped together in the valley of Pathros opposite Tachpanches.

26 And Balaam the son of Beor the Syrian was there in the camp of Zepho, for he came with the children of Chittim to the battle, and Balaam was a man highly honoured in the eyes of Zepho and his men.

27 And Zepho said unto Balaam, try by divination for us that we may know who will prevail in the battle, we or the Egyptians.

28 And Balaam rose up and tried the art of divination, and he was skilful in the knowledge of it, but he was confused, and the work was destroyed in his hand.

29 And he tried it again but it did not succeed, and Balaam despaired of it and left it and did not complete it, for this was from the Lord, in order to cause Zepho and his people to fall into the hand of the children of Israel, who had trusted in the Lord, the God of their ancestors, in their war.

30 And Zepho and Hadad put their forces in battle array, and all the Egyptians went alone against them, about three hundred thousand men, and not one man of Israel was with them.

31 And all the Egyptians fought with these kings opposite Pathros and Tachpanches, and the battle was severe against the Egyptians.

32 And the kings were stronger than the Egyptians in that battle, and about one hundred and eighty men of Egypt fell on that day, and about thirty men of the forces of the kings, and all the men of Egypt fled from before the kings, so the children of Esau and Ishmael pursued the Egyptians, continuing to smite them unto the place where was the camp of the children of Israel.

33 And all the Egyptians cried unto the children of Israel, saying, hasten to us and assist us and save us from the hand of Esau, Ishmael and the children of Chittim.

34 And the hundred and fifty men of the children of Israel ran from their station to the camps of these kings, and the children of Israel cried unto the Lord their God to deliver them.

35 And the Lord hearkened to Israel, and the Lord gave all the men of the kings into their hand, and the children of Israel fought against these kings, and the children of Israel smote about four thousand of the kings' men.

36 And the Lord threw a great consternation in the camp of the kings, so that the fear of the children of Israel fell upon them.

37 And all the hosts of the kings fled from before the children of Israel and the children of Israel pursued them continuing to smite them unto the borders of the land of Cush.

38 And the children of Israel slew of them in the road yet two thousand men, and of the children of Israel not one fell.

39 And when the Egyptians saw that the children of Israel had fought with such few men with the kings, and that the battle was so very severe against them,

40 All the Egyptians were greatly afraid of their lives on account of the strong battle, and all Egypt fled, every man hiding himself from the arrayed forces, and they hid themselves in the road, and they left the Israelites to fight.

41 And the children of Israel inflicted a terrible blow upon the kings' men, and they returned from them after they had driven them to the border of the land of Cush.

42 And all Israel knew the thing which the men of Egypt had done to them, that they had fled from them in battle, and had left them to fight alone.

43 So the children of Israel also acted with cunning, and as the children of Israel returned from battle, they found some of the Egyptians in the road and smote them there.

44 And whilst they slew them, they said unto them these words:

45 Wherefore did you go from us and leave us, being a few people, to fight against these kings who had a great people to smite us, that you might thereby deliver your own souls?

46 And of some which the Israelites met on the road, they the children of Israel spoke to each other, saying, Smite, smite, for he is an Ishmaelite, or an Edomite, or from the children of Chittim, and they stood over him and slew him, and they knew that he was an Egyptian.

47 And the children of Israel did these things cunningly against the Egyptians, because they had deserted them in battle and had fled from them.

48 And the children of Israel slew of the men of Egypt in the road in this manner, about two hundred men.

49 And all the men of Egypt saw the evil which the children of Israel had done to them, so all Egypt feared greatly the children of Israel, for they had seen their great power, and that not one man of them had fallen.

50 So all the children of Israel returned with joy on their road to Goshen, and the rest of Egypt returned each man to his place.

Chapter 65

1 And it came to pass after these things, that all the counsellors of Pharaoh, king of Egypt, and all the elders of Egypt assembled and came before the king and bowed down to the ground, and they sat before him.

2 And the counsellors and elders of Egypt spoke unto the king, saying,

3 Behold the people of the children of Israel is greater and mightier than we are, and thou know all the evil which they did to us in the road when we returned from battle.

4 And thou hast also seen their strong power, for this power is unto them from their fathers, for but a few men stood up against a people numerous as the sand, and smote them at the edge of the sword, and of themselves not one has fallen, so that if they had been numerous they would then have utterly destroyed them.

Comment:1: Here we see the Egyptians take counsel concerning the Israelites among them as they noticed that the children of Israel being few in number and yet much better fighters and warriors than they themselves. They are afraid that they will grow in numbers and one day totally overcome Egypt.

C.2 It is stated that Moses was born 60 years after the death of Joseph. It is also a fact that Moses was 80 when he went down to Egypt. We saw in the last chapter that it mentioned that there were only 150 men of Israel. I suppose with wives and children taken into consideration. Israel could have numbered 1000. How did the population of Israel get from 1000 to 3,000,000 in the next 60 years until Moses was born +80 years until Moses came to rebuke Pharaoh and deliver the children of Israel =140 years? Is that actually possible? Apparently, it is possible if every family had at least 5-10 children in a time period of 20 years generation then indeed 3,000,000 could have been the final number of the Children of Israel by the time Moses delivered God's people.

5 Now therefore give us counsel what to do with them, until we gradually destroy them from amongst us, lest they become too numerous for us in the land.

6 For if the children of Israel should increase in the land, they will become an obstacle to us, and if any war should happen to take place,

they with their great strength will join our enemy against us, and fight against us, destroy us from the land and go away from it.

7 So the king answered the elders of Egypt and said unto them, this is the plan advised against Israel, from which we will not depart,

8 Behold in the land are Pithom and Rameses, cities unfortified against battle, it behooves you and us to build them, and to fortify them.

9 Now therefore go you also and act cunningly toward them, and proclaim a voice in Egypt and in Goshen at the command of the king, saying,

10 All ye men of Egypt, Goshen, Pathros and all their inhabitants! the king has commanded us to build Pithom and Rameses, and to fortify them for battle; who amongst you of all Egypt, of the children of Israel and of all the inhabitants of the cities, are willing to build with us, shall each have his wages given to him daily at the king's order; so go you first and do cunningly, and gather yourselves and come to Pithom and Rameses to build.

11 And whilst you are building, cause a proclamation of this kind to be made throughout Egypt every day at the command of the king.

12 And when some of the children of Israel shall come to build with you, you shall give them their wages daily for a few days.

13 And after they shall have built with you for their daily hire, drag yourselves away from them daily one by one in secret, and then you shall rise up and become their task-masters and officers, and you shall leave them afterward to build without wages, and should they refuse, then force them with all your might to build.

14 And if you do this it will be well with us to strengthen our land against the children of Israel, for on account of the fatigue of the building and the work, the children of Israel will decrease, because you will deprive them from their wives day by day.

15 And all the elders of Egypt heard the counsel of the king, and the counsel seemed good in their eyes and in the eyes of the servants of Pharaoh, and in the eyes of all Egypt, and they did according to the word of the king.

16 And all the servants went away from the king, and they caused a proclamation to be made in all Egypt, in Tachpanches and in Goshen, and in all the cities which surrounded Egypt, saying,

17 You have seen what the children of Esau and Ishmael did to us, who came to war against us and wished to destroy us.

18 Now therefore the king commanded us to fortify the land, to build the cities Pithom and Rameses, and to fortify them for battle, if they should again come against us.

19 Whosoever of you from all Egypt and from the children of Israel will come to build with us, he shall have his daily wages given by the king, as his command is unto us.

20 And when Egypt and all the children of Israel heard all that the servants of Pharaoh had spoken, there came from the Egyptians, and the children of Israel to build with the servants of Pharaoh, Pithom and Rameses, but none of the children of Levi came with their brethren to build.

21 And all the servants of Pharaoh and his princes came at first with deceit to build with all Israel as daily hired laborers, and they gave to Israel their daily hire at the beginning.

22 And the servants of Pharaoh built with all Israel and were employed in that work with Israel for a month.

23 And at the end of the month, all the servants of Pharaoh began to withdraw secretly from the people of Israel daily.

24 And Israel went on with the work at that time, but they then received their daily hire, because some of the men of Egypt were yet carry- ing on the work with Israel at that time; therefore the Egyptians gave

Israel their hire in those days, in order that they, the Egyptians their fellow-workmen, might also take the pay for their labour.

25 And at the end of a year and four months all the Egyptians had withdrawn from the children of Israel, so that the children of Israel were left alone engaged in the work.

26 And after all the Egyptians had withdrawn from the children of Israel they returned and became oppressors and officers over them, and some of them stood over the children of Israel as task masters, to receive from them all that they gave them for the pay of their labour.

27 And the Egyptians did in this manner to the children of Israel day by day, in order to afflict in their work.

28 And all the children of Israel were alone engaged in the labour, and the Egyptians refrained from giving any pay to the children of Israel from that time forward.

29 And when some of the men of Israel refused to work on account of the wages not being given to them, then the exactors and the servants of Pharaoh oppressed them and smote them with heavy blows, and made them return by force, to labour with their brethren; thus did all the Egyptians unto the children of Israel all the days.

30 And all the children of Israel were greatly afraid of the Egyptians in this matter, and all the children of Israel returned and worked alone without pay.

31 And the children of Israel built Pithom and Rameses, and all the children of Israel did the work, some making bricks, and some building, and the children of Israel built and fortified all the land of Egypt and its walls, and the children of Israel were engaged in work for many years, until the time came when the Lord remembered them and brought them out of Egypt.

32 But the children of Levi were not employed in the work with their

brethren of Israel, from the beginning unto the day of their going forth from Egypt.

33 For all the children of Levi knew that the Egyptians had spoken all these words with deceit to the Israelites, therefore the children of Levi refrained from approaching to the work with their brethren.

34 And the Egyptians did not direct their attention to make the children of Levi work afterward, since they had not been with their brethren at the beginning, therefore the Egyptians left them alone.

35 And the hands of the men of Egypt were directed with continued severity against the children of Israel in that work, and the Egyptians made the children of Israel work with rigor.

36 And the Egyptians embittered the lives of the children of Israel with hard work, in mortar and bricks, and also in all manner of work in the field.

37 And the children of Israel called Melol the king of Egypt "Meror, king of Egypt," because in his days the Egyptians had embittered their lives with all manner of work.

38 And all the work wherein the Egyptians made the children of Israel labour, they exacted with rigor, in order to afflict the children of Israel, but the more they afflicted them, the more they increased and grew, and the Egyptians were grieved because of the children of Israel.

EXO.1:12 But the more they afflicted them, the more they multiplied and grew. And they were grieved because of the children of Israel.

EXO.1:13 And the Egyptians made the children of Israel to serve with rigour:

EXO.1:14 And they made their lives bitter with hard bondage, in mortar and in brick, and in all manner of service in the field: all their service, wherein they made them serve, was with rigour.

Chapter 66

1 At that time died Hadad the son of Bedad king of Edom, and Samlah from Mesrekah, from the country of the children of the east, reigned in his place.

2 In the thirteenth year of the reign of Pharaoh king of Egypt, which was the hundred and twenty-fifth year of the Israelites going down into Egypt, Samlah had reigned over Edom eighteen years.

3 And when he reigned, he drew forth his hosts to go and fight against Zepho the son of Eliphaz and the children of Chittim, because they had made war against Angeas king of Africa, and they destroyed his whole army.

4 But he did not engage with him, for the children of Esau prevented him, saying, He was their brother, so Samlah listened to the voice of the children of Esau, and turned back with all his forces to the land of Edom, and did not proceed to fight against Zepho the son of Eliphaz.

5 And Pharaoh king of Egypt heard this thing, saying, Samlah king of Edom has resolved to fight the children of Chittim, and afterward he will come to fight against Egypt.

6 And when the Egyptians heard this matter, they increased the labour upon the children of Israel, lest the Israelites should do unto them as they did unto them in their war with the children of Esau in the days of Hadad.

7 So the Egyptians said unto the children of Israel, Hasten and do your work, and finish your task, and strengthen the land, lest the children of Esau your brethren should come to fight against us, for on your account will they come against us.

8 And the children of Israel did the work of the men of Egypt day by day, and the Egyptians afflicted the children of Israel in order to lessen them in the land.

9 But as the Egyptians increased the labour upon the children of Israel, so did the children of Israel increase and multiply, and all Egypt was filled with the children of Israel.

10 And in the hundred and twenty-fifth year of Israel's going down into Egypt, all the Egyptians saw that their counsel did not succeed against Israel, but that they increased and grew, and the land of Egypt and the land of Goshen were filled with the children of Israel.

EXO.1:12 But the more they afflicted them, the more they multiplied and grew. And they were grieved because of the children of Israel.

11 So all the elders of Egypt and its wise men came before the king and bowed down to him and sat before him.

12 And all the elders of Egypt and the wise men thereof said unto the king, May the king live forever; thou didst counsel us the counsel against the children of Israel, and we did unto them according to the word of the king.

13 But in proportion to the increase of the labour so do they increase and grow in the land, and behold the whole country is filled with them.

14 Now therefore our lord and king, the eyes of all Egypt are upon thee to give them advice with thy wisdom, by which they may prevail over Israel to destroy them, or to diminish them from the land; and the king answered them saying, Give you counsel in this matter that we may know what to do unto them.

15 And an officer, one of the king's counsellors, whose name was Job, from Mesopotamia, in the land of Uz, answered the king, saying,

16 If it please the king, let him hear the counsel of his servant; and the king said unto him, Speak.

17 And Job spoke before the king, the princes, and before all the elders of Egypt, saying,

18 Behold the counsel of the king which he advised formerly respecting the labour of the children of Israel is very good, and you must not remove from them that labour forever.

19 But this is the advice counselled by which you may lessen them, if it seems good to the king to afflict them.

20 Behold we have feared war for a long time, and we said, When Israel becomes fruitful in the land, they will drive us from the land if a war should take place.

21 If it please the king, let a royal decree go forth, and let it be written in the laws of Egypt which shall not be revoked, that every male child born to the Israelites, his blood shall be spilled upon the ground.

Comment:1: BIRTH CONTROL

The children of Israel were multiplying so fast and filling up the land of Egypt, so that Pharaoh started to panic and after counselling with others, it was decided to start killing off the baby boys born in the land of Goshen where the Israelites lived. As this was also at the time when Moses was born, it is possible the population of Israel was already approx. 1.000.000. Although the population had grown so fast for the previous 60 years, now the population growth rate among the Israelites went down drastically for the next 80 years until Moses came to the rescue of Israel. The population went from around approx. 1.000.000 to 3.000.000 in the next 80 years. Notice that the birth rate of the Israelites in the first 100 years in Egypt was much lower. Jacob sons being 12 ended up being around 1000 souls after the first 100 years in Egypt. Once the children of Israel were afflicted until the time of the order given to slay the boy babies was around 60 years.

EXO.1:12 But the more they afflicted them, the more they multiplied and grew. And they were grieved because of the children of Israel.

C.2 Why did the Children of Israel's population grow at such a rate even though they were afflicted. I would suggest that as the men had to labour very hard every day in slave labour, that they needed the comfort of their wives at night-time, much more than normally they would. They didn't have any distractions and the only physical and emotional comfort was their wives. Thus, many more children were born unto them which was part of God's plan. God's first commandment both to Adam and Eve, and then later on after the Great flood to Noah and his sons was to 'Be fruitful and multiply. When much of the world is destroyed in the near future by first the Anti-Christ and his satanic forces, and then also by God Himself in the Wrath of God and in particular the Battle of Armageddon, then the number of men on the earth will be very few. There will many more women than men upon the earth. Again, at the start of the Millennium I am sure that God will be encouraging people to both marry and have large families and some men will probably have more than one wife, just as in the days of Jacob. With few men on the planet, then it is very likely.

ISA.4:1 And in that day seven women shall take hold of one man, saying, 'We will eat our own bread, and wear our own apparel: only let us be called by thy name, to take away our reproach'.

C.3 This means that the women want to be married and to have children. In the old days it was considered a curse if a woman couldn't have children. It was considered to be a blessing to have lots of children.

PSA.127:3 Lo, children are an heritage of the LORD: and the fruit of the womb is his reward.

PSA.127:4 As arrows are in the hand of a mighty man; so are children of the youth.

PSA.127:5 Happy is the man that hath his quiver full of them: they shall not be ashamed, but they shall speak with the enemies in the gate.

C.4 Many women in history have opted to have children even if they are not married and are alone.

ISA.54:1 Sing, O barren, thou that didst not bear; break forth into singing, and cry aloud, thou that didst not travail with child: for more are the children of the desolate than the children of the married wife, saith the LORD.

C.5 Today in our modern world, the Western peoples are not having enough children (1.3 /couple average, when the minimum should be 2.1) in order to sustain their races and are thus actually committing genocide without really realizing it. I would say the reason is that people have too many distractions, and they don't put enough emphasis on both marriage and building a family in obedience to God, as most of the world has become very ungodly, wicked and degenerate in their way of living, and are easily led astray by Satan and his Fallen angels and their sons the former giants, who are now the disembodies spirits of the Demons.

---

22 And by your doing this, when all the male children of Israel shall have died, the evil of their wars will cease; let the king do so and send for all the Hebrew midwives and order them in this matter to execute it; so the thing pleased the king and the princes, and the king did according to the word of Job.

23 And the king sent for the Hebrew midwives to be called, of which the name of one was Shephrah, and the name of the other Puah.

---

24 And the midwives came before the king and stood in his presence.

25 And the king said unto them, When you do the office of a midwife to the Hebrew women, and see them upon the stools, if it be a son, then you shall kill him, but if it be a daughter, then she shall live.

26 But if you will not do this thing, then will I burn you up and all your houses with fire.

27 But the midwives feared God and did not hearken to the king of Egypt nor to his words, and when the Hebrew women brought forth to the midwife son or daughter, then did the midwife do all that was necessary to the child and let it live; thus did the midwives all the days.

28 And this thing was told to the king, and he sent and called for the midwives and he said to them, Why have you done this thing and have saved the children alive?

29 And the midwives answered and spoke together before the king, saying,

30 Let not the king think that the Hebrew women are as the Egyptian women, for all the children of Israel are hale, and before the midwife comes to them they are delivered, and as for us thy handmaids, for many days no Hebrew woman has brought forth upon us, for all the Hebrew women are their own midwives, because they are hale.

31 And Pharaoh heard their words and believed them in this matter, and the midwives went away from the king, and God dealt well with them, and the people multiplied and waxed exceedingly.

EXO.1:19 And the midwives said unto Pharaoh, Because the Hebrew women are not as the Egyptian women; for they are lively and are delivered ere the midwives come in unto them.

EXO.1:20 Therefore God dealt well with the midwives: and the people multiplied and waxed very mighty.

EXO.1:22 And Pharaoh charged all his people, saying, 'Every son that is born ye shall cast into the river, and every daughter ye shall save alive.'

Chapter 67

1 There was a man in the land of Egypt of the seed of Levi, whose name was Amram, the son of Kehath, the son of Levi, the son of Israel.

2 And this man went and took a wife, namely Jochebed the daughter of Levi his father's sister, and she was one hundred and twenty-six years old, and he came unto her.

C.1 Amram's wife was not 126 years old when he married her according to the Bible. Consider that Joseph has died at only 110 years old, some 60 years earlier and of all his brothers at around 120 on average. God stated just before the Great Flood that He would reduce a man's life to only 120 years. The length of a man's life had been decreasing since the time of Noah. Noah died at 950, Shem his son at 600, Shem's son Arphaxad at 400, his great grandson Peleg 200, Peleg's great grandson Nahor 148, Nahor's great-great grandson Jacob 146, & Jacob's son Joseph 110. This age degeneration would continue to do so until the time of King David, who stated that a man's life shall be 70 years.

C.2 This all being the case, I think that the age stated here for Amram's wife Jocabed has to be incorrect. Perhaps we should take off 100 years and find out that Amram's wife was more like 26 which would be normal for a young wife.

C.3 We also find tampering in other books such as the Septuagint using +100 years to the ages of those coming after the Great flood such as Arphaxad down to about Terah. Why? Now that is a very good question which I have answered in the Appendix of this book.

3 And the woman conceived and bare a daughter, and she called her name Miriam, because in those days the Egyptians had embittered the lives of the children of Israel.

4 And she conceived again and bare a son and she called his name Aaron, for in the days of her conception, Pharaoh began to spill the blood of the male children of Israel.

5 In those days died Zepho the son of Eliphaz, son of Esau, king of Chittim, and Janeas reigned in his stead.

C.4 Here we finally see Zepho, the grandson of Esau finally dies after having been king over Chittim for 40 years

6 And the time that Zepho reigned over the children of Chittim was fifty years, and he died and was buried in the city of Nabna in the land of Chittim.

7 And Janeas, one of the mighty men of the children of Chittim, reigned after him and he reigned fifty years.

8 And it was after the death of the king of Chittim that Balaam the son of Beor fled from the land of Chittim, and he went and came to Egypt to Pharaoh king of Egypt.

C.5 Here again we here about that that long-lived Sorcerer Balaam moving down to Egypt to become one of Pharaoh's evil henchmen.

9 And Pharaoh received him with great honor, for he had heard of his wisdom, and he gave him presents and made him for a counsellor and aggrandized him.

10 And Balaam dwelt in Egypt, in honor with all the nobles of the king, and the nobles exalted him, because they all coveted to learn his wisdom.

11 And in the hundred and thirtieth year of Israel's going down to Egypt, Pharaoh dreamed that he was sitting upon his kingly throne, and lifted up his eyes and saw an old man standing before him, and there were scales in the hands of the old man, such scales as are used by merchants.

12 And the old man took the scales and hung them before Pharaoh.

13 And the old man took all the elders of Egypt and all its nobles and great men, and he tied them together and put them in one scale.

14 And he took a milk kid and put it into the other scale, and the kid preponderated over all.

15 And Pharaoh was astonished at this dreadful vision, why the kid should preponderate over all, and Pharaoh awoke and behold it was a dream.

186

16 And Pharaoh rose up early in the morning and called all his servants and related to them the dream, and the men were greatly afraid.

17 And the king said to all his wise men, Interpret I pray you the dream which I dreamed, that I may know it.

18 And Balaam the son of Beor answered the king and said unto him, This means nothing else but a great evil that will spring up against Egypt in the latter days.

19 For a son will be born to Israel who will destroy all Egypt and its inhabitants and bring forth the Israelites from Egypt with a mighty hand.

C.6 Balaam warns Pharaoh that a deliverer will be born into Israel who will deliver Israel out of Pharaoh's hand and will end up destroying Egypt.

C.7 It never ceases to amaze me how that God tried to warn so many of the rulers of the empires of man not to touch His people, but they always listened to evil advise because that was their 'bent', and because they always ended up rejecting God's counsel either through dreams or visions or directly through his prophets. Because of the ruler's rejection of the Spirit of God, the rulers ended up being destroyed or overthrown by another kingdom!

20 Now therefore, O king, take counsel upon this matter, that you may destroy the hope of the children of Israel and their expectation, before this evil arise against Egypt.

21 And the king said unto Balaam, And what shall we do unto Israel? surely after a certain manner did we at first counsel against them and could not prevail over them.

22 Now therefore give you also advice against them by which we may prevail over them.

23 And Balaam answered the king, saying, Send now and call thy two counsellors, and we will see what their advice is upon this matter and afterward thy servant will speak.

24 And the king sent and called his two counsellors Reuel the Midianite and Job the Uzite, and they came and sat before the king.

25 And the king said to them, Behold you have both heard the dream which I have dreamed, and the interpretation thereof; now therefore give counsel and know and see what is to be done to the children of Israel, whereby we may prevail over them, before their evil shall spring up against us.

26 And Reuel the Midianite answered the king and said, May the king live, may the king live forever.

27 If it seem good to the king, let him desist from the Hebrews and leave them, and let him not stretch forth his hand against them.

28 For these are they whom the Lord chose in days of old, and took as the lot of his inheritance from amongst all the nations of the earth and the kings of the earth; and who is there that stretched his hand against them with impunity, of whom their God was not avenged?

29 Surely thou know that when Abraham went down to Egypt, Pharaoh, the former king of Egypt, saw Sarah his wife, and took her for a wife, because Abraham said, She is my sister, for he was afraid, lest the men of Egypt should slay him on account of his wife.

30 And when the king of Egypt had taken Sarah then God smote him and his household with heavy plagues, until he restored unto Abraham his wife Sarah, then was he healed.

31 And Abimelech the Gerarite, king of the Philistines, God punished on account of Sarah wife of Abraham, in stopping up every womb from man to beast.

32 When their God came to Abimelech in the dream of night and terrified him in order that he might restore to Abraham Sarah whom he had taken, and afterward all the people of Gerar were punished on account of Sarah, and Abraham prayed to his God for them, and he was entreated of him, and he healed them.

33 And Abimelech feared all this evil that came upon him and his people, and he returned to Abraham his wife Sarah, and gave him with her many gifts.

34 He did so also to Isaac when he had driven him from Gerar, and God had done wonderful things to him, that all the water courses of Gerar were dried up, and their productive trees did not bring forth.

35 Until Abimelech of Gerar, and Ahuzzath one of his friends, and Pichol the captain of his host, went to him and they bent and bowed down before him to the ground.

36 And they requested of him to supplicate for them, and he prayed to the Lord for them, and the Lord was entreated of him and he healed them.

37 Jacob also, the plain man, was delivered through his integrity from the hand of his brother Esau, and the hand of Laban the Syrian his mother's brother, who had sought his life; likewise from the hand of all the kings of Canaan who had come together against him and his children to destroy them, and the Lord delivered them out of their hands, that they turned upon them and smote them, for who had ever stretched forth his hand against them with impunity?

38 Surely Pharaoh the former, thy father's father, raised Joseph the son of Jacob above all the princes of the land of Egypt, when he saw his wisdom, for through his wisdom he rescued all the inhabitants of the land from the famine.

39 After which he ordered Jacob and his children to come down to Egypt, in order that through their virtue, the land of Egypt and the land of Goshen might be delivered from the famine.

40 Now therefore if it seem good in thine eyes, cease from destroying the children of Israel, but if it be not thy will that they shall dwell in Egypt, send them forth from here, that they may go to the land of Canaan, the land where their ancestors sojourned.

41 And when Pharaoh heard the words of Jethro he was very angry with him, so that he rose with shame from the king's presence, and went to Midian, his land, and took Joseph's stick with him.

C.8 It is not surprising that Jethro said these words as he was the father in law to Moses, but obviously Pharaoh didn't perceive this.

> 42 And the king said to Job the Uzite, What say thou Job, and what is thy advice respecting the Hebrews?
>
> 43 So Job said to the king, 'Behold all the inhabitants of the land are in thy power, let the king do as it seems good in his eyes'.

C.9 According to the Bible, Job from the land of Uz was a good man, but of course there could have been many people from Uz with the same name.

> 44 And the king said unto Balaam, 'What dost thou say, Balaam, speak thy word that we may hear it'.
>
> 45 And Balaam said to the king, Of all that the king has counselled against the Hebrews will they be delivered, and the king will not be able to prevail over them with any counsel.
>
> 46 For if thou think to lessen them by the flaming fire, thou canst not prevail over them, for surely their God delivered Abraham their father from Ur of the Chaldeans; and if thou think to destroy them with a sword, surely Isaac their father was delivered from it, and a ram was placed in his stead.
>
> 47 And if with hard and rigorous labour thou think to lessen them, thou wilt not prevail even in this, for their father Jacob served Laban in all manner of hard work and prospered.
>
> 48 Now therefore, O King, hear my words, for this is the counsel which is counselled against them, by which thou wilt prevail over them, and from which thou should not depart.
>
> 49 If it please the king let him order all their children which shall be born from this day forward, to be thrown into the water, for by this canst thou wipe away their name, for none of them, nor of their fathers, were tried in this manner.
>
> 50 And the king heard the words of Balaam, and the thing pleased the king and the princes, and the king did according to the word of Balaam.

> 51 And the king ordered a proclamation to be issued and a law to be made throughout the land of Egypt, saying, 'Every male child born to the Hebrews from this day forward shall be thrown into the water'.

C.10 Thus, the expression 'To the Nile crocodile' as many are taught in Sunday school that Pharaoh caused all the baby Israelite baby boys to be thrown into the Nile river or estuary/Delta of Egypt and that the crocodiles would eat up and devour all the little babies. Now is that really a true picture? Couldn't God Himself have rescued the babies put upon the waters in the same way that He rescued those abandoned on the land by their mothers?

C.11 This is clearly shown in the Book of Revelations as both happening in the time of Moses and also in the time of Jesus. The following verses are talking about Satan. He tried to prevent Moses from being born, as he was foretold as the deliverer, and also baby Jesus was the foretold Messiah. Fortunately, on both occasions Satan failed in his attempt to get rid of God's Deliverer and Messiah:

REV.12:3 And there appeared another wonder in heaven; and behold a great red dragon (Satan), having seven heads and ten horns, and seven crowns upon his heads.

C.12 The 7 heads are Egypt. Assyria, Babylon, Medio-Persia, Greece, Rome & the 7th the coming Anti-Christ One World Government or New World Order.

REV.12:4 And his tail drew the third part of the stars of heaven and did cast them to the earth: and the Dragon stood before the woman which was ready to be delivered, for to devour her child as soon as it was born.

> 52 And Pharaoh called unto all his servants, saying, 'Go now and seek throughout the land of Goshen where the children of Israel are, and see that every son born to the Hebrews shall be cast into the river, but every daughter you shall let live'.
>
> 53 And when the children of Israel heard this thing which Pharaoh had commanded, to cast their male children into the river, some of the people separated from their wives and others adhered to them.

C.13 SUPERNATURAL PROTECTION Some of the Israelites had the faith that even if they continued to have their babies that God would somehow take care of them.

> 54 And from that day forward, when the time of delivery arrived to those women of Israel who had remained with their husbands, they went to the field to bring forth there, and they brought forth in the field, and left their children upon the field and returned home.

191

C.14 To avoid having their children slain by Pharaoh's soldiers they would give birth to their babies out in the field and abandon the babies, expecting God to take care of their babies. This was because God had sworn to Abraham that He Himself would multiply the seed of Abraham, therefore God sent His angels to take care of and to nurture the babies until they were old enough to go back to their families. Such a miraculous story that has been omitted from the Bible. After all if God could cause a big fish to swallow up His prophet in the story of Jonah and also use the ravens to feed Elijah and to open the mouth of Balaam's ass to speak to Balaam then what can't God do if it so suits His Almighty purpose. It is very important not to limit God by what we think He can or can't do!

> 55 And the Lord who had sworn to their ancestors to multiply them, sent one of his ministering angels which are in heaven to wash each child in water, to anoint and swathe it and to put into its hands two smooth stones from one of which it sucked milk and from the other honey, and he caused its hair to grow to its knees, by which it might cover itself; to comfort it and to cleave to it, through his compassion for it.

C.15 This is truly amazing that when the children of Israel chose to have babies anyway in spite of the Pharaoh's commands to throw the baby boys into the river that the women who were obedient to have children were protected by God. They who also tried to bear them away from the city in order to protect their lives. It is wonderful to hear that when the situation became impossible for the Children of Israel, then God Himself stepped in directly and sent his angels to minister unto the babies and to fully take care of them.

> 56 And when God had compassion over them and had desired to multiply them upon the face of the land, he ordered his earth to receive them to be preserved therein till the time of their growing up, after which the earth opened its mouth and vomited them forth and they sprouted forth from the city like the herb of the earth, and the grass of the forest, and they returned each to his family and to his father's house, and they remained with them.

C.16 Here it is referring to the earth as if it were alive or had a spirit by which it could understand God's commandment to it. The ancient Greeks believed that the earth was alive and called is Gaia. The earth opened up and received the babies and nurtured them until they had grown up sufficiently unto the earth vomited them forth and they sprouted forth like the herb of the earth and they returned to their families. What a miraculous description. So, if the situation is truly impossible, then God Himself will get directly involved and even order the earth itself to act as a mother. Thus, the name 'Mother Earth'. There is another book called Ezdras II which talks about the earth in the same way.

(See my book 'Ezdras Insights') Here is a relevant quote from it.

II Ezdras 5.48 'He said to me' I have given the womb of the earth to those who from time to time are sown in it.

C.17 Now speaking of Mother earth directly:

II Ezdras 5.50 'Is our Mother, of whom thou hast told me still young? Or is she now approaching old age?'

C.18 To get the answer to that question: **(See my book 'Ezdras Insights')**

C.19 Here is an even stranger miracle, that God *'ordered the earth'* to receive *the babies to be preserved until the time of their growing up'* - *'after which the earth opened its mouth and vomited them forth and they sprouted forth from the city like the herb of the earth, and the grass of the forest'.* We don't find miraculous stories like this in either the Bible or other religious books. I wonder why? Could be that the religious people don't really believe in God's miracles and that if He is the God of the universe then it is His privilege to do as He pleases and sees best to do upon any given occasion even if He has to command the earth to open up and nourish the new born babies one way or the other. There are many miraculous stories of human babies having been nourished by wolves and other animals- thus the story of Jungle Book. I maintain that this 'Book of Jasher' was intended as a report of everything that had happened of great importance from the time of the Creation unto the time of Joshua. I maintain that it was compiled and written by a very diligent scribe or scribes or in modern terms a diligent reporter, who wasn't influenced by others lack of faith and belief in the supernatural like so many religionists today who no longer believe in miracles at all!

---

57 And the babes of the children of Israel were upon the earth like the herb of the field, through God's grace to them.

58 And when all the Egyptians saw this thing, they went forth, each to his field with his yoke of oxen and his ploughshare, and they ploughed it up as one ploughs the earth at seed time.

59 And when they ploughed they were unable to hurt the infants of the children of Israel, so the people increased and waxed exceedingly.

60 And Pharaoh ordered his officers daily to go to Goshen to seek for the babes of the children of Israel.

61 And when they had sought and found one, they took it from its mother's bosom by force, and threw it into the river, but the female child they left with its mother; thus, did the Egyptians do to the Israelites all the days.

C.20 This explains something about this same story in the Bible, that until now I simply could not fully understand: If Pharaoh's soldiers had been faithfully slaying the babies of the children of Israel, why is it repeatedly mentioned that despite all that Pharaoh tried to do against the children of Israel, that they continued to multiply anyway. The Bible doesn't explain how, but this 67th chapter of Jasher explains it so well. God supernaturally protected the infants. Perhaps the soldiers managed to get a few of the baby boys thrown into Nile, but then who knows, perhaps God even rescued them as well? I am only theorizing here, but if God could have ordered the earth to open up and take care of the babies, then perhaps he ordered the herrings or flamingos to pick up the abandoned babies and to take them onto the land, where they would be taken care of by both God's angels and other helpers. Just a thought? The traditional picture, which is taught to children, of crocodiles chomping on the defenceless babies of the children of Israel after they had been chucked unto the Nile river by the Egyptian soldiers, might actually be incorrect. Whatever way we look at it, the truth is that God supernaturally rescued the babies from destruction no matter what tricks Pharaoh tried, as God Himself wanted the babies to live as, He had promised unto Abraham the father of Israel.

C.21 The Bible says that the Mid-wives feared God and would not kill the babies of the children of Israel:

EXO.1:17 But the midwives feared God and did not as the king of Egypt commanded them but saved the men children alive.

EXO.1:18 And the king of Egypt called for the midwives, and said unto them, 'Why have ye done this thing, and have saved the men children alive?'

EXO.1:19 And the midwives said unto Pharaoh, 'Because the Hebrew women are not as the Egyptian women; for they are lively and are delivered ere the midwives come in unto them.'

Chapter 68

1 And it was at that time the spirit of God was upon Miriam the daughter of Amram the sister of Aaron, and she went forth and prophesied about the house, saying, Behold a son will be born unto us from my father and mother this time, and he will save Israel from the hands of Egypt.

Comment:1: This a beautiful nugget stating that Miriam was perhaps the first mentioned woman prophet or prophetess in the Bible. This particular prophecy about Moses her brother that he would be the Deliverer is not mentioned, although other prophecies that she had are mentioned.

2 And when Amram heard the words of his daughter, he went and took his wife back to the house, after he had driven her away at the time when Pharaoh ordered every male child of the house of Jacob to be thrown into the water.

C.2 Imagine such a terrible time that a man (Amram) would drive away his wife (Jocabed) whom he loved away from him, as he no longer wanted her to conceive and have children because of the horrendous law made by Pharaoh to 'execute all baby boys' that would be born to the Israelites. I am surprised that he didn't know about the use of herbs to prevent conception, as was used by many before the Great Flood. Unless of course Amram considered that to be an ungodly practice which God would not bless?

JASHER 2.19 For in those days the sons of men began to trespass against God, and to transgress the commandments which he had commanded to Adam, to be fruitful and multiply in the earth.

JASHER 2. 20 And some of the sons of men caused their wives to drink a draught that would render them barren, in order that they might retain their figures and whereby their beautiful appearance might not fade.

3 So Amram took Jochebed his wife, three years after he had driven her away, and he came to her and she conceived.

C.3 Poor woman, to be treated so unkindly and abandoned for 3 years, although I am sure that she understood why! Sometimes things that happen to us in life seem very extreme and very painful to endure at the time when we have to go through them, but if God is the centre of our lives, then He always brings a wonderful victory in the end, as is clearly the case here. A godly man and his wife abstain from being together even though they loved each other as they waited on the Lord to find out what His will was to be in this horrendous situation that they found themselves in. On the one hand they both believed God's commandant 'To be fruitful and multiply' but felt that they were not in that privileged position because of the obvious danger to any male children born to them.

> 4 And at the end of seven months from her conception she brought forth a son, and the whole house was filled with great light as of the light of the sun and moon at the time of their shining.

ENOCH 66.1 And after some days my son Methuselah took a wife for his son Lamech,

and she became pregnant and bore him a son, and his body was white

as snow and red as the blooming of a rose, and the hair of his head and

his long locks were white as wool, and his eyes beautiful. And when he

opened his eyes he lighted up the whole house like the sun, and the whole house was very bright.

> 5 And when the woman saw the child that it was good and pleasing to the sight, she hid it for three months in an inner room.

C.3 Think of what great faith Amram and Jocabed had, in both deciding to have a baby anyway, in spite of the fairly recent order by Pharaoh himself to execute all male babies born to the Israelites and then hiding him as they saw that he was indeed a very special children where God himself had shown signs following at this very birth.

> 6 In those days the Egyptians conspired to destroy all the Hebrews there.

C.4 Apart from the Hebrews being so numerous, what was the other reason Pharaoh wanted the baby boys in particular executed? It was because it had been prophesied among the Israelites that a 'Deliverer would come' and set them free from Egypt.

C.5 This ordered execution by the world's first World Empire is mirrored in the birth of the Messiah the Saviour of all mankind by Herod the king over Israel at the time of Christ's birth when Herod tried to have baby Jesus killed, but Jesus and his parents escaped to Egypt from Israel due to the forewarning of God's angel.

C.6 Notice that the above-mentioned was repeated with king Herod in circa 4 B.C, being afraid of a prophesied 'mighty king and deliverer' being born in Israel and being accurately foreseen by the 3 Kings who visited Israel from the East who followed the bright star from their own countries in the East all the way to Israel. Here the star stopped right above the manger where the Saviour Jesus was born

7 And the Egyptian women went to Goshen where the children of Israel were, and they carried their young ones upon their shoulders, their babes who could not yet speak.

8 And in those days, when the women of the children of Israel brought forth, each woman had hidden her son from before the Egyptians, that the Egyptians might not know of their bringing forth and might not destroy them from the land.

9 And the Egyptian women came to Goshen and their children who could not speak were upon their shoulders, and when an Egyptian woman came into the house of a Hebrew woman her babe began to cry.

10 And when it cried the child that was in the inner room answered it, so the Egyptian women went and told it at the house of Pharaoh.

C.7 This was a clever ploy by the mid-wives of Pharoah to make use of the fact that very young children communicate with each other naturally and without any malice or intentions as they are completely innocent not understanding the dangerous predicament that they were in as the little ones talking to the babies of the Egyptian women could cause their own deaths.

11 And Pharoah sent his officers to take the children and slay them; thus, did the Egyptians to the Hebrew women all the days.

12 And it was at that time, about three months from Jochebed's concealment of her son, that the thing was known in Pharoah's house.

13 And the woman hastened to take away her son before the officers came, and she took for him an ark of bulrushes, and daubed it with slime and with pitch, and put the child therein, and she laid it in the flags by the river's brink.

14 And his sister Miriam stood afar off to know what would be done to him, and what would become of her words.

15 And God sent forth at that time a terrible heat in the land of Egypt, which burned up the flesh of man like the sun in his circuit, and it greatly oppressed the Egyptians.

16 And all the Egyptians went down to bathe in the river, on account of the consuming heat which burned up their flesh.

17 And Bithia, the daughter of Pharaoh, went also to bathe in the river, owing to the consuming heat, and her maidens walked at the river side, and all the women of Egypt as well.

18 And Bithia lifted up her eyes to the river, and she saw the ark upon the water, and sent her maid to fetch it.

19 And she opened it and saw the child, and behold the babe wept, and she had compassion on him, and she said, This is one of the Hebrew children.

20 And all the women of Egypt walking on the river side desired to give him suck, but he would not suck, for this thing was from the Lord, in order to restore him to his mother's breast.

21 And Miriam his sister was at that time amongst the Egyptian women at the river side, and she saw this thing and she said to Pharaoh's daughter, Shall I go and fetch a nurse of the Hebrew women, that she may nurse the child for thee?

22 And Pharaoh's daughter said to her, Go, and the young woman went and called the child's mother.

23 And Pharaoh's daughter said to Jochebed, Take this child away and suckle it for me, and I will pay thee thy wages, two bits of silver daily; and the woman took the child and nursed it.

24 And at the end of two years, when the child grew up, she brought him to the daughter of Pharaoh, and he was unto her as a son, and she called his name Moses, for she said, Because I drew him out of the water.

25 And Amram his father called his name Chadbar, for he said, It was for him that he associated with his wife whom he had turned away.

26 And Jochebed his mother called his name Jekuthiel, Because, she said, I have hoped for him to the Almighty, and God restored him unto me.

27 And Miriam his sister called him Jered, for she descended after him to the river to know what his end would be.

28 And Aaron his brother called his name Abi Zanuch, saying, My father left my mother and returned to her on his account.

29 And Kehath the father of Amram called his name Abigdor, because on his account did God repair the breach of the house of Jacob, that they could no longer throw their male children into the water.

30 And their nurse called him Abi Socho, saying, In his tabernacle was he hidden for three months, on account of the children of Ham.

31 And all Israel called his name Shemaiah, son of Nethanel, for they said, In his days has God heard their cries and rescued them from their oppressors.

32 And Moses was in Pharaoh's house, and was unto Bathia, Pharaoh's daughter, as a son, and Moses grew up amongst the king's children.

Chapter 69

1 And the king of Edom died in those days, in the eighteenth year of his reign, and was buried in his temple which he had built for himself as his royal residence in the land of Edom.

2 And the children of Esau sent to Pethor, which is upon the river, and they fetched from there a young man of beautiful eyes and comely aspect, whose name was Saul, and they made him king over them in the place of Samlah.

3 And Saul reigned over all the children of Esau in the land of Edom for forty years.

4 And when Pharaoh king of Egypt saw that the counsel which Balaam had advised respecting the children of Israel did not succeed, but that still they were fruitful, multiplied and increased throughout the land of Egypt,

5 Then Pharaoh commanded in those days that a proclamation should be issued throughout Egypt to the children of Israel, saying, 'No man shall diminish anything of his daily labour'.

6 And the man who shall be found deficient in his labour which he performs daily, whether in mortar or in bricks, then his youngest son shall be put in their place.

7 And the labour of Egypt strengthened upon the children of Israel in those days, and behold if one brick was deficient in any man's daily labour, the Egyptians took his youngest boy by force from his mother, and put him into the building in the place of the brick which his father had left wanting.

Comment:1: Now Pharaoh finds an even more satanic method for getting rid of the baby-boy children of the Children of Israel by turning them into bricks.

C.2 In modern terms it is called 'Cause and Effect': 1st of all, make it so hard on those trying to build the buildings. When the men fail to keep their 'quota of bricks' then the small children of those same slaves are then used as a brick to 'fill in' the 'hole in the wall'. If this was true, then being as diabolical as

Pharaoh was it is no wonder that Egypt ended up soon after this event being totally uprooted and destroyed.

8 And the men of Egypt did so to all the children of Israel day by day, all the days for a long period.

9 But the tribe of Levi did not at that time work with the Israelites their brethren, from the beginning, for the children of Levi knew the cunning of the Egyptians which they exercised at first toward the Israelites.

Chapter 70

1 And in the third year from the birth of Moses, Pharaoh was sitting at a banquet, when Alparanith the queen was sitting at his right and Bathia at his left, and the lad Moses was lying upon her bosom, and Balaam the son of Beor with his two sons, and all the princes of the kingdom were sitting at table in the king's presence.

2 And the lad stretched forth his hand upon the king's head and took the crown from the king's head and placed it on his own head.

3 And when the king and princes saw the work which the boy had done, the king and princes were terrified, and one man to his neighbor expressed astonishment.

4 And the king said unto the princes who were before him at table, What speak you and what say you, O ye princes, in this matter, and what is to be the judgment against the boy on account of this act?

5 And Balaam the son of Beor the magician answered before the king and princes, and he said, Remember now, O my lord and king, the dream which thou didst dream many days since, and that which thy servant interpreted unto thee.

Comment:1: Here we see Balaam the magician spouting off a whole 'bunch of lies' about Abraham and his descendants trying to paint them as the evil ones. This is so typical of Satan and his satanic entities like Balaam who think nothing about lying against their enemies being - the snake race or serpents that they are.

JOH.8:44 Ye are of your father the devil, and the lusts of your father ye will do. He was a murderer from the beginning, and abode not in the truth, because there is no truth in him. When he speaketh a lie, he speaketh of his own: for he is a liar, and the father of it.

6 Now therefore this is a child from the Hebrew children, in whom is the spirit of God, and let not my lord the king imagine that this youngster did this thing without knowledge.

7 For he is a Hebrew boy, and wisdom and understanding are with him,

although he is yet a child, and with wisdom has he done this and chosen unto himself the kingdom of Egypt.

8 For this is the manner of all the Hebrews to deceive kings and their nobles, to do all these things cunningly, in order to make the kings of the earth and their men tremble.

9 Surely thou knowest that Abraham their father acted thus, who deceived the army of Nimrod king of Babel, and Abimelech king of Gerar, and that he possessed himself of the land of the children of Heth and all the kingdoms of Canaan.

10 And that he descended into Egypt and said of Sarah his wife, she is my sister, in order to mislead Egypt and her king.

11 His son Isaac also did so when he went to Gerar and dwelt there, and his strength prevailed over the army of Abimelech king of the Philistines.

12 He also thought of making the kingdom of the Philistines stumble, in saying that Rebecca his wife was his sister.

13 Jacob also dealt treacherously with his brother, and took from his hand his birthright and his blessing.

14 He went then to Padan-aram to the house of Laban his mother's brother, and cunningly obtained from him his daughter, his cattle, and all belonging to him, and fled away and returned to the land of Canaan to his father.

15 His sons sold their brother Joseph, who went down into Egypt and became a slave, and was placed in the prison house for twelve years.

16 Until the former Pharaoh dreamed dreams, and withdrew him from the prison house, and magnified him above all the princes in Egypt on account of his interpreting his dreams to him.

17 And when God caused a famine throughout the land he sent for and brought his father and all his brothers, and the whole of his father's

household, and supported them without price or reward, and bought the Egyptians for slaves.

18 Now therefore my lord king behold this child has risen up in their stead in Egypt, to do according to their deeds and to trifle with every king, prince and judge.

19 If it please the king, let us now spill his blood upon the ground, lest he grow up and take away the government from thy hand, and the hope of Egypt perish after he shall have reigned.

20 And Balaam said to the king, Let us moreover call for all the judges of Egypt and the wise men thereof, and let us know if the judgment of death is due to this boy as thou didst say, and then we will slay him.

21 And Pharaoh sent and called for all the wise men of Egypt and they came before the king, and an angel of the Lord came amongst them, and he was like one of the wise men of Egypt.

22 And the king said to the wise men, Surely you have heard what this Hebrew boy who is in the house has done, and thus has Balaam judged in the matter.

23 Now judge you also and see what is due to the boy for the act he has committed.

24 And the angel, who seemed like one of the wise men of Pharaoh, answered and said as follows, before all the wise men of Egypt and before the king and the princes:

25 If it please the king let the king send for men who shall bring before him an onyx stone and a coal of fire, and place them before the child, and if the child shall stretch forth his hand and take the onyx stone, then shall we know that with wisdom has the youth done all that he has done, and we must slay him.

26 But if he stretch forth his hand upon the coal, then shall we know that it was not with knowledge that he did this thing, and he shall live.

27 And the thing seemed good in the eyes of the king and the princes, so the king did according to the word of the angel of the Lord.

28 And the king ordered the onyx stone and coal to be brought and placed before Moses.

29 And they placed the boy before them, and the lad endeavoured to stretch forth his hand to the onyx stone, but the angel of the Lord took his hand and placed it upon the coal, and the coal became extinguished in his hand, and he lifted it up and put it into his mouth, and burned part of his lips and part of his tongue, and he became heavy in mouth and tongue.

30 And when the king and princes saw this, they knew that Moses had not acted with wisdom in taking off the crown from the king's head.

31 So the king and princes refrained from slaying the child, so Moses remained in Pharaoh's house, growing up, and the Lord was with him.

32 And whilst the boy was in the king's house, he was robed in purple and he grew amongst the children of the king.

33 And when Moses grew up in the king's house, Bathia the daughter of Pharaoh considered him as a son, and all the household of Pharaoh honoured him, and all the men of Egypt were afraid of him.

34 And he daily went forth and came into the land of Goshen, where his brethren the children of Israel were, and Moses saw them daily in shortness of breath and hard labour.

35 And Moses asked them, saying, 'Wherefore is this labour meted out unto you day by day'?

36 And they told him all that had befallen them, and all the injunctions which Pharaoh had put upon them before his birth.

37 And they told him all the counsels which Balaam the son of Beor had counselled against them, and what he had also counselled against him in order to slay him when he had taken the king's crown from off his head.

38 And when Moses heard these things his anger was kindled against Balaam, and he sought to kill him, and he was in ambush for him day by day.

39 And Balaam was afraid of Moses, and he and his two sons rose up and went forth from Egypt, and they fled and delivered their souls and betook themselves to the land of Cush to Kikianus, king of Cush.

40 And Moses was in the king's house going out and coming in, the Lord gave him favour in the eyes of Pharaoh, and in the eyes of all his servants, and in the eyes of all the people of Egypt, and they loved Moses exceedingly.

41 And the day arrived when Moses went to Goshen to see his brethren, that he saw the children of Israel in their burdens and hard labour, and Moses was grieved on their account.

42 And Moses returned to Egypt and came to the house of Pharaoh, and came before the king, and Moses bowed down before the king.

43 And Moses said unto Pharaoh, I pray thee my lord, I have come to seek a small request from thee, turn not away my face empty; and Pharaoh said unto him, Speak.

44 And Moses said unto Pharaoh, 'Let there be given unto thy servants the children of Israel who are in Goshen, one day to rest therein from their labour'.

45 And the king answered Moses and said, Behold I have lifted up thy face in this thing to grant thy request.

46 And Pharaoh ordered a proclamation to be issued throughout Egypt and Goshen, saying,

47 To you, all the children of Israel, thus says the king, for six days you shall do your work and labour, but on the seventh day you shall rest, and shall not perform any work, thus shall you do all the days, as the king and Moses the son of Bathia have commanded.

48 And Moses rejoiced at this thing which the king had granted to him, and all the children of Israel did as Moses ordered them.

49 For this thing was from the Lord to the children of Israel, for the Lord had begun to remember the children of Israel to save them for the sake of their fathers.

50 And the Lord was with Moses and his fame went throughout Egypt.

51 And Moses became great in the eyes of all the Egyptians, and in the eyes of all the children of Israel, seeking good for his people Israel and speaking words of peace regarding them to the king.

Chapter 71

1 And when Moses was eighteen years old, he desired to see his father and mother and he went to them to Goshen, and when Moses had come near Goshen, he came to the place where the children of Israel were engaged in work, and he observed their burdens, and he saw an Egyptian smiting one of his Hebrew brethren.

2 And when the man who was beaten saw Moses he ran to him for help, for the man Moses was greatly respected in the house of Pharaoh, and he said to him, My lord attend to me, this Egyptian came to my house in the night, bound me, and came to my wife in my presence, and now he seeks to take my life away.

3 And when Moses heard this wicked thing, his anger was kindled against the Egyptian, and he turned this way and the other, and when he saw there was no man there he smote the Egyptian and hid him in the sand, and delivered the Hebrew from the hand of him that smote him.

4 And the Hebrew went to his house, and Moses returned to his home, and went forth and came back to the king's house.

5 And when the man had returned home, he thought of repudiating his wife, for it was not right in the house of Jacob, for any man to come to his wife after she had been defiled.

6 And the woman went and told her brothers, and the woman's brothers sought to slay him, and he fled to his house and escaped.

7 And on the second day Moses went forth to his brethren, and saw, and behold two men were quarreling, and he said to the wicked one, Why dost thou smite thy neighbor?

8 And he answered him and said to him, Who has set thee for a prince and judge over us? dost thou think to slay me as thou didst slay the Egyptian? and Moses was afraid and he said, Surely the thing is known?

9 And Pharaoh heard of this affair, and he ordered Moses to be slain, so God sent his angel, and he appeared unto Pharaoh in the likeness of a captain of the guard.

10 And the angel of the Lord took the sword from the hand of the captain of the guard, and took his head off with it, for the likeness of the captain of the guard was turned into the likeness of Moses.

Comment:1: This is indeed a very strange verse which I would also think is highly unlikely as generally God doesn't behave in such a manner. That is man's way to destroy everything just like Satan. So, this verse seems very out of place?

11 And the angel of the Lord took hold of the right hand of Moses, and brought him forth from Egypt, and placed him from without the borders of Egypt, a distance of forty days' journey.

12 And Aaron his brother alone remained in the land of Egypt, and he prophesied to the children of Israel, saying,

13 Thus says the Lord God of your ancestors, Throw away, each man, the abominations of his eyes, and do not defile yourselves with the idols of Egypt.

14 And the children of Israel rebelled and would not hearken to Aaron at that time.

15 And the Lord thought to destroy them, were it not that the Lord remembered the covenant which he had made with Abraham, Isaac and Jacob.

16 In those days the hand of Pharaoh continued to be severe against the children of Israel, and he crushed and oppressed them until the time when God sent forth his word and took notice of them.

Chapter 72

1 And it was in those days that there was a great war between the children of Cush and the children of the east and Aram, and they rebelled against the king of Cush in whose hands they were.

2 So Kikianus king of Cush went forth with all the children of Cush, a people numerous as the sand, and he went to fight against Aram and the children of the east, to bring them under subjection.

3 And when Kikianus went out, he left Balaam the magician, with his two sons, to guard the city, and the lowest sort of the people of the land.

4 So Kikianus went forth to Aram and the children of the east, and he fought against them and smote them, and they all fell down wounded before Kikianus and his people.

5 And he took many of them captives and he brought them under subjection as at first, and he encamped upon their land to take tribute from them as usual.

6 And Balaam the son of Beor, when the king of Cush had left him to guard the city and the poor of the city, he rose up and advised with the people of the land to rebel against king Kikianus, not to let him enter the city when he should come home.

7 And the people of the land hearkened to him, and they swore to him and made him king over them, and his two sons for captains of the army.

8 So they rose up and raised the walls of the city at the two corners, and they built an exceeding strong building.

9 And at the third corner they dug ditches without number, between the city and the river which surrounded the whole land of Cush, and they made the waters of the river burst forth there.

10 At the fourth corner they collected numerous serpents by their incantations and enchantments, and they fortified the city and dwelt therein, and no one went out or in before them.

11 And Kikianus fought against Aram and the children of the east and he subdued them as before, and they gave him their usual tribute, and he went and returned to his land.

12 And when Kikianus the king of Cush approached his city and all the captains of the forces with him, they lifted up their eyes and saw that the walls of the city were built up and greatly elevated, so the men were astonished at this.

13 And they said one to the other, It is because they saw that we were delayed, in battle, and were greatly afraid of us, therefore have they done this thing and raised the city walls and fortified them so that the kings of Canaan might not come in battle against them.

14 So the king and the troops approached the city door and they looked up and behold, all the gates of the city were closed, and they called out to the sentinels, saying, Open unto us, that we may enter the city.

15 But the sentinels refused to open to them by the order of Balaam the magician, their king, they suffered them not to enter their city.

16 So they raised a battle with them opposite the city gate, and one hundred and thirty men of the army at Kikianus fell on that day.

17 And on the next day they continued to fight, and they fought at the side of the river; they endeavoured to pass but were not able, so some of them sank in the pits and died.

18 So the king ordered them to cut down trees to make rafts, upon which they might pass to them, and they did so.

19 And when they came to the place of the ditches, the waters revolved by mills, and two hundred men upon ten rafts were drowned.

20 And on the third day they came to fight at the side where the serpents were, but they could not approach there, for the serpents slew of them one hundred and seventy men, and they ceased fighting against Cush, and they besieged Cush for nine years, no person came out or in.

21 At that time that the war and the siege were against Cush, Moses fled from Egypt from Pharaoh who sought to kill him for having slain the Egyptian.

22 And Moses was eighteen years old when he fled from Egypt from the presence of Pharaoh, and he fled and escaped to the camp of Kikianus, which at that time was besieging Cush.

23 And Moses was nine years in the camp of Kikianus king of Cush, all the time that they were besieging Cush, and Moses went out and came in with them.

24 And the king and princes and all the fighting men loved Moses, for he was great and worthy, his stature was like a noble lion, his face was like the sun, and his strength was like that of a lion, and he was counsellor to the king.

25 And at the end of nine years, Kikianus was seized with a mortal disease, and his illness prevailed over him, and he died on the seventh day.

26 So his servants embalmed him and carried him and buried him opposite the city gate to the north of the land of Egypt.

27 And they built over him an elegant strong and high building, and they placed great stones below.

28 And the king's scribes engraved upon those stones all the might of their king Kikianus, and all his battles which he had fought, behold they are written there at this day.

29 Now after the death of Kikianus king of Cush it grieved his men and troops greatly on account of the war.

30 So they said one to the other, Give us counsel what we are to do at this time, as we have resided in the wilderness nine years away from our homes.

31 If we say we will fight against the city many of us will fall wounded or killed, and if we remain here in the siege we shall also die.

32 For now all the kings of Aram and of the children of the east will hear that our king is dead, and they will attack us suddenly in a hostile manner, and they will fight against us and leave no remnant of us.

33 Now therefore let us go and make a king over us, and let us remain in the siege until the city is delivered up to us.

34 And they wished to choose on that day a man for king from the army of Kikianus, and they found no object of their choice like Moses to reign over them.

35 And they hastened and stripped off each man his garments and cast them upon the ground, and they made a great heap and placed Moses thereon.

36 And they rose up and blew with trumpets and called out before him, and said, May the king live, may the king live!

37 And all the people and nobles swore unto him to give him for a wife Adoniah the queen, the Cushite, wife of Kikianus, and they made Moses king over them on that day.

38 And all the people of Cush issued a proclamation on that day, saying, Every man must give something to Moses of what is in his possession.

39 And they spread out a sheet upon the heap, and every man cast into it something of what he had, one a gold earring and the other a coin.

40 Also of onyx stones, bdellium, pearls and marble did the children of Cush cast unto Moses upon the heap, also silver and gold in great abundance.

41 And Moses took all the silver and gold, all the vessels, and the bdellium and onyx stones, which all the children of Cush had given to him, and he placed them amongst his treasures.

42 And Moses reigned over the children of Cush on that day, in the place of Kikianus king of Cush.

Chapter 73

1 In the fifty-fifth year of the reign of Pharaoh king of Egypt, that is in the hundred and fifty-seventh year of the Israelites going down into Egypt, reigned Moses in Cush.

2 Moses was twenty-seven years old when he began to reign over Cush, and forty years did he reign.

3 And the Lord granted Moses favour and grace in the eyes of all the children of Cush, and the children of Cush loved him exceedingly, so Moses was favoured by the Lord and by men.

4 And in the seventh day of his reign, all the children of Cush assembled and came before Moses and bowed down to him to the ground.

5 And all the children spoke together in the presence of the king, saying, Give us counsel that we may see what is to be done to this city.

6 For it is now nine years that we have been besieging round about the city, and have not seen our children and our wives.

7 So the king answered them, saying, If you will hearken to my voice in all that I shall command you, then will the Lord give the city into our hands and we shall subdue it.

8 For if we fight with them as in the former battle which we had with them before the death of Kikianus, many of us will fall down wounded as before.

9 Now therefore behold here is counsel for you in this matter; if you will hearken to my voice, then will the city be delivered into our hands.

10 So all the forces answered the king, saying, All that our lord shall command that will we do.

11 And Moses said unto them, Pass through and proclaim a voice in the whole camp unto all the people, saying,

215

12 Thus says the king, Go into the forest and bring with you of the young ones of the stork, each man a young one in his hand.

13 And any person transgressing the word of the king, who shall not bring his young one, he shall die, and the king will take all belonging to him.

14 And when you shall bring them they shall be in your keeping, you shall rear them until they grow up, and you shall teach them to dart upon, as is the way of the young ones of the hawk.

15 So all the children of Cush heard the words of Moses, and they rose up and caused a proclamation to be issued throughout the camp, saying,

16 Unto you, all the children of Cush, the king's order is, that you go all together to the forest, and catch there the young storks each man his young one in his hand, and you shall bring them home.

17 And any person violating the order of the king shall die, and the king will take all that belongs to him.

18 And all the people did so, and they went out to the wood and they climbed the fir trees and caught, each man a young one in his hand, all the young of the storks, and they brought them into the desert and reared them by order of the king, and they taught them to dart upon, similar to the young hawks.

19 And after the young storks were reared, the king ordered them to be hungered for three days, and all the people did so.

20 And on the third day, the king said unto them, strengthen yourselves and become valiant men, and put on each man his armour and gird on his sword upon him, and ride each man his horse and take each his young stork in his hand.

21 And we will rise up and fight against the city at the place where the serpents are; and all the people did as the king had ordered.

22 And they took each man his young one in his hand, and they went away, and when they came to the place of the serpents the king said to them, Send forth each man his young stork upon the serpents.

23 And they sent forth each man his young stork at the king's order, and the young storks ran upon the serpents and they devoured them all and destroyed them out of that place.

24 And when the king and people had seen that all the serpents were destroyed in that place, all the people set up a great shout.

25 And they approached and fought against the city and took it and subdued it, and they entered the city.

26 And there died on that day one thousand and one hundred men of the people of the city, all that inhabited the city, but of the people besieging not one died.

27 So all the children of Cush went each to his home, to his wife and children and to all belonging to him.

28 And Balaam the magician, when he saw that the city was taken, he opened the gate and he and his two sons and eight brothers fled and returned to Egypt to Pharaoh king of Egypt.

29 They are the sorcerers and magicians who are mentioned in the book of the law, standing against Moses when the Lord brought the plagues upon Egypt.

30 So Moses took the city by his wisdom, and the children of Cush placed him on the throne instead of Kikianus king of Cush.

31 And they placed the royal crown upon his head, and they gave him for a wife Adoniah the Cushite queen, wife of Kikianus.

32 And Moses feared the Lord God of his fathers, so that he came not to her, nor did he turn his eyes to her.

Comment:1: This story about Moses being a king of Cush is not mentioned in the Bible at all and it is also difficult to fit into his life between the time of him fleeing Egypt to the Wilderness and meeting Jethro and his daughters and finally seeing the 'Burning Bush' on the mountain side before he was sent by God himself back to Egypt to confront Pharaoh. It was only 40 years from Moses leaving Egypt until he came back to Egypt this time as the Deliverer of the Children of Israel, so how could he have had time to be a king of Cush for 40 years?

33 For Moses remembered how Abraham had made his servant Eliezer swear, saying unto him, 'Thou shalt not take a woman from the daughters of Canaan for my son Isaac'.

34 Also what Isaac did when Jacob had fled from his brother, when he commanded him, saying, Thou shalt not take a wife from the daughters of Canaan, nor make alliance with any of the children of Ham.

35 For the Lord our God gave Ham the son of Noah, and his children and all his seed, as slaves to the children of Shem and to the children of Japheth, and unto their seed after them for slaves, forever.

36 Therefore Moses turned not his heart nor his eyes to the wife of Kikianus all the days that he reigned over Cush.

37 And Moses feared the Lord his God all his life, and Moses walked before the Lord in truth, with all his heart and soul, he turned not from the right way all the days of his life; he declined not from the way either to the right or to the left, in which Abraham, Isaac and Jacob had walked.

38 And Moses strengthened himself in the kingdom of the children of Cush, and he guided the children of Cush with his usual wisdom, and Moses prospered in his kingdom.

39 And at that time Aram and the children of the east heard that Kikianus king of Cush had died, so Aram and the children of the east rebelled against Cush in those days.

40 And Moses gathered all the children of Cush, a people very mighty,

about thirty thousand men, and he went forth to fight with Aram and the children of the east.

41 And they went at first to the children of the east, and when the children of the east heard their report, they went to meet them, and engaged in battle with them.

42 And the war was severe against the children of the east, so the Lord gave all the children of the east into the hand of Moses, and about three hundred men fell down slain.

43 And all the children of the east turned back and retreated, so Moses and the children of Cush followed them and subdued them, and put a tax upon them, as was their custom.

44 So Moses and all the people with him passed from there to the land of Aram for battle.

45 And the people of Aram also went to meet them, and they fought against them, and the Lord delivered them into the hand of Moses, and many of the men of Aram fell down wounded.

46 And Aram also were subdued by Moses and the people of Cush, and also gave their usual tax.

47 And Moses brought Aram and the children of the east under subjection to the children of Cush, and Moses and all the people who were with him, turned to the land of Cush.

48 And Moses strengthened himself in the kingdom of the children of Cush, and the Lord was with him, and all the children of Cush were afraid of him.

Chapter 74

1 In the end of years died Saul king of Edom, and Baal Chanan the son of Achbor reigned in his place.

2 In the sixteenth year of the reign of Moses over Cush, Baal Chanan the son of Achbor reigned in the land of Edom over all the children of Edom for thirty-eight years.

3 In his days Moab rebelled against the power of Edom, having been under Edom since the days of Hadad the son of Bedad, who smote them and Midian, and brought Moab under subjection to Edom.

4 And when Baal Chanan the son of Achbor reigned over Edom, all the children of Moab withdrew their allegiance from Edom.

5 And Angeas king of Africa died in those days, and Azdrubal his son reigned in his stead.

6 And in those days died Janeas king of the children of Chittim, and they buried him in his temple which he had built for himself in the plain of Canopia for a residence, and Latinus reigned in his stead.

7 In the twenty-second year of the reign of Moses over the children of Cush, Latinus reigned over the children of Chittim forty-five years.

8 And he also built for himself a great and mighty tower, and he built therein an elegant temple for his residence, to conduct his government, as was the custom.

9 In the third year of his reign he caused a proclamation to be made to all his skilful men, who made many ships for him.

10 And Latinus assembled all his forces, and they came in ships, and went therein to fight with Azdrubal son of Angeas king of Africa, and they came to Africa and engaged in battle with Azdrubal and his army.

11 And Latinus prevailed over Azdrubal, and Latinus took from

Azdrubal the aqueduct which his father had brought from the children of Chittim, when he took Janiah the daughter of Uzi for a wife, so Latinus overthrew the bridge of the aqueduct, and smote the whole army of Azdrubal a severe blow.

12 And the remaining strong men of Azdrubal strengthened themselves, and their hearts were filled with envy, and they courted death, and again engaged in battle with Latinus king of Chittim.

13 And the battle was severe upon all the men of Africa, and they all fell wounded before Latinus and his people, and Azdrubal the king also fell in that battle.

14 And the king Azdrubal had a very beautiful daughter, whose name was Ushpezena, and all the men of Africa embroidered her likeness on their garments, on account of her great beauty and comely appearance.

15 And the men of Latinus saw Ushpezena, the daughter of Azdrubal, and praised her unto Latinus their king.

16 And Latinus ordered her to be brought to him, and Latinus took Ushpezena for a wife, and he turned back on his way to Chittim.

17 And it was after the death of Azdrubal son of Angeas, when Latinus had turned back to his land from the battle, that all the inhabitants of Africa rose up and took Anibal the son of Angeas, the younger brother of Azdrubal, and made him king instead at his brother over the whole land at Africa.

18 And when he reigned, he resolved to go to Chittim to fight with the children of Chittim, to avenge the cause of Azdrubal his brother, and the cause of the inhabitants of Africa, and he did so.

19 And he made many ships, and he came therein with his whole army, and he went to Chittim.

20 So Anibal fought with the children of Chittim, and the children of Chittim fell wounded before Anibal and his army, and Anibal avenged his brother's cause.

21 And Anibal continued the war for eighteen years with the children of Chittim, and Anibal dwelt in the land of Chittim and encamped there for a long time.

22 And Anibal smote the children of Chittim very severely, and he slew their great men and princes, and of the rest of the people he smote about eighty thousand men.

23 And at the end of days and years, Anibal returned to his land of Africa, and he reigned securely in the place of Azdrubal his brother.

Chapter 75

1 At that time, in the hundred and eightieth year of the Israelites going down into Egypt, there went forth from Egypt valiant men, thirty thousand on foot, from the children of Israel, who were all of the tribe of Joseph, of the children of Ephraim the son of Joseph.

2 For they said the period was completed which the Lord had appointed to the children of Israel in the times of old, which he had spoken to Abraham.

3 And these men girded themselves, and they put each man his sword at his side, and every man his armour upon him, and they trusted to their strength, and they went out together from Egypt with a mighty hand.

4 But they brought no provision for the road, only silver and gold, not even bread for that day did they bring in their hands, for they thought of getting their provision for pay from the Philistines, and if not they would take it by force.

5 And these men were very mighty and valiant men, one man could pursue a thousand and two could rout ten thousand, so they trusted to their strength and went together as they were.

6 And they directed their course toward the land of Gath, and they went down and found the shepherds of Gath feeding the cattle of the children of Gath.

7 And they said to the shepherds, Give us some of the sheep for pay, that we may eat, for we are hungry, for we have eaten no bread this day.

8 And the shepherds said, Are they our sheep or cattle that we should give them to you even for pay? so the children of Ephraim approached to take them by force.

9 And the shepherds of Gath shouted over them that their cry was heard at a distance, so all the children of Gath went out to them.

10 And when the children of Gath saw the evil doings of the children of Ephraim, they returned and assembled the men of Gath, and they put on each man his armour, and came forth to the children of Ephraim for battle.

11 And they engaged with them in the valley of Gath, and the battle was severe, and they smote from each other a great many on that day.

12 And on the second day the children of Gath sent to all the cities of the Philistines that they should come to their help, saying,

13 Come up unto us and help us, that we may smite the children of Ephraim who have come forth from Egypt to take our cattle, and to fight against us without cause.

14 Now the souls of the children of Ephraim were exhausted with hunger and thirst, for they had eaten no bread for three days. And forty thousand men went forth from the cities of the Philistines to the assistance of the men of Gath.

15 And these men were engaged in battle with the children of Ephraim, and the Lord delivered the children of Ephraim into the hands of the Philistines.

16 And they smote all the children of Ephraim, all who had gone forth from Egypt, none were remaining but ten men who had run away from the engagement.

17 For this evil was from the Lord against the children of Ephraim, for they transgressed the word of the Lord in going forth from Egypt, before the period had arrived which the Lord in the days of old had appointed to Israel.

18 And of the Philistines also there fell a great many, about twenty thousand men, and their brethren carried them and buried them in their cities.

19 And the slain of the children of Ephraim remained forsaken in the

valley of Gath for many days and years, and were not brought to burial, and the valley was filled with men's bones.

20 And the men who had escaped from the battle came to Egypt, and told all the children of Israel all that had befallen them.

21 And their father Ephraim mourned over them for many days, and his brethren came to console him.

22 And he came unto his wife and she bare a son, and he called his name Beriah, for she was unfortunate in his house.

Chapter 76

1 And Moses the son of Amram was still king in the land of Cush in those days, and he prospered in his kingdom, and he conducted the government of the children of Cush in justice, in righteousness, and integrity.

2 And all the children of Cush loved Moses all the days that he reigned over them, and all the inhabitants of the land of Cush were greatly afraid of him.

3 And in the fortieth year of the reign of Moses over Cush, Moses was sitting on the royal throne whilst Adoniah the queen was before him, and all the nobles were sitting around him.

4 And Adoniah the queen said before the king and the princes, What is this thing which you, the children of Cush, have done for this long time?

5 Surely you know that for forty years that this man has reigned over Cush he has not approached me, nor has he served the gods of the children of Cush.

6 Now therefore hear, O ye children of Cush, and let this man no more reign over you as he is not of our flesh.

7 Behold Menacrus my son is grown up, let him reign over you, for it is better for you to serve the son of your lord, than to serve a stranger, slave of the king of Egypt.

8 And all the people and nobles of the children of Cush heard the words which Adoniah the queen had spoken in their ears.

9 And all the people were preparing until the evening, and in the morning they rose up early and made Menacrus, son of Kikianus, king over them.

10 And all the children of Cush were afraid to stretch forth their hand against Moses, for the Lord was with Moses, and the children of Cush remembered the oath which they swore unto Moses, therefore they did no harm to him.

11 But the children of Cush gave many presents to Moses, and sent him from them with great honor.

12 So Moses went forth from the land of Cush, and went home and ceased to reign over Cush, and Moses was sixty-six years old when he went out of the land of Cush, for the thing was from the Lord, for the period had arrived which he had appointed in the days of old, to bring forth Israel from the affliction of the children of Ham.

13 So Moses went to Midian, for he was afraid to return to Egypt on account of Pharaoh, and he went and sat at a well of water in Midian.

14 And the seven daughters of Reuel the Midianite went out to feed their father's flock.

15 And they came to the well and drew water to water their father's flock.

16 So the shepherds of Midian came and drove them away, and Moses rose up and helped them and watered the flock.

17 And they came home to their father Reuel, and told him what Moses did for them.

18 And they said, An Egyptian man has delivered us from the hands of the shepherds, he drew up water for us and watered the flock.

19 And Reuel said to his daughters, And where is he? wherefore have you left the man?

20 And Reuel sent for him and fetched him and brought him home, and he ate bread with him.

21 And Moses related to Reuel that he had fled from Egypt and that he reigned forty years over Cush, and that they afterward had taken the government from him, and had sent him away in peace with honor and with presents.

22 And when Reuel had heard the words of Moses, Reuel said within himself, I will put this man into the prison house, whereby I shall conciliate the children of Cush, for he has fled from them.

Comment: It does not make any sense that the future father in law of Moses and Zipporah's father would put Moses into jail. According to the Bible, Moses showed up from the dessert not long after having fled Egypt and was still dressed like an Egyptian.

23 And they took and put him into the prison house, and Moses was in prison ten years, and whilst Moses was in the prison house, Zipporah the daughter of Reuel took pity over him, and supported him with bread and water all the time.

24 And all the children of Israel were yet in the land of Egypt serving the Egyptians in all manner of hard work, and the hand of Egypt continued in severity over the children of Israel in those days.

25 At that time the Lord smote Pharaoh king of Egypt, and he afflicted with the plague of leprosy from the sole of his foot to the crown of his head; owing to the cruel treatment of the children of Israel was this plague at that time from the Lord upon Pharaoh king of Egypt.

26 For the Lord had hearkened to the prayer of his people the children of Israel, and their cry reached him on account of their hard work.

27 Still his anger did not turn from them, and the hand of Pharaoh was still stretched out against the children of Israel, and Pharaoh hardened his neck before the Lord, and he increased his yoke over the children of Israel, and embittered their lives with all manner of hard work.

28 And when the Lord had inflicted the plague upon Pharaoh king of Egypt, he asked his wise men and sorcerers to cure him.

29 And his wise men and sorcerers said unto him, That if the blood of little children were put into the wounds he would be healed.

30 And Pharaoh hearkened to them, and sent his ministers to Goshen to the children of Israel to take their little children.

31 And Pharaoh's ministers went and took the infants of the children of Israel from the bosoms of their mothers by force, and they brought them to Pharaoh daily, a child each day, and the physicians killed them and applied them to the plague; thus did they all the days.

32 And the number of the children which Pharaoh slew was three hundred and seventy-five.

33 But the Lord hearkened not to the physicians of the king of Egypt, and the plague went on increasing mightily.

34 And Pharaoh was ten years afflicted with that plague, still the heart of Pharaoh was more hardened against the children of Israel.

35 And at the end of ten years the Lord continued to afflict Pharaoh with destructive plagues.

36 And the Lord smote him with a bad tumour and sickness at the stomach, and that plague turned to a severe boil.

37 At that time the two ministers of Pharaoh came from the land of Goshen where all the children of Israel were, and went to the house of Pharaoh and said to him, 'We have seen the children of Israel slacken in their work and negligent in their labour'.

38 And when Pharaoh heard the words of his ministers, his anger was kindled against the children of Israel exceedingly, for he was greatly grieved at his bodily pain.

39 And he answered and said, Now that the children of Israel know that I am ill, they turn and scoff at us, now therefore harness my chariot for me, and I will betake myself to Goshen and will see the scoff of the children of Israel with which they are deriding me; so his servants harnessed the chariot for him.

40 And they took and made him ride upon a horse, for he was not able to ride of himself;

41 And he took with him ten horsemen and ten footmen, and went to the children of Israel to Goshen.

42 And when they had come to the border of Egypt, the king's horse passed into a narrow place, elevated in the hollow part of the vineyard, fenced on both sides, the low, plain country being on the other side.

43 And the horses ran rapidly in that place and pressed each other, and the other horses pressed the king's horse.

44 And the king's horse fell into the low plain whilst the king was riding upon it, and when he fell the chariot turned over the king's face and the horse lay upon the king, and the king cried out, for his flesh was very sore.

45 And the flesh of the king was torn from him, and his bones were broken and he could not ride, for this thing was from the Lord to him, for the Lord had heard the cries of his people the children of Israel and their affliction.

46 And his servants carried him upon their shoulders, a little at a time, and they brought him back to Egypt, and the horsemen who were with him came also back to Egypt.

47 And they placed him in his bed, and the king knew that his end was come to die, so Aparanith the queen his wife came and cried before the king, and the king wept a great weeping with her.

48 And all his nobles and servants came on that day and saw the king in that affliction, and wept a great weeping with him.

49 And the princes of the king and all his counsellors advised the king to cause one to reign in his stead in the land, whomsoever he should choose from his sons.

50 And the king had three sons and two daughters which Aparanith the queen his wife had borne to him, besides the king's children of concubines.

51 And these were their names, the firstborn Othri, the second Adikam, and the third Morion, and their sisters, the name of the elder Bathia and of the other Acuzi.

52 And Othri the first born of the king was an idiot, precipitate and hurried in his words.

53 But Adikam was a cunning and wise man and knowing in all the wisdom of Egypt, but of unseemly aspect, thick in flesh, and very short in stature; his height was one cubit.

54 And when the king saw Adikam his son intelligent and wise in all things, the king resolved that he should be king in his stead after his death.

55 And he took for him a wife Gedudah daughter of Abilot, and he was ten years old, and she bare unto him four sons.

56 And he afterward went and took three wives and begat eight sons and three daughters.

57 And the disorder greatly prevailed over the king, and his flesh stank like the flesh of a carcass cast upon the field in summer time, during the heat of the sun.

58 And when the king saw that his sickness had greatly strengthened itself over him, he ordered his son Adikam to be brought to him, and they made him king over the land in his place.

59 And at the end of three years, the king died, in shame, disgrace, and disgust, and his servants carried him and buried him in the sepulchre of the kings of Egypt in Zoan Mizraim.

60 But they embalmed him not as was usual with kings, for his flesh was putrid, and they could not approach to embalm him on account of the stench, so they buried him in haste.

61 For this evil was from the Lord to him, for the Lord had requited him evil for the evil which in his days he had done to Israel.

62 And he died with terror and with shame, and his son Adikam reigned in his place.<

Chapter 77

1 Adikam was twenty years old when he reigned over Egypt, he reigned four years.

2 In the two hundred and sixth year of Israel's going down to Egypt did Adikam reign over Egypt, but he continued not so long in his reign over Egypt as his fathers had continued their reigns.

3 For Melol his father reigned ninety-four years in Egypt, but he was ten years sick and died, for he had been wicked before the Lord.

4 And all the Egyptians called the name of Adikam Pharaoh like the name of his fathers, as was their custom to do in Egypt.

5 And all the wise men of Pharaoh called the name of Adikam Ahuz, for short is called Ahuz in the Egyptian language.

6 And Adikam was exceedingly ugly, and he was a cubit and a span and he had a great beard which reached to the soles of his feet.

7 And Pharaoh sat upon his father's throne to reign over Egypt, and he conducted the government of Egypt in his wisdom.

8 And whilst he reigned he exceeded his father and all the preceding kings in wickedness, and he increased his yoke over the children of Israel.

9 And he went with his servants to Goshen to the children of Israel, and he strengthened the labour over them and he said unto them, Complete your work, each day's task, and let not your hands slacken from our work from this day forward as you did in the days of my father.

10 And he placed officers over them from amongst the children of Israel, and over these officers he placed taskmasters from amongst his servants.

11 And he placed over them a measure of bricks for them to do according to that number, day by day, and he turned back and went to Egypt.

12 At that time the task-masters of Pharaoh ordered the officers of the children of Israel according to the command of Pharaoh, saying,

13 Thus says Pharaoh, Do your work each day, and finish your task, and observe the daily measure of bricks; diminish not anything.

14 And it shall come to pass that if you are deficient in your daily bricks, I will put your young children in their stead.

15 And the task-masters of Egypt did so in those days as Pharaoh had ordered them.

16 And whenever any deficiency was found in the children of Israel's measure of their daily bricks, the task-masters of Pharaoh would go to the wives of the children of Israel and take infants of the children of Israel to the number of bricks deficient, they would take them by force from their mother's laps, and put them in the building instead of the bricks;

17 Whilst their fathers and mothers were crying over them and weeping when they heard the weeping voices of their infants in the wall of the building.

18 And the task-masters prevailed over Israel, that the Israelites should place their children in the building, so that a man placed his son in the wall and put mortar over him, whilst his eyes wept over him, and his tears ran down upon his child.

19 And the task-masters of Egypt did so to the babes of Israel for many days, and no one pitied or had compassion over the babes of the children of Israel.

20 And the number of all the children killed in the building was two hundred and seventy, some whom they had built upon instead of the bricks which had been left deficient by their fathers, and some whom they had drawn out dead from the building.

21 And the labour imposed upon the children of Israel in the days of Adikam exceeded in hardship that which they performed in the days of his father.

22 And the children of Israel sighed every day on account of their heavy work, for they had said to themselves, Behold when Pharaoh shall die, his son will rise up and lighten our work!

23 But they increased the latter work more than the former, and the children of Israel sighed at this and their cry ascended to God on account of their labour.

24 And God heard the voice of the children of Israel and their cry, in those days, and God remembered to them his covenant which he had made with Abraham, Isaac and Jacob.

25 And God saw the burden of the children of Israel, and their heavy work in those days, and he determined to deliver them.

26 And Moses the son of Amram was still confined in the dungeon in those days, in the house of Reuel the Midianite, and Zipporah the daughter of Reuel did support him with food secretly day by day.

27 And Moses was confined in the dungeon in the house of Reuel for ten years.

28 And at the end of ten years which was the first year of the reign of Pharaoh over Egypt, in the place of his father,

29 Zipporah said to her father Reuel, No person inquires or seeks after the Hebrew man, whom thou didst bind in prison now ten years.

30 Now therefore, if it seem good in thy sight, let us send and see whether he is living or dead, but her father knew not that she had supported him.

31 And Reuel her father answered and said to her, Has ever such a thing happened that a man should be shut up in a prison without food for ten years, and that he should live?

32 And Zipporah answered her father, saying, Surely thou hast heard that the God of the Hebrews is great and awful, and does wonders for them at all times.

33 He it was who delivered Abraham from Ur of the Chaldeans, and Isaac from the sword of his father, and Jacob from the angel of the Lord who wrestled with him at the ford of Jabbuk.

34 Also with this man has he done many things, he delivered him from the river in Egypt and from the sword of Pharaoh, and from the children of Cush, so also can he deliver him from famine and make him live.

35 And the thing seemed good in the sight of Reuel, and he did according to the word of his daughter, and sent to the dungeon to ascertain what became of Moses.

36 And he saw, and behold the man Moses was living in the dungeon, standing upon his feet, praising and praying to the God of his ancestors.

37 And Reuel commanded Moses to be brought out of the dungeon, so they shaved him and he changed his prison garments and ate bread.

38 And afterward Moses went into the garden of Reuel which was behind the house, and he there prayed to the Lord his God, who had done mighty wonders for him.

39 And it was that whilst he prayed he looked opposite to him, and behold a sapphire stick was placed in the ground, which was planted in the midst of the garden.

40 And he approached the stick and he looked, and behold the name of the Lord God of hosts was engraved thereon, written and developed upon the stick.

41 And he read it and stretched forth his hand and he plucked it like a forest tree from the thicket, and the stick was in his hand.

42 And this is the stick with which all the works of our God were performed, after he had created heaven and earth, and all the host of them, seas, rivers and all their fishes.

43 And when God had driven Adam from the garden of Eden, he took the stick in his hand and went and tilled the ground from which he was taken.

44 And the stick came down to Noah and was given to Shem and his descendants, until it came into the hand of Abraham the Hebrew.

45 And when Abraham had given all he had to his son Isaac, he also gave to him this stick.

46 And when Jacob had fled to Padan-aram, he took it into his hand, and when he returned to his father he had not left it behind him.

47 Also when he went down to Egypt he took it into his hand and gave it to Joseph, one portion above his brethren, for Jacob had taken it by force from his brother Esau.

48 And after the death of Joseph, the nobles of Egypt came into the house of Joseph, and the stick came into the hand of Reuel the Midianite, and when he went out of Egypt, he took it in his hand and planted it in his garden.

49 And all the mighty men of the Kinites tried to pluck it when they endeavoured to get Zipporah his daughter, but they were unsuccessful.

50 So that stick remained planted in the garden of Reuel, until he came who had a right to it and took it.

51 And when Reuel saw the stick in the hand of Moses, he wondered at it, and he gave him his daughter Zipporah for a wife.

Chapter 78

1 At that time died Baal Channan son of Achbor, king of Edom, and was buried in his house in the land of Edom.

2 And after his death the children of Esau sent to the land of Edom, and took from there a man who was in Edom, whose name was Hadad, and they made him king over them in the place of Baal Channan, their king.

3 And Hadad reigned over the children of Edom forty-eight years.

4 And when he reigned he resolved to fight against the children of Moab, to bring them under the power of the children of Esau as they were before, but he was not able, because the children of Moab heard this thing, and they rose up and hastened to elect a king over them from amongst their brethren.

5 And they afterward gathered together a great people, and sent to the children of Ammon their brethren for help to fight against Hadad king of Edom.

6 And Hadad heard the thing which the children of Moab had done, and was greatly afraid of them, and refrained from fighting against them.

7 In those days Moses, the son of Amram, in Midian, took Zipporah, the daughter of Reuel the Midianite, for a wife.

8 And Zipporah walked in the ways of the daughters of Jacob, she was nothing short of the righteousness of Sarah, Rebecca, Rachel and Leah.

9 And Zipporah conceived and bare a son and he called his name Gershom, for he said, I was a stranger in a foreign land; but he circumcised not his foreskin, at the command of Reuel his father-in-law.

10 And she conceived again and bare a son, but circumcised his fore-

skin, and called his name Eliezer, for Moses said, Because the God of my fathers was my help, and delivered me from the sword of Pharaoh.

11 And Pharaoh king of Egypt greatly increased the labour of the children of Israel in those days and continued to make his yoke heavier upon the children of Israel.

12 And he ordered a proclamation to be made in Egypt, saying, Give no more straw to the people to make bricks with, let them go and gather themselves straw as they can find it.

13 Also the tale of bricks which they shall make let them give each day, and diminish nothing from them, for they are idle in their work.

14 And the children of Israel heard this, and they mourned and sighed, and they cried unto the Lord on account of the bitterness of their souls.

15 And the Lord heard the cries of the children of Israel, and saw the oppression with which the Egyptians oppressed them.

16 And the Lord was jealous of his people and his inheritance, and heard their voice, and he resolved to take them out of the affliction of Egypt, to give them the land of Canaan for a possession.

Chapter 79

1 And in those days Moses was feeding the flock of Reuel the Midianite his father-in-law, beyond the wilderness of Sin, and the stick which he took from his father-in-law was in his hand.

2 And it came to pass one day that a kid of goats strayed from the flock, and Moses pursued it and it came to the mountain of God to Horeb.

3 And when he came to Horeb, the Lord appeared there unto him in the bush, and he found the bush burning with fire, but the fire had no power over the bush to consume it.

4 And Moses was greatly astonished at this sight, wherefore the bush was not consumed, and he approached to see this mighty thing, and the Lord called unto Moses out of the fire and commanded him to go down to Egypt, to Pharaoh king of Egypt, to send the children of Israel from his service.

5 And the Lord said unto Moses, Go, return to Egypt, for all those men who sought thy life are dead, and thou shalt speak unto Pharaoh to send forth the children of Israel from his land.

6 And the Lord showed him to do signs and wonders in Egypt before the eyes of Pharaoh and the eyes of his subjects, in order that they might believe that the Lord had sent him.

7 And Moses hearkened to all that the Lord had commanded him, and he returned to his father-in-law and told him the thing, and Reuel said to him, Go in peace.

8 And Moses rose up to go to Egypt, and he took his wife and sons with him, and he was at an inn in the road, and an angel of God came down, and sought an occasion against him.

Comment:1: It was actually the 'Fallen angel' Satan that sought to slay Moses, as he didn't want Moses interfering with his satanic world empire of Egypt. Only the book of Jubilees gets this story of Moses returning to Egypt to chastise Pharaoh correct. Both the Bible and this Book of Jasher fail to mention that it was not an angel of God, but a Fallen angel that sought to slay Moses, which makes a lot more sense. Why would God one-minute command Moses to go to Egypt and the very next minute send an angel to slay Moses over a tiny detail such as circumcision? That does not may any sense. Satan was angry and was trying to get in the way of God's plan and slay Moses.

JUBILEES 48.3 And thou thyself know what He spake unto thee on [2410 A.M.] Mount Sinai, and what prince Mastema (Satan) desired to do with thee when thou was returning into Egypt.

JUBILEES 48.4 Did he not with all his power seek to slay thee and deliver the Egyptians out of thy hand when he saw that thou was sent to execute judgment and vengeance on the Egyptians.

---

9 And he wished to kill him on account of his first-born son, because he had not circumcised him, and had transgressed the covenant which the Lord had made with Abraham.

10 For Moses had hearkened to the words of his father-in-law which he had spoken to him, not to circumcise his first-born son, therefore he circumcised him not.

11 And Zipporah saw the angel of the Lord seeking an occasion against Moses, and she knew that this thing was owing to his not having circumcised her son Gershom.

C.2 Here we see Satan disguised as an Angel of Light.

2CO.11:14 And no marvel; for Satan himself is transformed into an angel of light.

---

12 And Zipporah hastened and took of the sharp rock stones that were there, and she circumcised her son, and delivered her husband and her son from the hand of the angel of the Lord.

C.3 Satan is a great 'Religionist' when it suits his purpose! He knew that God had sent Moses to Pharaoh and he was determined to stop Moses, so he used the 'letter of the Hebrew Law' that Moses had forgotten to circumcise his son, which was punishable by death according to Hebrew laws. Satan is a type of 'executioner of the Law' who goes before God in his courts and is always accusing the Saints before God day and night and seeks to slay the innocent by twisting the rules to his own advantage. Many millions of innocent people have been murdered because of Satan acting as the religious judge who is a persecutor and an executioner.

241

REV.12:10 And I heard a loud voice saying in heaven, Now is come salvation, and strength, and the kingdom of our God, and the power of his Christ: for the accuser of our brethren is cast down, which accused them before our God day and night.

13 And Aaron the son of Amram, the brother of Moses, was in Egypt walking at the river side on that day.

14 And the Lord appeared to him in that place, and he said to him, Go now toward Moses in the wilderness, and he went and met him in the mountain of God, and he kissed him.

15 And Aaron lifted up his eyes, and saw Zipporah the wife of Moses and her children, and he said unto Moses, Who are these unto thee?

16 And Moses said unto him, They are my wife and sons, which God gave to me in Midian; and the thing grieved Aaron on account of the woman and her children.

17 And Aaron said to Moses, Send away the woman and her children that they may go to her father's house, and Moses hearkened to the words of Aaron, and did so.

18 And Zipporah returned with her children, and they went to the house of Reuel, and remained there until the time arrived when the Lord had visited his people, and brought them forth from Egypt from the hand at Pharaoh.

19 And Moses and Aaron came to Egypt to the community of the children of Israel, and they spoke to them all the words of the Lord, and the people rejoiced an exceeding great rejoicing.

20 And Moses and Aaron rose up early on the next day, and they went to the house of Pharaoh, and they took in their hands the stick of God.

21 And when they came to the king's gate, two young lions were confined there with iron instruments, and no person went out or came in from before them, unless those whom the king ordered to come, when the conjurors came and withdrew the lions by their incantations, and this brought them to the king.

22 And Moses hastened and lifted up the stick upon the lions, and he loosed them, and Moses and Aaron came into the king's house.

23 The lions also came with them in joy, and they followed them and rejoiced as a dog rejoices over his master when he comes from the field.

24 And when Pharaoh saw this thing he was astonished at it, and he was greatly terrified at the report, for their appearance was like the appearance of the children of God.

25 And Pharaoh said to Moses, What do you require? and they answered him, saying, The Lord God of the Hebrews has sent us to thee, to say, Send forth my people that they may serve me.

26 And when Pharaoh heard their words he was greatly terrified before them, and he said to them, Go today and come back to me tomorrow, and they did according to the word of the king.

27 And when they had gone Pharaoh sent for Balaam the magician and to Jannes and Jambres his sons, and to all the magicians and conjurors and counsellors which belonged to the king, and they all came and sat before the king.

28 And the king told them all the words which Moses and his brother Aaron had spoken to him, and the magicians said to the king, But how came the men to thee, on account of the lions which were confined at the gate?

29 And the king said, Because they lifted up their rod against the lions and loosed them, and came to me, and the lions also rejoiced at them as a dog rejoices to meet his master.

30 And Balaam the son of Beor the magician answered the king, saying, These are none else than magicians like ourselves.

31 Now therefore send for them, and let them come and we will try them, and the king did so.

32 And in the morning Pharaoh sent for Moses and Aaron to come before the king, and they took the rod of God, and came to the king and spoke to him, saying,

33 Thus said the Lord God of the Hebrews, Send my people that they may serve me.

34 And the king said to them, But who will believe you that you are the messengers of God and that you come to me by his order?

35 Now therefore give a wonder or sign in this matter, and then the words which you speak will be believed.

36 And Aaron hastened and threw the rod out of his hand before Pharaoh and before his servants, and the rod turned into a serpent.

37 And the sorcerers saw this and they cast each man his rod upon the ground and they became serpents.

38 And the serpent of Aaron's rod lifted up its head and opened its mouth to swallow the rods of the magicians.

39 And Balaam the magician answered and said, This thing has been from the days of old, that a serpent should swallow its fellow, and that living things devour each other.

40 Now therefore restore it to a rod as it was at first, and we will also restore our rods as they were at first, and if thy rod shall swallow our rods, then shall we know that the spirit of God is in thee, and if not, thou art only an artificer like unto ourselves.

41 And Aaron hastened and stretched forth his hand and caught hold of the serpent's tail and it became a rod in his hand, and the sorcerers did the like with their rods, and they got hold, each man of the tail of his serpent, and they became rods as at first.

42 And when they were restored to rods, the rod of Aaron swallowed up their rods.

43 And when the king saw this thing, he ordered the book of records that related to the kings of Egypt, to be brought, and they brought the book of records, the chronicles of the kings of Egypt, in which all the idols of Egypt were inscribed, for they thought of finding therein the name of Jehovah, but they found it not.

44 And Pharaoh said to Moses and Aaron, Behold I have not found the name of your God written in this book, and his name I know not.

45 And the counsellors and wise men answered the king, We have heard that the God of the Hebrews is a son of the wise, the son of ancient kings.

46 And Pharaoh turned to Moses and Aaron and said to them, I know not the Lord whom you have declared, neither will I send his people.

47 And they answered and said to the king, The Lord God of Gods is his name, and he proclaimed his name over us from the days of our ancestors, and sent us, saying, Go to Pharaoh and say unto him, Send my people that they may serve me.

48 Now therefore send us, that we may take a journey for three days in the wilderness, and there may sacrifice to him, for from the days of our going down to Egypt, he has not taken from our hands either burnt offering, oblation or sacrifice, and if thou wilt not send us, his anger will be kindled against thee, and he will smite Egypt either with the plague or with the sword.

49 And Pharaoh said to them, Tell me now his power and his might; and they said to him, He created the heaven and the earth, the seas and all their fishes, he formed the light, created the darkness, caused rain upon the earth and watered it, and made the herbage and grass to sprout, he created man and beast and the animals of the forest, the birds of the air and the fish of the sea, and by his mouth they live and die.

50 Surely he created thee in thy mother's womb, and put into thee the breath of life, and reared thee and placed thee upon the royal throne of Egypt, and he will take thy breath and soul from thee, and return thee to the ground whence thou wast taken.

51 And the anger of the king was kindled at their words, and he said to them, But who amongst all the Gods of nations can do this? my river is mine own, and I have made it for myself.

52 And he drove them from him, and he ordered the labour upon Israel to be more severe than it was yesterday and before.

53 And Moses and Aaron went out from the king's presence, and they saw the children of Israel in an evil condition for the taskmasters had made their labour exceedingly heavy.

54 And Moses returned to the Lord and said, 'Why hast thou ill-treated thy people? for since I came to speak to Pharaoh what thou didst send me for, he has exceedingly ill-used the children of Israel.'

55 And the Lord said to Moses, 'Behold thou wilt see that with an outstretched hand and heavy plagues, Pharaoh will send the children of Israel from his land'.

56 And Moses and Aaron dwelt amongst their brethren the children of Israel in Egypt.

57 And as for the children of Israel the Egyptians embittered their lives, with the heavy work which they imposed upon them.

Chapter 80

Comment:1: This story is also told in the Bible in Exodus chapters 8-12, but the Book of Jasher has many extra *interesting details*:

1 And at the end of two years, the Lord again sent Moses to Pharaoh to bring forth the children of Israel, and to send them out of the land of Egypt.

2 And Moses went and came to the house of Pharaoh, and he spoke to him the words of the Lord who had sent him, but Pharaoh would not hearken to the voice of the Lord, and God roused his might in Egypt upon Pharaoh and his subjects, and God smote Pharaoh and his people with very great and sore plagues.

3 And the Lord sent by the hand of Aaron and turned all the waters of Egypt into blood, with all their streams and rivers.

4 And when an Egyptian came to drink and draw water, he looked into his pitcher, and behold all the water was turned into blood; and when he came to drink from his cup the water in the cup became blood.

5 And when a woman kneaded her dough and cooked her victuals, their appearance was turned to that of blood.

6 And the Lord sent again and caused all their waters to bring forth frogs, and all the frogs came into the houses of the Egyptians.

7 And when the Egyptians drank, their bellies were filled with frogs and they danced in their bellies as they dance when in the river.

8 And all their drinking water and cooking water turned to frogs, also when they lay in their beds their perspiration bred frogs.

9 Notwithstanding all this the anger of the Lord did not turn from them, and his hand was stretched out against all the Egyptians to smite them with every heavy plague.

247

10 And he sent and smote their dust to lice, and the lice became in Egypt to the height of two cubits upon the earth.

11 The lice were also very numerous, in the flesh of man and beast, in all the inhabitants of Egypt, also upon the king and queen the Lord sent the lice, and it grieved Egypt exceedingly on account of the lice.

12 Notwithstanding this, the anger of the Lord did not turn away, and his hand was still stretched out over Egypt.

13 And the Lord sent all kinds of beasts of the field into Egypt, and they came and destroyed all Egypt, man and beast, and trees, and all things that were in Egypt.

14 And the Lord sent fiery serpents, scorpions, mice, weasels, toads, together with others creeping in dust.

15 Flies, hornets, fleas, bugs and gnats, each swarm according to its kind.

16 And all reptiles and winged animals according to their kind came to Egypt and grieved the Egyptians exceedingly.

C.2 'Winged animals' are these birds or are they chimeras such as griffins (Lion with wings)? It is odd that griffins were sometimes used to depict ancient Babylon. Another chimera was the one mentioned as guarding the Assyrian Empire: Head of a man, body of a bull and the wings of an eagle

17 And the fleas and flies came into the eyes and ears of the Egyptians.

18 And the hornet came upon them and drove them away, and they removed from it into their inner rooms, and it pursued them.

19 And when the Egyptians hid themselves on account of the swarm of animals, they locked their doors after them, and God ordered the Sulanuth which was in the sea, to come up and go into Egypt.

C.3 This verse is truly incredible. So, God commanded some sort of sea monster, that sounds like a giant octopus, to come onto the dry land and both remove the roofing of the Egyptians houses and to open the locks to the barred doors. These are actions which are not normally associated with sea monsters! However, we all know that with God anything *is* possible and especially when He commands the creature to do His will.

LUK.1:37 For with God nothing shall be impossible.

JOHN.1:17 Now the LORD had prepared a great fish to swallow up Jonah. And Jonah was in the belly of the fish three days and three nights.

JOHN.2:10 And the LORD spake unto the fish, and it vomited out Jonah upon the dry land.

---

20 And she had long arms, ten cubits in length of the cubit of a man.

21 And she went upon the roofs and uncovered the raftering and flooring and cut them, and stretched forth her arm into the house and removed the lock and the bolt, and opened the houses of Egypt.

22 Afterward came the swarm of animals into the houses of Egypt, and the swarm of animals destroyed the Egyptians, and it grieved them exceedingly.

23 Notwithstanding this the anger of the Lord did not turn away from the Egyptians, and his hand was yet stretched forth against them.

24 And God sent the pestilence, and the pestilence pervaded Egypt, in the horses and asses, and in the camels, in herds of oxen and sheep and in man.

25 And when the Egyptians rose up early in the morning to take their cattle to pasture they found all their cattle dead.

26 And there remained of the cattle of the Egyptians only one in ten, and of the cattle belonging to Israel in Goshen not one died.

27 And God sent a burning inflammation in the flesh of the Egyptians, which burst their skins, and it became a severe itch in all the Egyptians from the soles of their feet to the crowns of their heads.

28 And many boils were in their flesh, that their flesh wasted away until they became rotten and putrid.

---

29 Notwithstanding this the anger of the Lord did not turn away, and his hand was still stretched out over all Egypt.

30 And the Lord sent a very heavy hail, which smote their vines and broke their fruit trees and dried them up that they fell upon them.

31 Also every green herb became dry and perished, for a mingling fire descended amidst the hail, therefore the hail and the fire consumed all things.

32 Also men and beasts that were found abroad perished of the flames of fire and of the hail, and all the young lions were exhausted.

33 And the Lord sent and brought numerous locusts into Egypt, the Chasel, Salom, Chargol, and Chagole, locusts each of its kind, which devoured all that the hail had left remaining.

34 Then the Egyptians rejoiced at the locusts, although they consumed the produce of the field, and they caught them in abundance and salted them for food.

35 And the Lord turned a mighty wind of the sea which took away all the locusts, even those that were salted, and thrust them into the Red Sea; not one locust remained within the boundaries of Egypt.

36 And God sent darkness upon Egypt, that the whole land of Egypt and Pathros became dark for three days, so that a man could not see his hand when he lifted it to his mouth.

37 At that time died many of the people of Israel who had rebelled against the Lord and who would not hearken to Moses and Aaron, and believed not in them that God had sent them.

38 And who had said, We will not go forth from Egypt lest we perish with hunger in a desolate wilderness, and who would not hearken to the voice of Moses.

39 And the Lord plagued them in the three days of darkness, and the Israelites buried them in those days, without the Egyptians knowing of them or rejoicing over them.

40 And the darkness was very great in Egypt for three days, and any person who was standing when the darkness came, remained standing in his place, and he that was sitting remained sitting, and he that was lying continued lying in the same state, and he that was walking remained sitting upon the ground in the same spot; and this thing happened to all the Egyptians, until the darkness had passed away.

41 And the days of darkness passed away, and the Lord sent Moses and Aaron to the children of Israel, saying, Celebrate your feast and make your Passover, for behold I come in the midst of the night amongst all the Egyptians, and I will smite all their first born, from the first born of a man to the first born of a beast, and when I see your Passover, I will pass over you.

42 And the children of Israel did according to all that the Lord had commanded Moses and Aaron, thus did they in that night.

43 And it came to pass in the middle of the night, that the Lord went forth in the midst of Egypt, and smote all the first born of the Egyptians, from the first born of man to the first born of beast.

44 And Pharaoh rose up in the night, he and all his servants and all the Egyptians, and there was a great cry throughout Egypt in that night, for there was not a house in which there was not a corpse.

45 Also the likenesses of the first born of Egypt, which were carved in the walls at their houses, were destroyed and fell to the ground.

46 Even the bones of their first born who had died before this and whom they had buried in their houses, were raked up by the dogs of Egypt on that night and dragged before the Egyptians and cast before them.

47 And all the Egyptians saw this evil which had suddenly come upon them, and all the Egyptians cried out with a loud voice.

48 And all the families of Egypt wept upon that night, each man for his son and each man for his daughter, being the first born, and the tumult of Egypt was heard at a distance on that night.

49 And Bithia the daughter of Pharaoh went forth with the king on that night to seek Moses and Aaron in their houses, and they found them in their houses, eating and drinking and rejoicing with all Israel.

50 And Bithia said to Moses, Is this the reward for the good which I have done to thee, who have reared thee and stretched thee out, and thou hast brought this evil upon me and my father's house?

51 And Moses said to her, Surely ten plagues did the Lord bring upon Egypt; did any evil accrue to thee from any of them? did one of them affect thee? and she said, No.

52 And Moses said to her, Although thou art the first born to thy mother, thou shalt not die, and no evil shall reach thee in the midst of Egypt.

53 And she said, What advantage is it to me, when I see the king, my brother, and all his household and subjects in this evil, whose first born perish with all the first born of Egypt?

54 And Moses said to her, Surely thy brother and his household, and subjects, the families of Egypt, would not hearken to the words of the Lord, therefore did this evil come upon them.

55 And Pharaoh king of Egypt approached Moses and Aaron, and some of the children of Israel who were with them in that place, and he prayed to them, saying,

56 Rise up and take your brethren, all the children of Israel who are in the land, with their sheep and oxen, and all belonging to them, they shall leave nothing remaining, only pray for me to the Lord your God.

57 And Moses said to Pharaoh, Behold though thou art thy mother's first born, yet fear not, for thou wilt not die, for the Lord has commanded

that thou shalt live, in order to show thee his great might and strong stretched out arm.

58 And Pharaoh ordered the children of Israel to be sent away, and all the Egyptians strengthened themselves to send them, for they said, We are all perishing.

59 And all the Egyptians sent the Israelites forth, with great riches, sheep and oxen and precious things, according to the oath of the Lord between him and our Father Abraham.

60 And the children of Israel delayed going forth at night, and when the Egyptians came to them to bring them out, they said to them, Are we thieves, that we should go forth at night?

61 And the children of Israel asked of the Egyptians, vessels of silver, and vessels of gold, and garments, and the children of Israel stripped the Egyptians.

62 And Moses hastened and rose up and went to the river of Egypt, and brought up from thence the coffin of Joseph and took it with him.

63 The children of Israel also brought up, each man his father's coffin with him, and each man the coffins of his tribe.

Chapter 81

1 And the children of Israel journeyed from Rameses to Succoth, about six hundred thousand men on foot, besides the little ones and their wives.

2 Also a mixed multitude went up with them, and flocks and herds, even much cattle.

3 And the sojourning of the children of Israel, who dwelt in the land of Egypt in hard labour, was two hundred and ten years.

Comment:1: Notice that it states that the time that the growing 'nation of Israel' had 'sojourned' in Egypt was only 210 years and not 430 years as often claimed by Bible students. See APPENDIX for details on the Timeframe discrepancy

4 And at the end of two hundred and ten years, the Lord brought forth the children of Israel from Egypt with a strong hand.

5 And the children of Israel travelled from Egypt and from Goshen and from Rameses, and encamped in Succoth on the fifteenth day of the first month.

6 And the Egyptians buried all their first born whom the Lord had smitten, and all the Egyptians buried their slain for three days.

7 And the children of Israel travelled from Succoth and encamped in Ethom, at the end of the wilderness.

8 And on the third day after the Egyptians had buried their first born, many men rose up from Egypt and went after Israel to make them return to Egypt, for they repented that they had sent the Israelites away from their servitude.

9 And one man said to his neighbor, Surely Moses and Aaron spoke to Pharaoh, saying, We will go a three days' journey in the wilderness and sacrifice to the Lord our God.

10 Now therefore let us rise up early in the morning and cause them to return, and it shall be that if they return with us to Egypt to their masters, then shall we know that there is faith in them, but if they will not return, then will we fight with them, and make them come back with great power and a strong hand.

11 And all the nobles of Pharaoh rose up in the morning, and with them about seven hundred thousand men, and they went forth from Egypt on that day, and came to the place where the children of Israel were.

12 And all the Egyptians saw and behold Moses and Aaron and all the children of Israel were sitting before Pi-hahiroth, eating and drinking and celebrating the feast of the Lord.

13 And all the Egyptians said to the children of Israel, Surely you said, We will go a journey for three days in the wilderness and sacrifice to our God and return.

14 Now therefore this day makes five days since you went, why do you not return to your masters?

15 And Moses and Aaron answered them, saying, Because the Lord our God has testified in us, saying, You shall no more return to Egypt, but we will betake ourselves to a land flowing with milk and honey, as the Lord our God had sworn to our ancestors to give to us.

16 And when the nobles of Egypt saw that the children of Israel did not hearken to them, to return to Egypt, they girded themselves to fight with Israel.

17 And the Lord strengthened the hearts of the children of Israel over the Egyptians, that they gave them a severe beating, and the battle was sore upon the Egyptians, and all the Egyptians fled from before the children of Israel, for many of them perished by the hand of Israel.

18 And the nobles of Pharaoh went to Egypt and told Pharaoh, saying, The children of Israel have fled, and will no more return to Egypt, and in this manner did Moses and Aaron speak to us.

19 And Pharaoh heard this thing, and his heart and the hearts of all his subjects were turned against Israel, and they repented that they had sent Israel; and all the Egyptians advised Pharaoh to pursue the children of Israel to make them come back to their burdens.

20 And they said each man to his brother, What is this which we have done, that we have sent Israel from our servitude?

21 And the Lord strengthened the hearts of all the Egyptians to pursue the Israelites, for the Lord desired to overthrow the Egyptians in the Red Sea.

22 And Pharaoh rose up and harnessed his chariot, and he ordered all the Egyptians to assemble, not one man was left excepting the little ones and the women.

23 And all the Egyptians went forth with Pharaoh to pursue the children of Israel, and the camp of Egypt was an exceedingly large and heavy camp, about ten hundred thousand men.

24 And the whole of this camp went and pursued the children of Israel to bring them back to Egypt, and they reached them encamping by the Red Sea.

25 And the children of Israel lifted up their eyes, and beheld all the Egyptians pursuing them, and the children of Israel were greatly terrified at them, and the children of Israel cried to the Lord.

26 And on account of the Egyptians, the children of Israel divided themselves into four divisions, and they were divided in their opinions, for they were afraid of the Egyptians, and Moses spoke to each of them.

27 The first division was of the children of Reuben, Simeon, and Issachar, and they resolved to cast themselves into the sea, for they were exceedingly afraid of the Egyptians.

28 And Moses said to them, Fear not, stand still and see the salvation of the Lord which He will effect this day for you.

29 The second division was of the children of Zebulun, Benjamin and Naphtali, and they resolved to go back to Egypt with the Egyptians.

30 And Moses said to them, Fear not, for as you have seen the Egyptians this day, so shall you see them no more for ever.

31 The third division was of the children of Judah and Joseph, and they resolved to go to meet the Egyptians to fight with them.

32 And Moses said to them, Stand in your places, for the Lord will fight for you, and you shall remain silent.

33 And the fourth division was of the children of Levi, Gad, and Asher, and they resolved to go into the midst of the Egyptians to confound them, and Moses said to them, Remain in your stations and fear not, only call unto the Lord that he may save you out of their hands.

34 After this Moses rose up from amidst the people, and he prayed to the Lord and said,

35 O Lord God of the whole earth, save now thy people whom thou didst bring forth from Egypt, and let not the Egyptians boast that power and might are theirs.

36 So the Lord said to Moses, Why dost thou cry unto me? speak to the children of Israel that they shall proceed, and do thou stretch out thy rod upon the sea and divide it, and the children of Israel shall pass through it.

37 And Moses did so, and he lifted up his rod upon the sea and divided it.

38 And the waters of the sea were divided into twelve parts, and the children of Israel passed through on foot, with shoes, as a man would pass through a prepared road.

39 And the Lord manifested to the children of Israel his wonders in Egypt and in the sea by the hand of Moses and Aaron.

40 And when the children of Israel had entered the sea, the Egyptians came after them, and the waters of the sea resumed upon them, and they all sank in the water, and not one man was left excepting Pharaoh, who gave thanks to the Lord and believed in him, therefore the Lord did not cause him to perish at that time with the Egyptians.

C.2 Finally, Pharaoh says 'uncle to God', or he submits to God and therefore God does not allow him to die with all the other Egyptian soldiers who were drowned in the Sea.

41 And the Lord ordered an angel to take him from amongst the Egyptians, who cast him upon the land of Ninevah and he reigned over it for a long time.

C.3 This verse stating that Pharaoh was taken by the hand of an angel and cast him on the land of Nineveh is highly unlikely. This is certainly not biblical. According to factual History, Pharaoh returned to Egypt, practically in disgrace. However, his son became a believer in the God of Israel.

42 And on that day the Lord saved Israel from the hand of Egypt, and all the children of Israel saw that the Egyptians had perished, and they beheld the great hand of the Lord, in what he had performed in Egypt and in the sea.

43 Then sang Moses and the children of Israel this song unto the Lord, on the day when the Lord caused the Egyptians to fall before them.

44 And all Israel sang in concert, saying, I will sing to the Lord for He is greatly exalted, the horse and his rider has he cast into the sea; behold it is written in the book of the law of God.

45 After this the children of Israel proceeded on their journey, and encamped in Marah, and the Lord gave to the children of Israel statutes and judgments in that place in Marah, and the Lord commanded the children of Israel to walk in all his ways and to serve him.

46 And they journeyed from Marah and came to Elim, and in Elim were twelve springs of water and seventy date trees, and the children encamped there by the waters.

47 And they journeyed from Elim and came to the wilderness of Sin, on the fifteenth day of the second month after their departure from Egypt.

48 At that time the Lord gave the manna to the children of Israel to eat, and the Lord caused food to rain from heaven for the children of Israel day by day.

49 And the children of Israel ate the manna for forty years, all the days that they were in the wilderness, until they came to the land of Canaan to possess it.

50 And they proceeded from the wilderness of Sin and encamped in Alush.

51 And they proceeded from Alush and encamped in Rephidim.

52 And when the children of Israel were in Rephidim, Amalek the son of Eliphaz, the son of Esau, the brother of Zepho, came to fight with Israel.

53 And he brought with him eight hundred and one thousand men, magicians and conjurers, and he prepared for battle with Israel in Rephidim.

54 And they carried on a great and severe battle against Israel, and the Lord delivered Amalek and his people into the hands of Moses and the children of Israel, and into the hand of Joshua, the son of Nun, the Ephrathite, the servant of Moses.

55 And the children of Israel smote Amalek and his people at the edge of the sword, but the battle was very sore upon the children of Israel.

56 And the Lord said to Moses, Write this thing as a memorial for thee in a book, and place it in the hand of Joshua, the son of Nun, thy servant, and thou shalt command the children of Israel, saying, When thou shalt come to the land of Canaan, thou shalt utterly efface the remembrance of Amalek from under heaven.

57 And Moses did so, and he took the book and wrote upon it these words, saying,

58 Remember what Amalek has done to thee in the road when thou wentest forth from Egypt.

59 Who met thee in the road and smote thy rear, even those that were feeble behind thee when thou wast faint and weary.

60 Therefore it shall be when the Lord thy God shall have given thee rest from all thine enemies round about in the land which the Lord thy God giveth thee for an inheritance, to possess it, that thou shalt blot out the remembrance of Amalek from under heaven, thou shalt not forget it.

61 And the king who shall have pity on Amalek, or upon his memory or upon his seed, behold I will require it of him, and I will cut him off from amongst his people.

62 And Moses wrote all these things in a book, and he enjoined the children of Israel respecting all these matters.

Chapter 82

1 And the children of Israel proceeded from Rephidim and they encamped in the wilderness of Sinai, in the third month from their going forth from Egypt.

2 At that time came Reuel the Midianite, the father-in-law of Moses, with Zipporah his daughter and her two sons, for he had heard of the wonders of the Lord which he had done to Israel, that he had delivered them from the hand of Egypt.

3 And Reuel came to Moses to the wilderness where he was encamped, where was the mountain of God.

4 And Moses went forth to meet his father-in-law with great honor, and all Israel was with him.

5 And Reuel and his children remained amongst the Israelites for many days, and Reuel knew the Lord from that day forward.

6 And in the third month from the children of Israel's departure from Egypt, on the sixth day thereof, the Lord gave to Israel the ten commandments on Mount Sinai.

7 And all Israel heard all these commandments, and all Israel rejoiced exceedingly in the Lord on that day.

8 And the glory of the Lord rested upon Mount Sinai, and he called to Moses, and Moses came in the midst of a cloud and ascended the mountain.

9 And Moses was upon the mount forty days and forty nights; he ate no bread and drank no water, and the Lord instructed him in the statutes and judgments in order to teach the children of Israel.

10 And the Lord wrote the ten commandments which he had commanded the children of Israel upon two tablets of stone, which he gave to Moses to command the children of Israel.

11 And at the end of forty days and forty nights, when the Lord had finished speaking to Moses on Mount Sinai, then the Lord gave to Moses the tablets of stone, written with the finger of God.

12 And when the children of Israel saw that Moses tarried to come down from the mount, they gathered round Aaron, and said, As for this man Moses we know not what has become of him.

13 Now therefore rise up, make unto us a god who shall go before us, so that thou shalt not die.

14 And Aaron was greatly afraid of the people, and he ordered them to bring him gold and he made it into a molten calf for the people.

15 And the Lord said to Moses, before he had come down from the mount, Get thee down, for thy people whom thou didst bring forth from Egypt have corrupted themselves.

16 They have made to themselves a molten calf, and have bowed down to it, now therefore leave me, that I may consume them from off the earth, for they are a stiff-necked people.

17 And Moses besought the countenance of the Lord, and he prayed to the Lord for the people on account of the calf which they had made, and he afterward descended from the mount and in his hands were the two tablets of stone, which God had given him to command the Israelites.

18 And when Moses approached the camp and saw the calf which the people had made, the anger of Moses was kindled and he broke the tablets under the mount.

19 And Moses came to the camp and he took the calf and burned it with fire, and ground it till it became fine dust, and strewed it upon the water and gave it to the Israelites to drink.

20 And there died of the people by the swords of each other about three thousand men who had made the calf.

21 And on the morrow Moses said to the people, I will go up to the Lord, peradventure I may make atonement for your sins which you have sinned to the Lord.

22 And Moses again went up to the Lord, and he remained with the Lord forty days and forty nights.

23 And during the forty days did Moses entreat the Lord in behalf of the children of Israel, and the Lord hearkened to the prayer of Moses, and the Lord was entreated of him in behalf of Israel.

24 Then spake the Lord to Moses to hew two stone tablets and to bring them up to the Lord, who would write upon them the ten commandments.

25 Now Moses did so, and he came down and hewed the two tablets and went up to Mount Sinai to the Lord, and the Lord wrote the ten commandments upon the tablets.

26 And Moses remained yet with the Lord forty days and forty nights, and the Lord instructed him in statutes and judgments to impart to Israel.

27 And the Lord commanded him respecting the children of Israel that they should make a sanctuary for the Lord, that his name might rest therein, and the Lord showed him the likeness of the sanctuary and the likeness of all its vessels.

28 And at the end of the forty days, Moses came down from the mount and the two tablets were in his hand.

29 And Moses came to the children of Israel and spoke to them all the words of the Lord, and he taught them laws, statutes and judgments which the Lord had taught him.

30 And Moses told the children of Israel the word of the Lord, that a sanctuary should be made for him, to dwell amongst the children of Israel.

31 And the people rejoiced greatly at all the good which the Lord had spoken to them, through Moses, and they said, We will do all that the Lord has spoken to thee.

32 And the people rose up like one man and they made generous offerings to the sanctuary of the Lord, and each man brought the offering of the Lord for the work of the sanctuary, and for all its service.

33 And all the children of Israel brought each man of all that was found in his possession for the work of the sanctuary of the Lord, gold, silver and brass, and everything that was serviceable for the sanctuary.

34 And all the wise men who were practiced in work came and made the sanctuary of the Lord, according to all that the Lord had commanded, every man in the work in which he had been practiced; and all the wise men in heart made the sanctuary, and its furniture and all the vessels for the holy service, as the Lord had commanded Moses.

35 And the work of the sanctuary of the tabernacle was completed at the end of five months, and the children of Israel did all that the Lord had commanded Moses.

36 And they brought the sanctuary and all its furniture to Moses; like unto the representation which the Lord had shown to Moses, so did the children of Israel.

37 And Moses saw the work, and behold they did it as the Lord had commanded him, so Moses blessed them.

Chapter 83

1 And in the twelfth month, in the twenty-third day of the month, Moses took Aaron and his sons, and he dressed them in their garments, and anointed them and did unto them as the Lord had commanded him, and Moses brought up all the offerings which the Lord had on that day commanded him.

2 Moses afterward took Aaron and his sons and said to them, For seven days shall you remain at the door of the tabernacle, for thus am I commanded.

3 And Aaron and his sons did all that the Lord had commanded them through Moses, and they remained for seven days at the door of the tabernacle.

4 And on the eighth day, being the first day of the first month, in the second year from the Israelites' departure from Egypt, Moses erected the sanctuary, and Moses put up all the furniture of the tabernacle and all the furniture of the sanctuary, and he did all that the Lord had commanded him.

5 And Moses called to Aaron and his sons, and they brought the burnt offering and the sin offering for themselves and the children of Israel, as the Lord had commanded Moses.

6 On that day the two sons of Aaron, Nadab and Abihu, took strange fire and brought it before the Lord who had not commanded them, and a fire went forth from before the Lord, and consumed them, and they died before the Lord on that day.

LEV.10:1 And Nadab and Abihu, the sons of Aaron, took either of them his censer, and put fire therein, and put incense thereon, and offered strange fire before the LORD, which he commanded them not.

LEV.10:2 And there went out fire from the LORD, and devoured them, and they died before the LORD.

Comment: 1: What was this 'strange fire'? We simply don't know. Perhaps rather than the word 'strange' it should read 'unauthorized'.

7 Then on the day when Moses had completed to erect the sanctuary, the princes of the children of Israel began to bring their offerings before the Lord for the dedication of the altar.

8 And they brought up their offerings each prince for one day, a prince each day for twelve days.

9 And all the offerings which they brought, each man in his day, one silver charger weighing one hundred and thirty shekels, one silver bowl of seventy shekels after the shekel of the sanctuary, both of them full of fine flour, mingled with oil for a meat offering.

10 One spoon, weighing ten shekels of gold, full of incense.

11 One young bullock, one ram, one lamb of the first year for a burnt offering.

12 And one kid of the goats for a sin offering.

13 And for a sacrifice of peace offering, two oxen, five rams, five he-goats, five lambs of a year old.

14 Thus did the twelve princes of Israel day by day, each man in his day.

15 And it was after this, in the thirteenth day of the month, that Moses commanded the children of Israel to observe the Passover.

16 And the children of Israel kept the Passover in its season in the fourteenth day of the month, as the Lord had commanded Moses, so did the children of Israel.

17 And in the second month, on the first day thereof, the Lord spoke unto Moses, saying,

18 Number the heads of all the males of the children of Israel from twenty years old and upward, thou and thy brother Aaron and the twelve princes of Israel.

19 And Moses did so, and Aaron came with the twelve princes of Israel, and they numbered the children of Israel in the wilderness of Sinai.

20 And the numbers of the children of Israel by the houses of their fathers, from twenty years old and upward, were six hundred and three thousand, five hundred and fifty.

21 But the children of Levi were not numbered amongst their brethren the children of Israel.

22 And the number of all the males of the children of Israel from one month old and upward, was twenty-two thousand, two hundred and seventy-three.

23 And the number of the children of Levi from one month old and above, was twenty-two thousand.

24 And Moses placed the priests and the Levites each man to his service and to his burden to serve the sanctuary of the tabernacle, as the Lord had commanded Moses.

25 And on the twentieth day of the month, the cloud was taken away from the tabernacle of testimony.

26 At that time the children of Israel continued their journey from the wilderness of Sinai, and they took a journey of three days, and the cloud rested upon the wilderness of Paran; there the anger of the Lord was kindled against Israel, for they had provoked the Lord in asking him for meat, that they might eat.

27 And the Lord hearkened to their voice, and gave them meat which they ate for one month.

28 But after this the anger of the Lord was kindled against them, and he smote them with a great slaughter, and they were buried there in that place.

29 And the children of Israel called that place Kebroth Hattaavah, because there they buried the people that lusted flesh.

30 And they departed from Kebroth Hattaavah and pitched in Hazeroth, which is in the wilderness of Paran.

31 And whilst the children of Israel were in Hazeroth, the anger of the Lord was kindled against Miriam on account of Moses, and she became leprous, white as snow.

32 And she was confined without the camp for seven days, until she had been received again after her leprosy.

33 The children of Israel afterward departed from Hazeroth, and pitched in the end of the wilderness of Paran.

34 At that time, the Lord spoke to Moses to send twelve men from the children of Israel, one man to a tribe, to go and explore the land of Canaan.

35 And Moses sent the twelve men, and they came to the land of Canaan to search and examine it, and they explored the whole land from the wilderness of Sin to Rechob as thou comest to Chamoth.

36 And at the end of forty days they came to Moses and Aaron, and they brought him word as it was in their hearts, and ten of the men brought up an evil report to the children of Israel, of the land which they had explored, saying, It is better for us to return to Egypt than to go to this land, a land that consumes its inhabitants.

37 But Joshua the son of Nun, and Caleb the son of Jephuneh, who were of those that explored the land, said, The land is exceedingly good.

38 If the Lord delight in us, then he will bring us to this land and give it to us, for it is a land flowing with milk and honey.

39 But the children of Israel would not hearken to them, and they hearkened to the words of the ten men who had brought up an evil report of the land.

40 And the Lord heard the murmurings of the children of Israel and he was angry and swore, saying,

41 Surely not one man of this wicked generation shall see the land from twenty years old and upward excepting Caleb the son of Jephuneh and Joshua the son of Nun.

42 But surely this wicked generation shall perish in this wilderness, and their children shall come to the land and they shall possess it; so the anger of the Lord was kindled against Israel, and he made them wander in the wilderness for forty years until the end of that wicked generation, because they did not follow the Lord.

43 And the people dwelt in the wilderness of Paran a long time, and they afterward proceeded to the wilderness by the way of the Red Sea.

Chapter 84

1 At that time Korah the son of Jetzer the son of Kehath the son of Levi, took many men of the children of Israel, and they rose up and quarrelled with Moses and Aaron and the whole congregation.

2 And the Lord was angry with them, and the earth opened its mouth, and swallowed them up, with their houses and all belonging to them, and all the men belonging to Korah.

3 And after this God made the people go round by the way of Mount Seir for a long time.

4 At that time the Lord said unto Moses, Provoke not a war against the children of Esau, for I will not give to you of anything belonging to them, as much as the sole of the foot could tread upon, for I have given Mount Seir for an inheritance to Esau.

5 Therefore did the children of Esau fight against the children of Seir in former times, and the Lord had delivered the children of Seir into the hands of the children of Esau, and destroyed them from before them, and the children of Esau dwelt in their stead unto this day.

6 Therefore the Lord said to the children of Israel, Fight not against the children of Esau your brethren, for nothing in their land belongs to you, but you may buy food of them for money and eat it, and you may buy water of them for money and drink it.

7 And the children of Israel did according to the word of the Lord.

8 And the children of Israel went about the wilderness, going round by the way of Mount Sinai for a long time, and touched not the children of Esau, and they continued in that district for nineteen years.

9 At that time died Latinus king of the children of Chittim, in the forty-fifth year of his reign, which is the fourteenth year of the children of Israel's departure from Egypt.

10 And they buried him in his place which he had built for himself in the land of Chittim, and Abimnas reigned in his place for thirty-eight years.

11 And the children of Israel passed the boundary of the children of Esau in those days, at the end of nineteen years, and they came and passed the road of the wilderness of Moab.

12 And the Lord said to Moses, besiege not Moab, and do not fight against them, for I will give you nothing of their land.

13 And the children of Israel passed the road of the wilderness of Moab for nineteen years, and they did not fight against them.

14 And in the thirty-sixth year of the children of Israel's departing from Egypt the Lord smote the heart of Sihon, king of the Amorites, and he waged war, and went forth to fight against the children of Moab.

15 And Sihon sent messengers to Beor the son of Janeas, the son of Balaam, counsellor to the king of Egypt, and to Balaam his son, to curse Moab, in order that it might be delivered into the hand of Sihon.

16 And the messengers went and brought Beor the son of Janeas, and Balaam his son, from Pethor in Mesopotamia, so Beor and Balaam his son came to the city of Sihon and they cursed Moab and their king in the presence of Sihon king of the Amorites.

17 So Sihon went out with his whole army, and he went to Moab and fought against them, and he subdued them, and the Lord delivered them into his hands, and Sihon slew the king of Moab.

18 And Sihon took all the cities of Moab in the battle; he also took Heshbon from them, for Heshbon was one of the cities of Moab, and Sihon placed his princes and his nobles in Heshbon, and Heshbon belonged to Sihon in those days.

19 Therefore the parable speakers Beor and Balaam his son uttered these words, saying, Come unto Heshbon, the city of Sihon will be built and established.

20 Woe unto thee Moab! thou art lost, O people of Kemosh! behold it is written upon the book of the law of God.

21 And when Sihon had conquered Moab, he placed guards in the cities which he had taken from Moab, and a considerable number of the children of Moab fell in battle into the hand of Sihon, and he made a great capture of them, sons and daughters, and he slew their king; so Sihon turned back to his own land.

22 And Sihon gave numerous presents of silver and gold to Beor and Balaam his son, and he dismissed them, and they went to Mesopotamia to their home and country.

23 At that time all the children of Israel passed from the road of the wilderness of Moab, and returned and surrounded the wilderness of Edom.

24 So the whole congregation came to the wilderness of Sin in the first month of the fortieth year from their departure from Egypt, and the children of Israel dwelt there in Kadesh, of the wilderness of Sin, and Miriam died there and she was buried there.

25 At that time Moses sent messengers to Hadad king of Edom, saying, Thus says thy brother Israel, Let me pass I pray thee through thy land, we will not pass through field or vineyard, we will not drink the water of the well; we will walk in the king's road.

26 And Edom said to him, Thou shalt not pass through my country, and Edom went forth to meet the children of Israel with a mighty people.

27 And the children of Esau refused to let the children of Israel pass through their land, so the Israelites removed from them and fought not against them.

28 For before this the Lord had commanded the children of Israel, saying, You shall not fight against the children of Esau, therefore the Israelites removed from them and did not fight against them.

29 So the children of Israel departed from Kadesh, and all the people came to Mount Hor.

30 At that time the Lord said to Moses, Tell thy brother Aaron that he shall die there, for he shall not come to the land which I have given to the children of Israel.

31 And Aaron went up, at the command of the Lord, to Mount Hor, in the fortieth year, in the fifth month, in the first day of the month.

32 And Aaron was one hundred and twenty-three years old when he died in Mount Hor.

Chapter 85

1 And king Arad the Canaanite, who dwelt in the south, heard that the Israelites had come by the way of the spies, and he arranged his forces to fight against the Israelites.

2 And the children of Israel were greatly afraid of him, for he had a great and heavy army, so the children of Israel resolved to return to Egypt.

3 And the children of Israel turned back about the distance of three days' journey unto Maserath Beni Jaakon, for they were greatly afraid on account of the king Arad.

4 And the children of Israel would not get back to their places, so they remained in Beni Jaakon for thirty days.

5 And when the children of Levi saw that the children of Israel would not turn back, they were jealous for the sake of the Lord, and they rose up and fought against the Israelites their brethren, and slew of them a great body, and forced them to turn back to their place, Mount Hor.

6 And when they returned, king Arad was still arranging his host for battle against the Israelites.

7 And Israel vowed a vow, saying, If thou wilt deliver this people into my hand, then I will utterly destroy their cities.

8 And the Lord hearkened to the voice of Israel, and he delivered the Canaanites into their hand, and he utterly destroyed them and their cities, and he called the name of the place Hormah.

9 And the children of Israel journeyed from Mount Hor and pitched in Oboth, and they journeyed from Oboth and they pitched at Ije-abarim, in the border of Moab.

10 And the children of Israel sent to Moab, saying, Let us pass now through thy land into our place, but the children of Moab would not

suffer the children of Israel to pass through their land, for the children of Moab were greatly afraid lest the children of Israel should do unto them as Sihon king of the Amorites had done to them, who had taken their land and had slain many of them.

11 Therefore Moab would not suffer the Israelites to pass through his land, and the Lord commanded the children of Israel, saying, That they should not fight against Moab, so the Israelites removed from Moab.

12 And the children of Israel journeyed from the border of Moab, and they came to the other side of Arnon, the border of Moab, between Moab and the Amorites, and they pitched in the border of Sihon, king of the Amorites, in the wilderness of Kedemoth.

13 And the children of Israel sent messengers to Sihon, king of the Amorites, saying,

14 Let us pass through thy land, we will not turn into the fields or into the vineyards, we will go along by the king's highway until we shall have passed thy border, but Sihon would not suffer the Israelites to pass.

15 So Sihon collected all the people of the Amorites and went forth into the wilderness to meet the children of Israel, and he fought against Israel in Jahaz.

16 And the Lord delivered Sihon king of the Amorites into the hand of the children of Israel, and Israel smote all the people of Sihon with the edge of the sword and avenged the cause of Moab.

17 And the children of Israel took possession of the land of Sihon from Aram unto Jabuk, unto the children of Ammon, and they took all the spoil of the cities.

18 And Israel took all these cities, and Israel dwelt in all the cities of the Amorites.

19 And all the children of Israel resolved to fight against the children of Ammon, to take their land also.

20 So the Lord said to the children of Israel, Do not besiege the children of Ammon, neither stir up battle against them, for I will give nothing to you of their land, and the children of Israel hearkened to the word of the Lord, and did not fight against the children of Ammon.

21 And the children of Israel turned and went up by the way of Bashan to the land of Og, king of Bashan, and Og the king of Bashan went out to meet the Israelites in battle, and he had with him many valiant men, and a very strong force from the people of the Amorites.

22 And Og king of Bashan was a very powerful man, but Naaron his son was exceedingly powerful, even stronger than he was.

23 And Og said in his heart, Behold now the whole camp of Israel takes up a space of three parsa, now will I smite them at once without sword or spear.

24 And Og went up Mount Jahaz, and took therefrom one large stone, the length of which was three parsa, and he placed it on his head, and resolved to throw it upon the camp of the children of Israel, to smite all the Israelites with that stone.

25 And the angel of the Lord came and pierced the stone upon the head of Og, and the stone fell upon the neck of Og that Og fell to the earth on account of the weight of the stone upon his neck.

26 At that time the Lord said to the children of Israel, Be not afraid of him, for I have given him and all his people and all his land into your hand, and you shall do to him as you did to Sihon.

27 And Moses went down to him with a small number of the children of Israel, and Moses smote Og with a stick at the ankles of his feet and slew him.

28 The children of Israel afterward pursued the children of Og and all his people, and they beat and destroyed them till there was no remnant left of them.

29 Moses afterward sent some of the children of Israel to spy out Jaazer, for Jaazer was a very famous city.

30 And the spies went to Jaazer and explored it, and the spies trusted in the Lord, and they fought against the men of Jaazer.

31 And these men took Jaazer and its villages, and the Lord delivered them into their hand, and they drove out the Amorites who had been there.

32 And the children of Israel took the land of the two kings of the Amorites, sixty cities which were on the other side of Jordan, from the brook of Arnon unto Mount Herman.

33 And the children of Israel journeyed and came into the plain of Moab which is on this side of Jordan, by Jericho.

34 And the children of Moab heard all the evil which the children of Israel had done to the two kings of the Amorites, to Sihon and Og, so all the men of Moab were greatly afraid of the Israelites.

35 And the elders of Moab said, Behold the two kings of the Amorites, Sihon and Og, who were more powerful than all the kings of the earth, could not stand against the children of Israel, how then can we stand before them?

36 Surely they sent us a message before now to pass through our land on their way, and we would not suffer them, now they will turn upon us with their heavy swords and destroy us; and Moab was distressed on account of the children of Israel, and they were greatly afraid of them, and they counselled together what was to be done to the children of Israel.

37 And the elders of Moab resolved and took one of their men, Balak the son of Zippor the Moabite, and made him king over them at that time, and Balak was a very wise man.

38 And the elders of Moab rose up and sent to the children of Midian to make peace with them, for a great battle and enmity had been in

those days between Moab and Midian, from the days of Hadad the son of Bedad king of Edom, who smote Midian in the field of Moab, unto these days.

39 And the children of Moab sent to the children of Midian, and they made peace with them, and the elders of Midian came to the land of Moab to make peace in behalf of the children of Midian.

40 And the elders of Moab counselled with the elders of Midian what to do in order to save their lives from Israel.

41 And all the children of Moab said to the elders of Midian, Now therefore the children of Israel lick up all that are round about us, as the ox licks up the grass of the field, for thus did they do to the two kings of the Amorites who are stronger than we are.

42 And the elders of Midian said to Moab, We have heard that at the time when Sihon king of the Amorites fought against you, when he prevailed over you and took your land, he had sent to Beor the son of Janeas and to Balaam his son from Mesopotamia, and they came and cursed you; therefore did the hand of Sihon prevail over you, that he took your land.

43 Now therefore send you also to Balaam his son, for he still remains in his land, and give him his hire, that he may come and curse all the people of whom you are afraid; so the elders of Moab heard this thing, and it pleased them to send to Balaam the son of Beor.

44 So Balak the son of Zippor king of Moab sent messengers to Balaam, saying,

45 Behold there is a people come out from Egypt, behold they cover the face of the earth, and they abide over against me.

46 Now therefore come and curse this people for me, for they are too mighty for me, peradventure I shall prevail to fight against them, and drive them out, for I heard that he whom thou blessest is blessed, and whom thou cursest is cursed.

NUM.22:5 He sent messengers therefore unto Balaam the son of Beor to Pethor, which is by the river of the land of the children of his people, to call him, saying, Behold, there is a people come out from Egypt: behold, they cover the face of the earth, and they abide over against me:

NUM.22:6 Come now therefore, I pray thee, curse me this people; for they are too mighty for me: peradventure I shall prevail, that we may smite them, and that I may drive them out of the land: for I wot that he whom thou blesses is blessed, and he whom thou curses is cursed.

---

47 So the messengers of Balak went to Balaam and brought Balaam to curse the people to fight against Moab.

48 And Balaam came to Balak to curse Israel, and the Lord said to Balaam, 'Curse not this people for it is blessed'.

NUM.22:12 And God said unto Balaam, 'Thou shalt not go with them; thou shalt not curse the people: for they are blessed'.

NUM.23:19 God is not a man, that he should lie; neither the son of man, that he should repent: hath he said, and shall he not do it? or hath he spoken, and shall he not make it good?

NUM.23:20 Behold, I (Balaam) have received commandment to bless: and he hath blessed; and I cannot reverse it.

NUM.23:21 He hath not beheld iniquity in Jacob, neither hath he seen perverseness in Israel: the LORD his God is with him, and the shout of a king is among them.

NUM.23:22 God brought them out of Egypt; he hath as it were the strength of an unicorn.

NUM.23:23 Surely there is no enchantment against Jacob, neither is there any divination against Israel: according to this time it shall be said of Jacob and of Israel, 'What hath God wrought!'

NUM.23:24 Behold, the people shall rise up as a great lion, and lift up himself as a young lion: he shall not lie down until he eat of the prey and drink the blood of the slain.

---

49 And Balak urged Balaam day by day to curse Israel, but Balaam hearkened not to Balak on account of the word of the Lord which he had spoken to Balaam.

50 And when Balak saw that Balaam would not accede to his wish, he rose up and went home, and Balaam also returned to his land and he went from there to Midian.

279

51 And the children of Israel journeyed from the plain of Moab, and pitched by Jordan from Beth-jesimoth even unto Abel-shittim, at the end of the plains of Moab.

52 And when the children of Israel abode in the plain of Shittim, they began to commit whoredom with the daughters of Moab.

53 And the children of Israel approached Moab, and the children of Moab pitched their tents opposite to the camp of the children of Israel.

54 And the children of Moab were afraid of the children of Israel, and the children of Moab took all their daughters and their wives of beautiful aspect and comely appearance, and dressed them in gold and silver and costly garments.

55 And the children of Moab seated those women at the door of their tents, in order that the children of Israel might see them and turn to them, and not fight against Moab.

56 And all the children of Moab did this thing to the children of Israel, and every man placed his wife and daughter at the door of his tent, and all the children of Israel saw the act of the children of Moab, and the children of Israel turned to the daughters of Moab and coveted them, and they went to them.

57 And it came to pass that when a Hebrew came to the door of the tent of Moab, and saw a daughter of Moab and desired her in his heart, and spoke with her at the door of the tent that which he desired, whilst they were speaking together the men of the tent would come out and speak to the Hebrew like unto these words:

58 Surely you know that we are brethren, we are all the descendants of Lot and the descendants of Abraham his brother, wherefore then will you not remain with us, and wherefore will you not eat our bread and our sacrifice?

59 And when the children of Moab had thus overwhelmed him with their speeches, and enticed him by their flattering words, they seated

him in the tent and cooked and sacrificed for him, and he ate of their sacrifice and of their bread.

60 They then gave him wine and he drank and became intoxicated, and they placed before him a beautiful damsel, and he did with her as he liked, for he knew not what he was doing, as he had drunk plentifully of wine.

61 Thus did the children of Moab to Israel in that place, in the plain of Shittim, and the anger of the Lord was kindled against Israel on account of this matter, and he sent a pestilence amongst them, and there died of the Israelites twenty-four thousand men.

62 Now there was a man of the children of Simeon whose name was Zimri, the son of Salu, who connected himself with the Midianite Cosbi, the daughter of Zur, king of Midian, in the sight of all the children of Israel.

63 And Phineas the son of Elazer, the son of Aaron the priest, saw this wicked thing which Zimri had done, and he took a spear and rose up and went after them, and pierced them both and slew them, and the pestilence ceased from the children of Israel.

Chapter 86

1 At that time after the pestilence, the Lord said to Moses, and to Eleazer the son of Aaron the priest, saying,

2 Number the heads of the whole community of the children of Israel, from twenty years old and upward, all that went forth in the army.

NUM.26:1 And it came to pass after the plague, that the LORD spoke unto Moses and unto Eleazar the son of Aaron the priest, saying,

NUM.26:2 Take the sum of all the congregation of the children of Israel, from twenty years old and upward, throughout their fathers' house, all that are able to go to war in Israel.

3 And Moses and Elazer numbered the children of Israel after their families, and the number of all Israel was seven hundred thousand, seven hundred and thirty.

4 And the number of the children of Levi, from one month old and upward, was twenty-three thousand, and amongst these there was not a man of those numbered by Moses and Aaron in the wilderness of Sinai.

5 For the Lord had told them that they would die in the wilderness, so they all died, and not one had been left of them excepting Caleb the son of Jephuneh, and Joshua the son of Nun.

6 And it was after this that the Lord said to Moses, Say unto the children of Israel to avenge upon Midian the cause of their brethren the children of Israel.

7 And Moses did so, and the children of Israel chose from amongst them twelve thousand men, being one thousand to a tribe, and they went to Midian.

8 And the children of Israel warred against Midian, and they slew every male, also the five princes of Midian, and Balaam the son of Beor did they slay with the sword.

9 And the children of Israel took the wives of Midian captive, with their little ones and their cattle, and all belonging to them.

10 And they took all the spoil and all the prey, and they brought it to Moses and to Elazer to the plains of Moab.

11 And Moses and Eleazer and all the princes of the congregation went forth to meet them with joy.

12 And they divided all the spoil of Midian, and the children of Israel had been revenged upon Midian for the cause of their brethren the children of Israel.

Chapter 87

1 At that time the Lord said to Moses, Behold thy days are approaching to an end, take now Joshua the son of Nun thy servant and place him in the tabernacle, and I will command him, and Moses did so.

2 And the Lord appeared in the tabernacle in a pillar of cloud, and the pillar of cloud stood at the entrance of the tabernacle.

3 And the Lord commanded Joshua the son of Nun and said unto him, Be strong and courageous, for thou shalt bring the children of Israel to the land which I swore to give them, and I will be with thee.

4 And Moses said to Joshua, Be strong and courageous, for thou wilt make the children of Israel inherit the land, and the Lord will be with thee, he will not leave thee nor forsake thee, be not afraid nor disheartened.

5 And Moses called to all the children of Israel and said to them, You have seen all the good which the Lord your God has done for you in the wilderness.

6 Now therefore observe all the words of this law, and walk in the way of the Lord your God, turn not from the way which the Lord has commanded you, either to the right or to the left.

7 And Moses taught the children of Israel statutes and judgments and laws to do in the land as the Lord had commanded him.

8 And he taught them the way of the Lord and his laws; behold they are written upon the book of the law of God which he gave to the children of Israel by the hand of Moses.

9 And Moses finished commanding the children of Israel, and the Lord said to him, saying, Go up to the Mount Abarim and die there, and be gathered unto thy people as Aaron thy brother was gathered.

10 And Moses went up as the Lord had commanded him, and he died

there in the land of Moab by the order of the Lord, in the fortieth year from the Israelites going forth from the land of Egypt.

11 And the children of Israel wept for Moses in the plains of Moab for thirty days, and the days of weeping and mourning for Moses were completed.

Chapter 88

1 And it was after the death of Moses that the Lord said to Joshua the son of Nun, saying,

2 Rise up and pass the Jordan to the land which I have given to the children of Israel, and thou shalt make the children of Israel inherit the land.

3 Every place upon which the sole of your feet shall tread shall belong to you, from the wilderness of Lebanon unto the great river the river of Perath shall be your boundary.

4 No man shall stand up against thee all the days of thy life; as I was with Moses, so will I be with thee, only be strong and of good courage to observe all the law which Moses commanded thee, turn not from the way either to the right or to the left, in order that thou mayest prosper in all that thou doest.

5 And Joshua commanded the officers of Israel, saying, Pass through the camp and command the people, saying, Prepare for yourselves provisions, for in three days more you will pass the Jordan to possess the land.

6 And the officers of the children of Israel did so, and they commanded the people and they did all that Joshua had commanded.

7 And Joshua sent two men to spy out the land of Jericho, and the men went and spied out Jericho.

8 And at the end of seven days they came to Joshua in the camp and said to him, The Lord has delivered the whole land into our hand, and the inhabitants thereof are melted with fear because of us.

9 And it came to pass after that, that Joshua rose up in the morning and all Israel with him, and they journeyed from Shittim, and Joshua and all Israel with him passed the Jordan; and Joshua was eighty-two years old when he passed the Jordan with Israel.

10 And the people went up from Jordan on the tenth day of the first month, and they encamped in Gilgal at the eastern corner of Jericho.

11 And the children of Israel kept the Passover in Gilgal, in the plains of Jericho, on the fourteenth day at the month, as it is written in the law of Moses.

12 And the manna ceased at that time on the morrow of the Passover, and there was no more manna for the children of Israel, and they ate of the produce of the land of Canaan.

13 And Jericho was entirely closed against the children of Israel, no one came out or went in.

14 And it was in the second month, on the first day of the month, that the Lord said to Joshua, Rise up, behold I have given Jericho into thy hand with all the people thereof; and all your fighting men shall go round the city, once each day, thus shall you do for six days.

15 And the priests shall blow upon trumpets, and when you shall hear the sound of the trumpet, all the people shall give a great shouting, that the walls of the city shall fall down; all the people shall go up every man against his opponent.

16 And Joshua did so according to all that the Lord had commanded him.

17 And on the seventh day they went round the city seven times, and the priests blew upon trumpets.

18 And at the seventh round, Joshua said to the people, Shout, for the Lord has delivered the whole city into our hands.

19 Only the city and all that it contains shall be accursed to the Lord, and keep yourselves from the accursed thing, lest you make the camp of Israel accursed and trouble it.

20 But all the silver and gold and brass and iron shall be consecrated to the Lord, they shall come into the treasury of the Lord.

21 And the people blew upon trumpets and made a great shouting, and the walls of Jericho fell down, and all the people went up, every man straight before him, and they took the city and utterly destroyed all that was in it, both man and woman, young and old, ox and sheep and ass, with the edge of the sword.

22 And they burned the whole city with fire; only the vessels of silver and gold, and brass and iron, they put into the treasury of the Lord.

23 And Joshua swore at that time, saying, Cursed be the man who builds Jericho; he shall lay the foundation thereof in his first-born, and in his youngest son shall he set up the gates thereof.

24 And Achan the son of Carmi, the son of Zabdi, the son of Zerah, son of Judah, dealt treacherously in the accursed thing, and he took of the accursed thing and hid it in the tent, and the anger of the Lord was kindled against Israel.

25 And it was after this when the children of Israel had returned from burning Jericho, Joshua sent men to spy out also Ai, and to fight against it.

26 And the men went up and spied out Ai, and they returned and said, Let not all the people go up with thee to Ai, only let about three thousand men go up and smite the city, for the men thereof are but few.

27 And Joshua did so, and there went up with him of the children of Israel about three thousand men, and they fought against the men of Ai.

28 And the battle was severe against Israel, and the men of Ai smote thirty-six men of Israel, and the children of Israel fled from before the men of Ai.

29 And when Joshua saw this thing, he tore his garments and fell upon his face to the ground before the Lord, he, with the elders of Israel, and they put dust upon their heads.

30 And Joshua said, Why O Lord didst thou bring this people over the Jordan? what shall I say after the Israelites have turned their backs against their enemies?

31 Now therefore all the Canaanites, inhabitants of the land, will hear this thing, and surround us and cut off our name.

32 And the Lord said to Joshua, Why dost thou fall upon thy face? rise, get thee off, for the Israelites have sinned, and taken of the accursed thing; I will no more be with them unless they destroy the accursed thing from amongst them.

33 And Joshua rose up and assembled the people, and brought the Urim by the order of the Lord, and the tribe of Judah was taken, and Achan the son of Carmi was taken.

34 And Joshua said to Achan, Tell me my son, what hast thou done, and Achan said, I saw amongst the spoil a goodly garment of Shinar and two hundred shekels of silver, and a wedge of gold of fifty shekels weight; I coveted them and took them, and behold they are all hid in the earth in the midst of the tent.

35 And Joshua sent men who went and took them from the tent of Achan, and they brought them to Joshua.

36 And Joshua took Achan and these utensils, and his sons and daughters and all belonging to him, and they brought them into the valley of Achor.

37 And Joshua burned them there with fire, and all the Israelites stoned Achan with stones, and they raised over him a heap of stones, therefore did he call that place the valley of Achor, so the Lord's anger was appeased, and Joshua afterward came to the city and fought against it.

38 And the Lord said to Joshua, Fear not, neither be thou dismayed, behold I have given into thy hand Ai, her king and her people, and thou shalt do unto them as thou didst to Jericho and her king, only the spoil thereof and the cattle thereof shall you take for a prey for yourselves; lay an ambush for the city behind it.

39 So Joshua did according to the word of the Lord, and he chose from amongst the sons of war thirty thousand valiant men, and he sent them, and they lay in ambush for the city.

40 And he commanded them, saying, When you shall see us we will flee before them with cunning, and they will pursue us, you shall then rise out of the ambush and take the city, and they did so.

41 And Joshua fought, and the men of the city went out toward Israel, not knowing that they were lying in ambush for them behind the city.

42 And Joshua and all the Israelites feigned themselves wearied out before them, and they fled by the way of the wilderness with cunning.

43 And the men of Ai gathered all the people who were in the city to pursue the Israelites, and they went out and were drawn away from the city, not one remained, and they left the city open and pursued the Israelites.

44 And those who were lying in ambush rose up out of their places, and hastened to come to the city and took it and set it on fire, and the men of Ai turned back, and behold the smoke of the city ascended to the skies, and they had no means of retreating either one way or the other.

45 And all the men of Ai were in the midst of Israel, some on this side and some on that side, and they smote them so that not one of them remained.

46 And the children of Israel took Melosh king of Ai alive, and they brought him to Joshua, and Joshua hanged him on a tree and he died.

47 And the children of Israel returned to the city after having burned it, and they smote all those that were in it with the edge of the sword.

48 And the number of those that had fallen of the men of Ai, both man and woman, was twelve thousand; only the cattle and the spoil of the city they took to themselves, according to the word of the Lord to Joshua.

49 And all the kings on this side Jordan, all the kings of Canaan, heard of the evil which the children of Israel had done to Jericho and to Ai, and they gathered themselves together to fight against Israel.

50 Only the inhabitants of Gibeon were greatly afraid of fighting against the Israelites lest they should perish, so they acted cunningly, and they came to Joshua and to all Israel, and said unto them, We have come from a distant land, now therefore make a covenant with us.

51 And the inhabitants of Gibeon over-reached the children of Israel, and the children of Israel made a covenant with them, and they made peace with them, and the princes of the congregation swore unto them, but afterward the children of Israel knew that they were neighbours to them and were dwelling amongst them.

52 But the children of Israel slew them not; for they had sworn to them by the Lord, and they became hewers of wood and drawers of water.

53 And Joshua said to them, Why did you deceive me, to do this thing to us? and they answered him, saying, Because it was told to thy servants all that you had done to all the kings of the Amorites, and we were greatly afraid of our lives, and we did this thing.

54 And Joshua appointed them on that day to hew wood and to draw water, and he divided them for slaves to all the tribes of Israel.

55 And when Adonizedek king of Jerusalem heard all that the children of Israel had done to Jericho and to Ai, he sent to Hoham king of Hebron and to Piram king at Jarmuth, and to Japhia king of Lachish and to Deber king of Eglon, saying,

56 Come up to me and help me, that we may smite the children of Israel and the inhabitants of Gibeon who have made peace with the children of Israel.

57 And they gathered themselves together and the five kings of the Amorites went up with all their camps, a mighty people numerous as the sand of the sea shore.

58 And all these kings came and encamped before Gibeon, and they began to fight against the inhabitants of Gibeon, and all the men of Gibeon sent to Joshua, saying, Come up quickly to us and help us, for all the kings of the Amorites have gathered together to fight against us.

59 And Joshua and all the fighting people went up from Gilgal, and Joshua came suddenly to them, and smote these five kings with a great slaughter.

60 And the Lord confounded them before the children at Israel, who smote them with a terrible slaughter in Gibeon, and pursued them along the way that goes up to Beth Horon unto Makkedah, and they fled from before the children of Israel.

61 And whilst they were fleeing, the Lord sent upon them hailstones from heaven, and more of them died by the hailstones, than by the slaughter of the children of Israel.

62 And the children of Israel pursued them, and they still smote them in the road, going on and smiting them.

63 And when they were smiting, the day was declining toward evening, and Joshua said in the sight of all the people, Sun, stand thou still upon Gibeon, and thou moon in the valley of Ajalon, until the nation shall have revenged itself upon its enemies.

64 And the Lord hearkened to the voice of Joshua, and the sun stood still in the midst of the heavens, and it stood still six and thirty moments, and the moon also stood still and hastened not to go down a whole day.

65 And there was no day like that, before it or after it, that the Lord hearkened to the voice of a man, for the Lord fought for Israel.

C.1 This is a very revealing verse: no day like that, before it or after it, that the Lord hearkened to the voice of a man, for the Lord fought for Israel.

Chapter 89

1 Then spoke Joshua this song, on the day that the Lord had given the Amorites into the hand of Joshua and the children of Israel, and he said in the sight of all Israel,

2 Thou hast done mighty things, O Lord, thou hast performed great deeds; who is like unto thee? my lips shall sing to thy name.

3 My goodness and my fortress, my high tower, I will sing a new song unto thee, with thanksgiving will I sing to thee, thou art the strength of my salvation.

4 All the kings of the earth shall praise thee, the princes of the world shall sing to thee, the children of Israel shall rejoice in thy salvation, they shall sing and praise thy power.

5 To thee, O Lord, did we confide; we said thou art our God, for thou wast our shelter and strong tower against our enemies.

6 To thee we cried and were not ashamed, in thee we trusted and were delivered; when we cried unto thee, thou didst hear our voice, thou didst deliver our souls from the sword, thou didst show unto us thy grace, thou didst give unto us thy salvation, thou didst rejoice our hearts with thy strength.

7 Thou didst go forth for our salvation, with thine arm thou didst redeem thy people; thou didst answer us from the heavens of thy holiness, thou didst save us from ten thousands of people.

8 The sun and moon stood still in heaven, and thou didst stand in thy wrath against our oppressors and didst command thy judgments over them.

9 All the princes of the earth stood up, the kings of the nations had gathered themselves together, they were not moved at thy presence, they desired thy battles.

10 Thou didst rise against them in thine anger, and didst bring down thy wrath upon them; thou didst destroy them in thine anger, and cut them off in thine heart.

11 Nations have been consumed with thy fury, kingdoms have declined because of thy wrath, thou didst wound kings in the day of thine anger.

12 Thou didst pour out thy fury upon them, thy wrathful anger took hold of them; thou didst turn their iniquity upon them, and didst cut them off in their wickedness.

13 They did spread a trap, they fell therein, in the net they hid, their foot was caught.

14 Thine hand was ready for all thine enemies who said, Through their sword they possessed the land, through their arm they dwelt in the city; thou didst fill their faces with shame, thou didst bring their horns down to the ground, thou didst terrify them in thy wrath, and didst destroy them in thine anger.

15 The earth trembled and shook at the sound of thy storm over them, thou didst not withhold their souls from death, and didst bring down their lives to the grave.

16 Thou didst pursue them in thy storm, thou didst consume them in thy whirlwind, thou didst turn their rain into hail, they fell in deep pits so that they could not rise.

17 Their carcasses were like rubbish cast out in the middle of the streets.

18 They were consumed and destroyed in thine anger, thou didst save thy people with thy might.

19 Therefore our hearts rejoice in thee, our souls exalt in thy salvation.

20 Our tongues shall relate thy might, we will sing and praise thy wondrous works.

21 For thou didst save us from our enemies, thou didst deliver us from those who rose up against us, thou didst destroy them from before us and depress them beneath our feet.

22 Thus shall all thine enemies perish O Lord, and the wicked shall be like chaff driven by the wind, and thy beloved shall be like trees planted by the waters.

23 So Joshua and all Israel with him returned to the camp in Gilgal, after having smitten all the kings, so that not a remnant was left of them.

24 And the five kings fled alone on foot from battle, and hid themselves in a cave, and Joshua sought for them in the field of battle, and did not find them.

25 And it was afterward told to Joshua, saying, The kings are found and behold they are hidden in a cave.

26 And Joshua said, Appoint men to be at the mouth of the cave, to guard them, lest they take themselves away; and the children of Israel did so.

27 And Joshua called to all Israel and said to the officers of battle, Place your feet upon the necks of these kings, and Joshua said, So shall the Lord do to all your enemies.

28 And Joshua commanded afterward that they should slay the kings and cast them into the cave, and to put great stones at the mouth of the cave.

29 And Joshua went afterward with all the people that were with him on that day to Makkedah, and he smote it with the edge of the sword.

30 And he utterly destroyed the souls and all belonging to the city, and he did to the king and people thereof as he had done to Jericho.

31 And he passed from there to Libnah and he fought against it, and the Lord delivered it into his hand, and Joshua smote it with the edge of the sword, and all the souls thereof, and he did to it and to the king thereof as he had done to Jericho.

32 And from there he passed on to Lachish to fight against it, and Horam king of Gaza went up to assist the men of Lachish, and Joshua smote him and his people until there was none left to him.

33 And Joshua took Lachish and all the people thereof, and he did to it as he had done to Libnah.

34 And Joshua passed from there to Eglon, and he took that also, and he smote it and all the people thereof with the edge of the sword.

35 And from there he passed to Hebron and fought against it and took it and utterly destroyed it, and he returned from there with all Israel to Debir and fought against it and smote it with the edge of the sword.

36 And he destroyed every soul in it, he left none remaining, and he did to it and the king thereof as he had done to Jericho.

37 And Joshua smote all the kings of the Amorites from Kadesh-barnea to Azah, and he took their country at once, for the Lord had fought for Israel.

38 And Joshua with all Israel came to the camp to Gilgal.

39 When at that time Jabin king of Chazor heard all that Joshua had done to the kings of the Amorites, Jabin sent to Jobat king of Midian, and to Laban king of Shimron, to Jephal king of Achshaph, and to all the kings of the Amorites, saying,

40 Come quickly to us and help us, that we may smite the children of Israel, before they come upon us and do unto us as they have done to the other kings of the Amorites.

41 And all these kings hearkened to the words of Jabin, king of Chazor, and they went forth with all their camps, seventeen kings, and their people were as numerous as the sand on the sea shore, together with horses and chariots innumerable, and they came and pitched together at the waters of Merom, and they were met together to fight against Israel.

42 And the Lord said to Joshua, Fear them not, for tomorrow about this time I will deliver them up all slain before you, thou shalt hough their horses and burn their chariots with fire.

43 And Joshua with all the men of war came suddenly upon them and smote them, and they fell into their hands, for the Lord had delivered them into the hands of the children of Israel.

44 So the children of Israel pursued all these kings with their camps, and smote them until there was none left of them, and Joshua did to them as the Lord had spoken to him.

45 And Joshua returned at that time to Chazor and smote it with the sword and destroyed every soul in it and burned it with fire, and from Chazor, Joshua passed to Shimron and smote it and utterly destroyed it.

46 From there he passed to Achshaph and he did to it as he had done to Shimron.

47 From there he passed to Adulam and he smote all the people in it, and he did to Adulam as he had done to Achshaph and to Shimron.

48 And he passed from them to all the cities of the kings which he had smitten, and he smote all the people that were left of them and he utterly destroyed them.

49 Only their booty and cattle the Israelites took to themselves as a prey, but every human being they smote, they suffered not a soul to live.

50 As the Lord had commanded Moses so did Joshua and all Israel, they failed not in anything.

51 So Joshua and all the children of Israel smote the whole land of Canaan as the Lord had commanded them, and smote all their kings, being thirty and one kings, and the children of Israel took their whole country.

52 Besides the kingdoms of Sihon and Og which are on the other side Jordan, of which Moses had smitten many cities, and Moses gave them to the Reubenites and the Gadites and to half the tribe of Manasseh.

> 53 And Joshua smote all the kings that were on this side Jordan to the west, and gave them for an inheritance to the nine tribes and to the half tribe of Israel.
>
> 54 For five years did Joshua carry on the war with these kings, and he gave their cities to the Israelites, and the land became tranquil from battle throughout the cities of the Amorites and the Canaanites.

JOSH.11:6 And the LORD said unto Joshua, 'Be not afraid because of them: for tomorrow about this time will I deliver them up all slain before Israel: thou shalt hough their horses and burn their chariots with fire'.

JOSH.11:7 So Joshua came, and all the people of war with him, against them by the waters of Merom suddenly; and they fell upon them.

JOSH.11:8 And the LORD delivered them into the hand of Israel, who smote them, and chased them unto great Zidon, and unto Misrephothmaim, and unto the valley of Mizpah eastward; and they smote them, until they left them none remaining.

JOSH.11:9 And Joshua did unto them as the LORD bade him: he houghed their horses and burnt their chariots with fire.

JOSH.11:10 And Joshua at that time turned back, and took Hazor, and smote the king thereof with the sword: for Hazor beforetime was the head of all those kingdoms.

JOSH.11:11 And they smote all the souls that were therein with the edge of the sword, utterly destroying them: there was not any left to breathe: and he burnt Hazor with fire.

JOSH.11:12 And all the cities of those kings, and all the kings of them, did Joshua take, and smote them with the edge of the sword, and he utterly destroyed them, as Moses the servant of the LORD commanded.

Comment:1: There are many people who think that Israel was totally barbaric in ancient times and that they descended down from their mountainous forts and slaughtered everything in sight without any sense of discrimination and no regard for human life, even killing all the women, children and babies.

C.2 Something so abhorrent to us in modern times we would simply not tolerate it, if we had the power to do something about it!

C.3 What was so different back then that even God Himself through the mouth of Moses commanded the people to totally destroy the Canaanites and all the nations that occupied all the lands that God had in fact given to the descendants of Shem or Israel?

C.4 As I mentioned before, it stemmed back to the time of Noah when Noah had put a curse on any of his sons who would steal the lands of his brethren.

C.5 Well, Canaan the fore-father of the Canaanites that lived in the lands of

Shem for one 1000 years was the one who defied his father Ham's command also. So that Canaan and his descendants were indeed cursed and eventually totally driven out of the lands of Shem.

C.6 The main reason God curses the Canaanites and their relatives was because their blood was mixed with the Nephilim Giant D.N.A which kept popping up somewhere. Four years after Joshua's time there were still some giants among the Philistines and they had a very bad attitude.

C.7 It is only a fairy tale that there used to be 'good giants' None of the Nephilim giants were good and in fact they were cannibals.

C.8 Nephilim blood made people depraved & literally behave like demons especially in their times of ritual and licentious orgies dancing to demons, such as occurred when the children of Israel went whoring after other gods at the time of the Golden Calf. Those that were guilty of the 'Children of Israel' were killed by God when Moses came back down the mountain from receiving the 10 Commandments.

C.9 Thus, in the eyes of God it was necessary to destroy all the descendants of the Nephilim. And in particular the Canaanites.

C.10 Notice in all the stories of this Book of Jasher, how that the Canaanites were Idol Worshippers which is the same as worshipping demons and devils and demi-gods (the disembodied spirits of the Giants)

C.11 Don't think for a moment that anything has changed concerning Idol worship and demon worship. The world today is rife with it. Jesus mentioned that when He returned to our planet the 2nd time that 'As it was in the days of Noah so will it be in the days of the coming of the son of Man'.

MAT.24:37 But as the days of Noe were, so shall also the coming of the Son of man be.

MAT.24:38 For as in the days that were before the flood they were eating and drinking, marrying and giving in marriage, until the day that Noe entered into the ark,

C.12 What does *'eating and drinking, marrying and giving in marriage'* mean? It just means that everyone *'keeps on doing what they have always been doing'* in their continual wickedness until they will all be swept away not by a Great Flood next time but by 'Fire And Brimstone' at 'The Wrath Of God' as described so well in Revelations 16.

MAT.24:39 And knew not until the flood came, and took them all away; so, shall also the coming of the Son of man be.

C.13 Under the coming worldwide satanic New World Order men will become just as bad as those before the Great Flood and will therefore will largely wiped out again in the Wrath of God again because of Idol and demon worship under the Anti-Christ.

REV.9:20 And the rest of the men which were not killed by these plagues yet repented not of the works of their hands, that they should not worship devils, and idols of gold, and silver, and brass, and stone, and of wood: which neither can see, nor hear, nor walk:

REV.9:21 Neither repented they of their murders, nor of their sorceries, nor of their fornication, nor of their thefts.

Chapter 90

1 At that time in the fifth year after the children of Israel had passed over Jordan, after the children of Israel had rested from their war with the Canaanites, at that time great and severe battles arose between Edom and the children of Chittim, and the children of Chittim fought against Edom.

2 And Abianus king of Chittim went forth in that year, that is in the thirty-first year of his reign, and a great force with him of the mighty men of the children of Chittim, and he went to Seir to fight against the children of Esau.

3 And Hadad the king of Edom heard of his report, and he went forth to meet him with a heavy people and strong force, and engaged in battle with him in the field of Edom.

4 And the hand of Chittim prevailed over the children of Esau, and the children of Chittim slew of the children of Esau, two and twenty thousand men, and all the children of Esau fled from before them.

5 And the children of Chittim pursued them and they reached Hadad king of Edom, who was running before them and they caught him alive, and brought him to Abianus king of Chittim.

6 And Abianus ordered him to be slain, and Hadad king of Edom died in the forty-eighth year of his reign.

7 And the children of Chittim continued their pursuit of Edom, and they smote them with a great slaughter and Edom became subject to the children of Chittim.

8 And the children of Chittim ruled over Edom, and Edom became under the hand of the children of Chittim and became one kingdom from that day.

9 And from that time they could no more lift up their heads, and their kingdom became one with the children of Chittim.

10 And Abianus placed officers in Edom and all the children of Edom became subject and tributary to Abianus, and Abianus turned back to his own land, Chittim.

11 And when he returned he renewed his government and built for himself a spacious and fortified palace for a royal residence, and reigned securely over the children of Chittim and over Edom.

12 In those days, after the children of Israel had driven away all the Canaanites and the Amorites, Joshua was old and advanced in years.

13 And the Lord said to Joshua, 'Thou art old, advanced in life, and a great part of the land remains to be possessed'.

JOS.23:1 And it came to pass a long time after that the LORD had given rest unto Israel from all their enemies round about, that Joshua waxed old and stricken in age.

JOS.23:2 And Joshua called for all Israel, and for their elders, and for their heads, and for their judges, and for their officers, and said unto them, I am old and stricken in age:

JOS.23:3 And ye have seen all that the LORD your God hath done unto all these nations because of you; for the LORD your God is he that hath fought for you.

JOS.23:4 Behold, I have divided unto you by lot these nations that remain, to be an inheritance for your tribes, from Jordan, with all the nations that I have cut off, even unto the great sea westward.

JOS.23:5 And the LORD your God, he shall expel them from before you, and drive them from out of your sight; and ye shall possess their land, as the LORD your God hath promised unto you.

JOS.23:6 Be ye therefore very courageous to keep and to do all that is written in the book of the law of Moses, that ye turn not aside therefrom to the right hand or to the left;

14 Now therefore divide this land for an inheritance to the nine tribes and to the half tribe of Manasseh, and Joshua rose up and did as the Lord had spoken to him.

15 And he divided the whole land to the tribes of Israel as an inheritance according to their divisions.

16 But to the tribe at Levi he gave no inheritance, the offerings of the Lord are their inheritance as the Lord had spoken of them by the hand of Moses.

17 And Joshua gave Mount Hebron to Caleb the son of Jephuneh, one portion above his brethren, as the Lord had spoken through Moses.

18 Therefore Hebron became an inheritance to Caleb and his children unto this day.

19 And Joshua divided the whole land by lots to all Israel for an inheritance, as the Lord had commanded him.

20 And the children of Israel gave cities to the Levites from their own inheritance, and suburbs for their cattle, and property, as the Lord had commanded Moses so did the children of Israel, and they divided the land by lot whether great or small.

21 And they went to inherit the land according to their boundaries, and the children of Israel gave to Joshua the son of Nun an inheritance amongst them.

22 By the word of the Lord did they give to him the city which he required, Timnath-serach in Mount Ephraim, and he built the city and dwelt therein.

23 These are the inheritances which Elazer the priest and Joshua the son of Nun and the heads of the fathers of the tribes portioned out to the children of Israel by lot in Shiloh, before the Lord, at the door of the tabernacle, and they left off dividing the land.

24 And the Lord gave the land to the Israelites, and they possessed it as the Lord had spoken to them, and as the Lord had sworn to their ancestors.

25 And the Lord gave to the Israelites rest from all their enemies around them, and no man stood up against them, and the Lord delivered all their enemies into their hands, and not one thing failed of all the good which the Lord had spoken to the children of Israel, yea the Lord performed everything.

JOS.23:14 And, behold, this day I am going the way of all the earth: and ye know in all your hearts and in all your souls, that not one thing hath failed of all the good things which the LORD your God spoke concerning you; all are come to pass unto you, and not one thing hath failed thereof.

Comment:1: Finally, the great promise to Abraham by God Himself that after 400 years of Abraham's descendants being in bondage that finally God would bring them into their own land is fulfilled.

26 And Joshua called to all the children of Israel and he blessed them, and commanded them to serve the Lord, and he afterward sent them away, and they went each man to his city, and each man to his inheritance.

27 And the children of Israel served the Lord all the days of Joshua, and the Lord gave them rest from all around them, and they dwelt securely in their cities.

28 And it came to pass in those days, that Abianus king of Chittim died, in the thirty-eighth year of his reign, that is the seventh year of his reign over Edom, and they buried him in his place which he had built for himself, and Latinus reigned in his stead fifty years.

29 And during his reign he brought forth an army, and he went and fought against the inhabitants of Britannia and Kernania, the children of Elisha son of Javan, and he fought over them and made them tributary.

30 He then heard that Edom had revolted from under the hand of Chittim, and Latinus went to them and smote them and subdued them, and placed them under the hand of the children of Chittim, and Edom became one kingdom with the children of Chittim all the days.

31 And for many years there was no king in Edom, and their government was with the children of Chittim and their king.

32 And it was in the twenty-sixth year after the children of Israel had passed the Jordan, that is the sixty-sixth year after the children of Israel had departed from Egypt, that Joshua was old, advanced in years, being one hundred and eight years old in those days.

33 And Joshua called to all Israel, to their elders, their judges and officers, after the Lord had given to all the Israelites rest from all their enemies round about, and Joshua said to the elders of Israel, and to their judges, Behold I am old, advanced in years, and you have seen what the Lord has done to all the nations whom he has driven away from before you, for it is the Lord who has fought for you.

34 Now therefore strengthen yourselves to keep and to do all the words of the law of Moses, not to deviate from it to the right or to the left, and not to come amongst those nations who are left in the land; neither shall you make mention of the name of their gods, but you shall cleave to the Lord your God, as you have done to this day.

35 And Joshua greatly exhorted the children of Israel to serve the Lord all their days.

36 And all the Israelites said, We will serve the Lord our God all our days, we and our children, and our children's children, and our seed for ever.

37 And Joshua made a covenant with the people on that day, and he sent away the children of Israel, and they went each man to his inheritance and to his city.

C.2 From the Bible we have the last deeds of Joshua when he was at the ripe old age of 110, which was incidentally the same age that Joseph had died at 400 years before Joshua.

C.3 That is interesting, as the lifespan of mankind stayed around 110-120 years from the time of Jacob's sons (1850 BCE) until the times of Moses (1450 BCE). However sometime between the times of Joshua and King David mankind's lifespan dropped another 40 years to only an average lifespan of 70 just 450 years later in King David's time. This average of around 70 years has been the same now most of the time for the past 3000 years.

C.4 Joshua assembled all the 'Children of Israel' in their new lands to 'Shechem'. Here, Joshua gave the 'Children of Israel' another 'history lesson' as to how God had taken very good care of Israel and an admonition for Israel 'not to turn to the worship of Idols & devils', but to continue to worship the 'Living God'.

JOSH.24:1 And Joshua gathered all the tribes of Israel to Shechem, and called for the elders of Israel, and for their heads, and for their judges, and for their officers; and they presented themselves before God.

JOSH.24:2 And Joshua said unto all the people, 'Thus saith the LORD God of Israel, Your fathers dwelt on the other side of the flood in old time, even Terah, the father of Abraham, and the father of Nahor: and they served other gods'.

JOSH.24:3 'And I took your father Abraham from the other side of the flood, and led him throughout all the land of Canaan, and multiplied his seed, and gave him Isaac'.

JOSH.24:4 'And I gave unto Isaac Jacob and Esau: and I gave unto Esau mount Seir, to possess it; but Jacob and his children went down into Egypt'.

JOSH.24:5 'I sent Moses also and Aaron, and I plagued Egypt, according to that which I did among them: and afterward I brought you out'.

JOSH.24:6 'And I brought your fathers out of Egypt: and ye came unto the sea; and the Egyptians pursued after your fathers with chariots and horsemen unto the Red sea.'

JOS.24:7 'And when they cried unto the LORD, he put darkness between you and the Egyptians, and brought the sea upon them, and covered them; and your eyes have seen what I have done in Egypt: and ye dwelt in the wilderness a long season.'

JOSH.24:8 'And I brought you into the land of the Amorites, which dwelt on the other side Jordan; and they fought with you: and I gave them into your hand, that ye might possess their land; and I destroyed them from before you.'

JOSH.24:9 'Then Balak the son of Zippor, king of Moab, arose and warred against Israel, and sent and called Balaam the son of Beor to curse you':

JOSH.24:10 'But I would not hearken unto Balaam; therefore, he blessed you still: so, I delivered you out of his hand'.

JOSH.24:11 'And you went over Jordan, and came unto Jericho: and the men of Jericho fought against you, the Amorites, and the Perizzites, and the Canaanites, and the Hittites, and the Girgashites, the Hivites, and the Jebusites; and I delivered them into your hand'.

JOSH.24:12 'And I sent the hornet before you, which drove them out from before you, even the two kings of the Amorites; but not with thy sword, nor with thy bow'.

JOSH.24:13 'And I have given you a land for which ye did not labour, and cities which ye built not, and ye dwell in them; of the vineyards and olive-yards which ye planted not do ye eat'.

JOSH.24:14 'Now therefore fear the LORD and serve him in sincerity and in truth: and put away the gods which your fathers served on the other side of the flood, and in Egypt; and serve ye the LORD'.

---

38 And it was in those days, when the children of Israel were dwelling securely in their cities, that they buried the coffins of the tribes of their

---

ancestors, which they had brought up from Egypt, each man in the inheritance of his children, the twelve sons of Jacob did the children of Israel bury, each man in the possession of his children.

39 And these are the names of the cities wherein they buried the twelve sons of Jacob, whom the children of Israel had brought up from Egypt.

40 And they buried Reuben and Gad on this side Jordan, in Romia, which Moses had given to their children.

41 And Simeon and Levi they buried in the city Mauda, which he had given to the children of Simeon, and the suburb of the city was for the children of Levi.

42 And Judah they buried in the city of Benjamin opposite Bethlehem.

43 And the bones of Issachar and Zebulun they buried in Zidon, in the portion which fell to their children.

44 And Dan was buried in the city of his children in Eshtael, and Naphtali and Asher they buried in Kadesh-naphtali, each man in his place which he had given to his children.

45 And the bones of Joseph they buried in Shechem, in the part of the field which Jacob had purchased from Hamor, and which became to Joseph for an inheritance.

46 And they buried Benjamin in Jerusalem opposite the Jebusite, which was given to the children of Benjamin; the children of Israel buried their fathers each man in the city of his children.

47 And at the end of two years, Joshua the son of Nun died, one hundred and ten years old, and the time which Joshua judged Israel was twenty-eight years, and Israel served the Lord all the days of his life.

48 And the other affairs of Joshua and his battles and his reproofs with which he reproved Israel, and all which he had commanded them, and the names of the cities which the children of Israel possessed in his days, behold they are written in the book of the words of Joshua to

the children of Israel, and in the book of the wars of the Lord, which Moses and Joshua and the children of Israel had written.

49 And the children of Israel buried Joshua in the border of his inheritance, in Timnath-serach, which was given to him in Mount Ephraim.

50 And Elazer the son of Aaron died in those days, and they buried him in a hill belonging to Phineas his son, which was given him in Mount Ephraim.

Chapter 91

1 At that time, after the death of Joshua, the children of the Canaanites were still in the land, and the Israelites resolved to drive them out.

2 And the children of Israel asked of the Lord, saying, Who shall first go up for us to the Canaanites to fight against them? and the Lord said, Judah shall go up.

3 And the children of Judah said to Simeon, Go up with us into our lot, and we will fight against the Canaanites and we likewise will go up with you, in your lot, so the children of Simeon went with the children of Judah.

4 And the children of Judah went up and fought against the Canaanites, so the Lord delivered the Canaanites into the hands of the children of Judah, and they smote them in Bezek, ten thousand men.

5 And they fought with Adonibezek in Bezek, and he fled from before them, and they pursued him and caught him, and they took hold of him and cut off his thumbs and great toes.

6 And Adonibezek said, Three score and ten kings having their thumbs and great toes cut off, gathered their meat under my table, as I have done, so God has requited me, and they brought him to Jerusalem and he died there.

7 And the children of Simeon went with the children of Judah, and they smote the Canaanites with the edge of the sword.

8 And the Lord was with the children of Judah, and they possessed the mountain, and the children of Joseph went up to Bethel, the same is Luz, and the Lord was with them.

9 And the children of Joseph spied out Bethel, and the watchmen saw a man going forth from the city, and they caught him and said unto him, Show us now the entrance of the city and we will show kindness to thee.

10 And that man showed them the entrance of the city, and the children of Joseph came and smote the City with the edge of the sword.

11 And the man with his family they sent away, and he went to the Hittites and he built a city, and he called the name thereof Luz, so all the Israelites dwelt in their cities, and the children at Israel dwelt in their cities, and the children of Israel served the Lord all the days of Joshua, and all the days of the elders, who had lengthened their days after Joshua, and saw the great work of the Lord, which he had performed for Israel.

12 And the elders judged Israel after the death of Joshua for seventeen years.

JOSHUA 24:31 And Israel served the LORD all the days of Joshua, and all the days of the elders that over-lived Joshua, and which had known all the works of the LORD, that he had done for Israel.

13 And all the elders also fought the battles of Israel against the Canaanites and the Lord drove the Canaanites from before the children of Israel, in order to place the Israelites in their land.

14 And he accomplished all the words which he had spoken to Abraham, Isaac, and Jacob, and the oath which he had sworn, to give to them and to their children, the land of the Canaanites.

15 And the Lord gave to the children of Israel the whole land of Canaan, as he had sworn to their ancestors, and the Lord gave them rest from those around them, and the children of Israel dwelt securely in their cities.

Comment: Thus, it was indeed fulfilled what God had originally promised to Abraham that the Canaanites would all be driven out of the land, and that the land would become the land of Israel given to Abraham's descendants. It took around a total of 500 years altogether from Abraham's time to just after the time of Joshua until the Canaanites had been totally dispersed from the land of Israel.

JOS.24:29 And it came to pass after these things, that Joshua the son of Nun, the servant of the LORD, died, being a hundred and ten years old.

JOS.24:30 And they buried him in the border of his inheritance in Timnathserah, which is in mount Ephraim, on the north side of the hill of Gaash.

JOS.24:31 And Israel served the LORD all the days of Joshua, and all the days of the elders that overlived Joshua, and which had known all the works of the LORD, that he had done for Israel.

JOS.24:32 And the bones of Joseph, which the children of Israel brought up out of Egypt, buried they in Shechem, in a parcel of ground which Jacob bought of the sons of Hamor the father of Shechem for an hundred pieces of silver: and it became the inheritance of the children of Joseph.

---

16 Blessed be the Lord for ever, amen, and amen.

17 Strengthen yourselves and let the hearts of all you that trust in the Lord be of good courage.

THE END

SALVATION

JOH.3:36 He that believeth on the Son hath everlasting life: and he that believeth not the Son shall not see life; but the wrath of God abides on him.

Finally, I challenge you, that if you have not already prayed to receive Jesus into your heart, so that you can have eternal life, & be guaranteed a an eternal place in Heaven, then please do so immediately, to keep you safe from what is soon coming upon the earth!

Jesus stated in Revelations 3.20 "Behold, I stand at the door and knock, if any man hear my voice, and open the door, I will come into him and live with him and him with me".

"He who believes on the Son of God has eternal life." John 3.36. That means right now!

Once saved, you are eternally saved, and here is a very simple prayer to help you to get saved: -

"Dear Jesus,

Please come into my heart, forgive me all of my sins, give me eternal life, and fill me with your Holy Spirit. Please help me to love others and to read the Word of God in Jesus name, Amen.

Once you've prayed that little prayer sincerely, then you are guaranteed a wonderful future in Heaven for eternity with your creator and loved ones. "For God is Love" (1 John 4.16)

As I mentioned earlier in this book, your Salvation does not depend on you going to church, and your good works. Titus 3.5 states "Not by works of righteousness which we have done, but according to His mercy he saved us".

Your salvation only depends on receiving Christ as your saviour, not on church or religion!

(Steve: If I could get saved having been an atheist and an evolutionist whilst at university, then anyone can get saved! Just challenge God to prove He exists & ask Him into your heart! He will show up in your life & teach you the truth!) (John 14.6)

"He that comes unto Me I will in no wise cast out"- Jesus

Jesus explained that unless you become as a child you won't even understand the Kingdom of Heaven. (John 3.3)

MORE ON SALVATION: http://www.outofthebottomlesspit.co.uk/418605189

APPENDICES

I BACKGROUND INFORMATION ABOUT THE BOOK OF JASHER

'The **Book of Jasher'** is mentioned twice in the Bible. For this reason, a number of Bible teachers and others consider it to be as reliable and/or inspired as the Old Testament. Is this true?

Comment:1: I believe that there was an 'original' Book of Jasher which was probably an excellent book; but the copy that we have today has unfortunately been *altered to some extent*, although I would say that most of it is still inspired. The first mention of the Book of Jasher is in the Old Testament book of **Joshua 10.13**

JOS.10:13 And the sun stood still, and the moon stayed, until the people had avenged themselves upon their enemies. Is not this *written in the book of Jasher*? So, the sun stood still in the midst of heaven, and hasted not to go down about a whole day.

The second mention is in **2 Samuel 1:18**.

2SA.1:18 (Also he bade them teach the children of Judah the use of the bow: behold, it is *written in the book of Jasher*.)

C.2 Obviously from reading these scriptures from the Old Testament, it is clear that at one time there used to be a **Book of Jasher** that was reliable, otherwise it would not have been mentioned in both the time of Joshua and in the time of King David. As I mentioned in the Introduction of my 2nd Book '**Enoch Insights'** we *must not automatically throw out the Apocryphal Books* just because they are not perfect. Maybe they were excellent books at one time, but some powerful persons have altered the texts at some time or other.

In Conclusion, I would say that most of the Apocryphal books are largely accurate in content with a few mostly 'time discrepancies.

Unlike the Old Testament books, we have *no access to any manuscript of Jasher dating before 100 AD.*

Why that date? *Because the book we have is written in modern, square Hebrew characters without the vowel points.* The earliest manuscripts from this time are also missing the vowel points. *This points directly to Rabbi Akiba and his group's efforts to promote rabbinical leadership over Scripture.* His group, referred to as the Council of Jamnia, wanted to produce a foundation copy of the Scriptures as the original had been burned by the Romans when Jerusalem and the Temple were destroyed in 70AD. They made a number of *changes in the Scriptures* (which have come down to us as the *Masoretic Text*).'

C.3 It sounds to me, like this guy Rabbi Akiba in 100 A.D was very bitter because of the destruction of Israel in 70 A.D, in the which 100,000 Jews were crucified around Jerusalem alone, and millions driven out of the country in the famous 'Diaspora'. That was a direct fulfilment of a prophecy given by Jesus Himself 40 years earlier.

C.4 Jesus warned Israel that because they had rejected Him, as their Messiah, and that they had killed all the prophets that God had sent unto them, that *Israel would be destroyed.*

MAT.23:37 O Jerusalem, Jerusalem, thou that kills the prophets, and stones them which are sent unto thee, how often would I have gathered thy children together, even as a hen gathers her chickens under her wings, and ye would not!

MAT.23:38 Behold, your house is left unto you desolate.

C.5 The Romans came in their full might and fury in 70 AD, in the figure of general Titus, to destroy Israel completely. Normally, throughout history, when an emperor has done something like that, it is simply because that particular nation is being very difficult, rebellious & totally impossible to deal with, and this particular case, being stubbornly unwilling to submit to the Roman Rule. The same thing happened to Jerusalem in the time of Nebuchadnezzar and the Babylonian Empire, some 600 years earlier. It was much worse under the Romans though, as Israel ceased to be a nation for almost 2000 years until 1948.

C.6 What did Israel expect? They murdered their own Saviour Jesus Christ! It looks to me as if *God Himself allowed Israel to be severely judged*, and its people *cast out* for their *blatant rebellion against God Himself and His Son Jesus.* It was necessary for trials and tribulations to happen to the Messiah in order for Him to fulfil His mission on earth., but woe was unto them by whom the tribulations came. *Israel was itself annihilated* for almost 2000 years.

C.7 Apparently because Israel did get destroyed, this Rabbi Akiba obviously blamed Jesus and Christianity for the destruction of Israel and decided to try and eradicate all mention of Jesus in the Old Testament, by altering the Old Hebrew version of the Septuagint. He did this because Christians were using the Septuagint versions of the Old testament, to actually prove that Jesus was in fact mentioned in the Old Testament as the Messiah and prophesied about hundreds and even thousands of years before His actual birth on earth. Here are a couple of examples: **Isaiah 53** (whole chapter) and **Psalm 22:16.**

ISA.53:5 But he was *wounded* for our *transgressions*, he was *bruised* for our *iniquities*: the *chastisement* of *our peace* was *upon him*; and with *his stripes we are healed.*

C.8 I can't think of anyone, other than Jesus Christ himself, who could have fulfilled this Old testament verse in Isaiah written over 700 years before the birth of Christ!

PSA.22:16 For dogs have compassed me: the assembly of the wicked have enclosed me: they *pierced my hands and my feet.*

C.9 The discovery of the Dead Sea Scrolls really exposed this fake Masoretic text by clearly showing that the Septuagint version of the Old Testament is by far the most accurate, and that the Masoretic text had altered many scriptures.

SOURCE: https://theorthodoxlife.wordpress.com/2012/03/12/masoretic-text-vs-original-hebrew/

The Masoretic text has a different wording in Deuteronomy 32:43 and Psalm 40:6. In addition chapters 5 and 11 of Genesis have a much-shortened chronology. Therefore, given these and the other variations, it is a simple matter to determine if the text of a Scripture version is following that of the ancient (Septuagint LXX), used by the Apostles and Church fathers, or is following the Masoretic text which came about 400 years later. If the Bible text does not have the full chronology in Genesis 5 & 11, or the full rendering of Deuteronomy 32:43 or the correct wording for Psalm 40:6 (39:6), then it is *not following the ancient text*, but is from the *changed Masoretic text*.

C.10 The Bible is 100% accurate when it comes to the 'New Testament', but concerning the KJV of the Old Testament, which is translated from the Masoretic Text, and therefore some important things were altered, as those who devised the Masoretic text wanted to expunge all references to Jesus as mentioned in the Old Testament, as their position was anti-Christ. The only solution today in 2018 is for people to read the *Septuagint* versions of the *Old Testament* which was compiled much earlier than the infamous Masoretic text. The Septuagint was put together in around 300 BCE and the Masoretic text around 100 A.D http://www.ecclesia.org/truth/comparisons.html

C.11 Here is a website which offers the Septuagint Text alongside the King James version which I personally have found very useful: http://ecmarsh.com/lxx-kjv/

C.12 Is the real date today 5993? [See this story on my website which is taken from the APPENDIX of my other book **JUBILEES INSIGHTS**: http://www.outofthebottomlesspit.co.uk/413438217}

C.13 Is it true that it is 5993 years after Creation at this moment in this year of 2018 or is more likely around 650 years older at around 6643 years old? Find out with the following excellent thought-provoking video: https://youtu.be/VI1yRTC6kGE?t=4

II MORE BACKGROUND INFO INTO THE BOOK OF JASHER

The first mention of the Book of Jasher is in the Old Testament book of **Joshua 10.13.**

JOSH.10:13 And the sun stood still, and the moon stayed, until the people had avenged themselves upon their enemies. *Is not this written in the book of Jasher?* So, the sun stood still in the midst of heaven, and hasted not to go down about a whole day.

The second mention is in **2 Samuel 1:18**.

2SA.1:18 (Also he bade them teach the children of Judah the use of the bow: behold, it is *written in the book of Jasher*.)

Some writers minimize or make light of these two verses mentioned above, but with a deeper examination, one finds out *that these two verses* are the *perfect verses* to describe the Book of Jasher and I will now explain why:

'USE OF THE BOW'
In this Book of Jasher in Chapter 56 verses 7-9 it states:

JASHER 56.7 And on the next day Jacob again called for his sons, and they all assembled and came to him and sat before him, and Jacob on that day blessed his sons before his death, each man did he bless according to his blessing; behold it is written in the book of the law of the Lord appertaining to Israel.

JASHER 56.8 And Jacob said unto Judah, I know my son that thou art a mighty man for thy brethren; reign over them, and thy sons shall reign over their sons forever.

JASHER 56.9 Only teach thy sons the bow and all the weapons of war, in order that they may fight the battles of their brother who will rule over his enemies.

C.1 The first important thing to notice is that Jacob the old Patriarch of Israel was on his deathbed and was giving his last 'Blessing' to his family.

Second: He chose Judah to be the *leader* over all of his brethren even though he wasn't the eldest. Judah from that time on (circa 1900 BC) became the leading tribe of Israel and eventually the Royal tribe from which proceeded the Kings of Judah & Israel.

Third: Let's examine the major events happening in 2SA.1:18 (Also he bade them teach the children of Judah the use of the bow: behold, it is *written in the book of Jasher*). This verse unlike the other verses in this chapter is in (brackets), as though the Old Testament writers are pausing for a moment, to *interject the importance of the Book of Jasher* although the content of the verse does not *seem to have anything to do with the other verses around it*:

2SA.1:17 And David lamented with this lamentation over Saul and over Jonathan his son:

2SA.1:18 (Also he bade them teach the children of Judah the use of the bow: behold, it is written in the book of Jasher.)

2SA.1:19 The beauty of Israel is slain upon thy high places: how are the mighty fallen!

C.2 King David later went on to capture Jerusalem and made it his own capital city.

2SA.5:7 Nevertheless David took the strong hold of Zion: the same is the city of David

1CH.11:4,7 And David and all Israel went to Jerusalem; And David dwelt in the castle; therefore, they called it the city of David.

C.3 What is the link between 'Use of the Bow' & Leadership?

REV.6:2 And I saw and behold a white horse: and he that sat on him had a bow; and a crown was given unto him: and he went forth conquering, and to conquer.

C.4 Fourth: Let's look at:

JOSH.10:13 'And the sun stood still, and the moon stayed, until the people had avenged themselves upon their enemies. Is not this *written in the book of Jasher*? So, the sun stood still in the midst of heaven, and hasted not to go down about a whole day'.

C.5 Both of the verses mentioning the Book of Jasher are in effect pointing to the importance of *Warrior Kings* starting with Jacob, then Judah not to mention Joshua. Then the capital *Jerusalem* conquered by 'Warrior King' David

IN CONCLUSION: WHY WERE THESE PARTICULAR TWO BIBLE VERSES THAT MENTION THE BOOK OF JASHER SO IMPORTANT?

C.6 Both verses occurred at *very critical times* in Ancient Israel's History. At actual turning points that would decide the very future of the nation of Israel.

In **Joshua 10.13** a decisive battle was occurring, and Joshua asked God to do a miracle and cause the Sun to stand still over Gibeon. He did this so that he would have enough time to defeat his enemies before the sun would have set.

2SA.1:18 In the story about David, it was when King Saul and his sons were killed in battle & just before David was made King.

C.7 The implication from the two verses mentioning the Book of Jasher in the Bible is for all to read the Book of Jasher as it talks about the beginning and fulfilment of Israel in History all the way to the founding of the city of Jerusalem in King David's time. Jerusalem is also to be the capital of the King of Kings in the future. So, in effect those two verses with the relevant verses in the Book of Jasher paint the picture of God's promises to Abraham fulfilled in Jacob, Judah, Jerusalem as Israel's capital city, & eventually the Coming of Jesus (King of Kings) & New Jerusalem. As Jesus said about Himself, I am the Alpha and the Omega.

C.8 The two verses mentioning the Book of Jasher are doing exactly that: pointing to the beginning and fulfilment of Israel as God's people and nation.

C.9 Those reading those verses in the Bible about the Book of Joshua and taking the time to research the Book of Jasher would end up reading Chapter 56 verses7-9 to get the point that Jacob on his deathbed was fulfilling the promises made to his grand-father Abraham and Isaac by choosing Judah to be the Warrior King and leader of his brethren but much more importantly that *Judah* was to be the most important *Leadership* tribe of the Kings of Israel

III NUMEROLOGY

THE IMPORTANCE OF THE LETTER J AS IN FOUND IN BOTH LEADERSHIP & WARRIOR KINGS.

C.1 The first leader mentioned in the Bible with a name beginning a J was Jared. 'For in his days the fallen angels descended upon the earth'. Jared was also the father of the great patriarch Enoch. Enoch became a King of Kings, where according to this Book of Jasher, all the Kings of the earth were afraid of him for his Godly aura and were obedient to him. So much of that Evil was kept in check whilst Enoch lived. Enoch was in a sense the 1st Warrior King. (The greatest Pre-Flood spiritual Warrior)

THE LETTER J HOWEVER DID NOT EXIST IN OLD HEBREW.

C.2 The letter J was invented by the Romans. However, it is *God who designs languages and letters*, and it is truly amazing that the tenth letter in the modern English language has such significance.

BIBLE NUMEROLOGY

C.3 The letter J is the 10th letter in the modern English Alphabet. The number 10 in Biblical numerology stands for leadership.

In the Bible, the number 10 is used 242 times. The designation "10th" is used 79 times. Ten is also *viewed as a complete and perfect number*, as is *3, 7* and *12*. It is made up of 4, the number of the physical creation, and 6, the number of man. As such, it signifies testimony, law, responsibility (leadership) and the completeness of order. <SOURCE: http://www.biblestudy.org/bibleref/meaning-of-numbers-in-bible/10.html>

THE FOLLOWING NAMES IN 'ENGLISH' ALL BEGIN WITH A J

C.4

JEHOVAH (Name of God)

JAWEH (Jewish Name of God)

JARED (Father of Enoch who was a King of Kings and a great Spiritual Warrior)

JACOB (Patriarch and Warrior)

JUDAH (Appointed to be leader over his brethren)

JEW (To lead people to the one true God)

JOSHUA (Warrior King)

JASHER (Book of Warrior Kings and leaders)

JUDGES (Book of Warrior leaders such as Samson)

JERUSALEM (Captured by 'WARRIOR KING' David)

JONATHAN (Prince, mighty warrior & close friend of King David)

JOSIAH (Good king of Judah)

JEHOSOPHAT (Good king of Judah)

JEREMIAH (Major prophet of Warning & JUDGEMENT)

JESUS (SAVIOUR & WARRIOR KING- JUSTICE-JUDGEMENT-JOY- for TRUE saved JEWS)

JOHN (BOOK OF REVELATIONS – Judgement & The 2nd Coming of Christ-New Heaven New Earth)

JERUSALEM (NEW) The Heavenly City.

IV Certainly, many serious scholars have concluded that this Book of Jasher is authentic. The well-known Hebraist and Rabbinic Scholar (and translator of the 1840 Book of Jasher) Moses Samuel wrote of Jasher: "...the book is, with the exception of some doubtful parts, a venerable monument of antiquity; and that, notwithstanding some few additions have been made to it in comparatively modern times, it still retains sufficient to prove it a copy of the book referred to in Joshua, Ch. x, and 2 Samuel, Ch. 1." - Moses Samuel - Hebraist and Rabbinic Scholar And my old friend and mentor, the late Dr Cyrus Gordon (who was the world's leading Semitist until his death) said: "There can be little doubt that the book of Jasher was a national epic... The time is ripe for a fresh investigation of such genuine sources of Scripture, particularly against the background of the Dead Sea Scrolls." - Dr Cyrus Gordon

SOURCE: http://nazarenespace.ning.com/group/bookofjasher

V THE BOOK OF JASHER

"The Book of Jasher," rendered in the LXX (Septuagint). "The Book of the *Upright One*," by the Vulgate "The Book of Just Ones," was probably a kind of national sacred songbook, a collection of songs in praise of the heroes of Israel, a "Book of golden deeds," a national anthology. We have only two specimens from the book, (1) the words of Joshua which he spake to the Lord at the crisis of the battle of Beth-horon (Joshua 10:12 Joshua 10:13); and (2) "the Song of the Bow," that beautiful and touching mournful elegy which David composed on the occasion of the death of Saul and Jonathan (2 Samuel 1:18-27).

C.1 Author of 'Jasher Insights': I would like to add that the Book of Jasher is *not* mentioned in the Septuagint version of Joshua 10:12 &13. In 2 Samuel 1:18-27 of the Septuagint the Book of Jasher is also *not* mentioned but only a reference to the 'Book of Right'.

SOURCE: (https://www.biblestudytools.com/dictionary/jasher/)

VI LAND OF NOD:

DEFINITIONS: https://en.wikipedia.org/wiki/Land_of_Nod

HOLLOW EARTH: WAS THE LAND OF NOD HELL? OR THE BEGINNING OF IT?

http://www.echoesofenoch.com/a_hollow_earth.htm

NAZI RELATIVES? CAIN'S DESCENDANTS!

INNER EARTH: If Nod is east of Eden and Eden is inside the earth...that means Nod is inside the earth too? Gen 4:11-16, "And now art thou cursed *from* the earth, which hath opened up her mouth to receive thy brother's blood from thy hand. When thou till the ground, it shall not henceforth yield unto thee her strength; a fugitive and a vagabond shalt thou be 'In the earth'. And Cain said unto the Lord, my punishment is greater than I can bear. Behold, thou hast driven me this day from the face (surface) of the earth; and I shall be a fugitive and a vagabond in the earth; and it shall come to pass, that every one that finds me shall slay me. And the Lord said unto him, Therefore, whosoever slays Cain, vengeance shall be taken on him sevenfold, and the Lord set a mark upon Cain, lest any finding him should kill him. And Cain went out from the presence of the Lord, and dwelt in the land of Nod, East of Eden."

It is interesting to note that in the many translations of the Bible, only the older English versions the King James and the American Standard use the translation "in the earth". All of the more recent translations simply say, "on the earth". A big liberty of translation placed upon God's word because of the assumption that the earth is solid and therefore could not contain life inside. The only other translation I am aware of that agrees with the older versions is the Torah. This is the Old Testament translated into the English by the Jews themselves! Regardless of this compromise of interpretation, from prior scriptures the Bible clearly establishes that Eden or Paradise and Hell are two separate chambers inside the earth. With that firmly established, (at least according to the Bible itself) the only word that could be used in context is "*in*"!

CAIN WAS REMOVED FROM THE SURFACE OF THE EARTH INTO A SUBTERRANEAN REALM. He was given a " mark" that he would not be killed by others. This Hebrew word *owth* means an identifying mark in the sense of an agreement. When translated into the Greek, the word used is *semion,* in the sense of a supernatural sign of some type. When Cain killed Abel, it was in the "process of time" this actually means in the last days. This would be referring to a time just prior to the great flood. The soil not yielding her strength may not mean an agricultural problem, but rather a genetic defect of some type. Soil, seed land and fruit have always, in the

320

scriptures been used to refer to the literal geographical elements, spiritual conditions or physical bloodline. Cain's bloodline may be the seed of the serpent mentioned in Gen 3. Cain was a bad guy. The Bible says so.

I Jn 3:12 "Not as Cain, who was of that wicked one,"

In context here this statement about Cain can mean more than the fact he was of the wicked one because he committed murder. It might also imply he was actually from the wicked one. It was in his blood. This was the same lineage Goliath came from, he was a big white guy with a bad attitude! The word Giant has another meaning as a tyrant or bully and can mean much more than physical stature. The Physical stature although is clearly defined in the OT. Numbers 13:33, Deu2:11, 20, 3:11,13 Josh 12:4, 13:12,15:8,17:15 and18:16.

As strange as this all sounds the Bible stands true upon itself. The worldwide legends of "white" tribes and ascended "masters" may not be myth at all but the continual encounters with a race from within. The search by Hitler and the Nazi's for blood relations from an inner earth may have a thread of truth. If Hitler came to his own to proclaim Satan's seed, in the same but opposite pattern, it could mean that the modern-day Philistines may be the Germanic lineage. Now not to condemn anyone by their race or national bloodline, I must say I am a Caucasian of Germanic descent and I love the Lord! God has made a provision for salvation that is no longer based on anything but faith. In Isaiah 14 there is an end time prophecy that indicates a genetic tampering involving the Philistines and a tribe used to punish them continually, this would be the tribe of Dan. This genetic tampering started with Nazi Germany and is continued in America.

VII CAIN

Cain was also viewed as a type of 'utter perverseness', an 'offspring of Satan', "a son of wrath", 'a lawless rebel' who said, "There is neither a divine judgment nor a judge", whose words of repentance were insincere whose fleeing from God was a denial of His omnipresence (and all his generations must be exterminated "the desire of the spirit of sin" He is the first of those who have no share in the world to come

GENERATIONS OF CAIN

The seven generations of Cain, as the brood of Satan, are accordingly represented as types of rebels .While the pious men all descended from Seth, there sprang from Cain all the wicked ones who rebelled against God and whose perverseness and corruption brought on the flood: they committed all abominations and incestuous crimes in public without shame. The daughters of Cain were those "fair daughters of men" who by their lasciviousness caused the fall of the "sons of God"., but were attracted by the gay and sensuous mode of life in which the children of Cain indulged; the latter spending their days at the foot of the mountain, in wild orgies, accompanied by the music of instruments invented by Jubal, and by women, in gorgeous attire, seducing the men to commit the most abominable practises. Also speaks of the excessive wickedness of the posterity of Cain, which grew in vehemence with every generation; while the posterity of Seth remained virtuous during seven generations, after which the fall of the angels ensued who produced gigantic offspring in making love with the women on earth. The antidomestic pagan Gnostics declared Cain and other rebels or sinners to be their prototypes of evil and licentiousness.

Cain, Esau, Korah, the Sodomites, and even Judas Iscariot, were made by these Gnostics expounders of the "wisdom" of the serpent in rebellion against God. **SOURCE:** http://www.jewishencyclopedia.com/articles/3904-cain

CONCLUSION about THE CAINITE DOCTRINE

C.1 It would appear that, once God banished Cain, and sent him to the Land of Nod, (Nod means sleep or delusions), that there he sought to do everything in direct rebellion to God. For example, if God's law said one thing, then Cain sought to do the exact opposite, being an actual son of Satan himself. The Cainite women, or descendants of Cain, are the ones who attracted the Fallen Angels some centuries after Cain's 'Fall from Grace'.

C.2 CAINITE ORGIES: Cainites were known to have orgies with women in public, flaunting it. They were the origin of lustfulness and licentiousness. They would also pillage their neighbours bringing random disorder instead of order.

C.3 REBELLION: Every law of God, Cain and his descendants 'tore apart' and deliberately 'did the exact opposite', exactly as one would expect a demon or devil to do, which Cain was. In Cain's time him being a physical being he was not restricted. With the Judgement of the Great Flood more restrictions were put on both men and demons to limit total anarchy & random disorder. Even more restrictions were put on Satan and his Fallen angels after the destruction of the tower of Babel. After Babel we saw 6 empires of man that were much better organized and had less chaos. So, has it been since the Tower of Babel until now that there has been 'Law & Order' of some sort at least?

SATAN'S EMPIRES: 1) EGYPT 2) ASSYRIA 3) BABYLON 4) MEDIO-PERSIA 5) GREECE 6) ROME 7) COMING NEW WORLD ORDER-ANTI-CHRIST

C.4 Maybe God Himself prefers even the Devil himself ruling the planet earth for the time being through his governments and World Empires, rather than the Total Chaos that developed during the hundreds of years prior to the Great Flood. Total chaos and *unrest* will return in the time period known as the Last Days or during the last days of the Great Tribulation just before Christ Returns for the Rapture of all of the Saved on the planet.

CAIN - A FORE-RUNNER OF THE ANTI-CHRIST

.5 Cain was literally an 'In the flesh Demon' as he was a son of Satan born through Eve. This is exactly how the coming infamous Anti-Christ will be. Just like Cain seeking to destroy all the laws of God and thus to abolish all religions with his eventual aim to cause all the inhabitants on earth to worship him - the Devil himself, in the flesh of the Anti-Christ.

VIII LUCIFER & THE FALLEN ANGELS

THE FALL OF SATAN & 1/3 OF THE ANGELS OF GOD.

.1 Many of us have written about the Fallen angels and even Lucifer's Fall, but with this little essay, I would like to put certain things into perspective.

.2 In studying ancient history at length and in particular Bible history from pre-Flood times until the time of Christ. Then moving on through the 20 centuries since... In fact, in examining the pre-Flood times, along with the immediate post-flood times and the tower of Babel. then moving on to the first world empire of mankind: the Egyptian dynasties & the Assyrian empire then the Babylonian empire - the Medio Persian empire - the Greek empire -the Roman empire - the last 2000 year - the coming world empire of the Anti-Christ - the following becomes apparent:

1) The forces of evil had more freedom before the Great Flood

2) God severely restricted the Forces of Evil after the Great Flood

3) After the Tower of Babel both Satan and his Fallen angels as well as mankind were all even more restricted as to what would now be permitted.

4) It is my conviction that right after the Tower of Babel, that God Himself called Satan onto the carpet before His throne and gave him a good tongue-lashing and stated to Satan: 'From now on I will not permit the *random*

chaos that you Lucifer and your roaming band of fallen angels have committed both on the earth and in the heavenlies (More on this later). From now on you must become a 'Law and Order' enforcer. This could also be when Satan became the *'Accuser of the Saints'* by twisting the law or at least trying to do so.

5) How have I come to this conclusion?

Well, look at the 6 World empires that followed the Towel of Babel. What was very different about their organization? Notice that the way the rulers went about doing things was somehow very different and much more organized and disciplined. Generally speaking, there was no longer the random chaos and the restless spirit that existed in pre-Flood times and that had even come back to some extent at the time of the Tower of Babel. Why? Because of the 'Return of the Nephilim'!

6) It is clear that Satan and his Powers have been somewhat held back and restricted to some degree ever since.

7) We do know that one day 'random chaos' will indeed return, but probably not until all light of God's Spirit has left the planet temporarily, at the very end of the Great Tribulation, and the Rapture of all of the saved.

8) The famous oriental prophet Avak stated that the original creation made by God was destroyed by Lucifer when he first rebelled. Then God re-created order out of the chaos that Lucifer had made. Some state that this is clearly shown in **Genesis 1.1** and **1.2**

GEN.1:1 In the beginning God created the heaven and the earth.

GEN.1:2 And the earth was without form, and void; and darkness was upon the face of the deep. And the Spirit of God moved upon the face of the waters.

9) What other writers have stated is that perhaps something happened between these two verses. Could that be? That first there was the Creation - then Chaos brought about by Satan - then Re-Creation by God Himself?

10) In spite of Satan's having tried relentlessly to defeat God's plan of Salvation by trying to insert Satan's Seed from the very beginning of Creation as in Cain and later in the seed of his Fallen Angels into humanity, & then for the millennia leading up to the coming of Jesus the Messiah – Satan failed miserably, although he got pretty close to destroying all of God's Creation when only Noah and his 3 sons and their wives were found righteous and survived the Great Flood judgement by God Himself.

11) SATAN IS THE ACCUSER. First, he tempted Fallen angels to Fall and then Adam and Eve and then the descendants of Cain and soon there was total chaos within a few hundred years of Enoch having been translated.

REV.12:9 And the great dragon was cast out, that old serpent, called the Devil, and Satan, which deceiveth the whole world: he was cast out into the earth, and his angels were cast out with him.

REV.12:10 And I heard a loud voice saying in heaven, Now is come salvation, and strength, and the kingdom of our God, and the power of his Christ: for the accuser of our brethren is cast down, which accused them before our God day and night.

C.3 SATAN IS SUCH A TWISTED TRICKSTER! First, he tempts people. Then when they do the wrong thing – he goes to the Courts of heaven acting as the Prosecuting Lawyer and accuses people before the throne of God. He then tells God that He must condemn mankind and judge them. We know from the Book of Job that God even uses the Devil himself to carry out some of His Judgements. At other times He uses His own angels to carry out Judgments:

JOB.1:6 Now there was a day when the sons of God came to present themselves before the LORD, and Satan came also among them.

JOB.1:7 And the LORD said unto Satan, Whence comest thou? Then Satan answered the LORD, and said, From going to and fro in the earth, and from walking up and down in it.

324

JOB.1:8 And the LORD said unto Satan, Hast thou considered my servant Job, that there is none like him in the earth, a perfect and an upright man, one that feareth God, and escheweth evil?

JOB.1:9 Then Satan answered the LORD, and said, Doth Job fear God for nought?

JOB.1:10 Hast not thou made an hedge about him, and about his house, and about all that he hath on every side? thou hast blessed the work of his hands, and his substance is increased in the land.

JOB.1:11 But put forth thine hand now, and touch all that he hath, and he will curse thee to thy face.

JOB.1:12 And the LORD said unto Satan, Behold, all that he hath is in thy power; only upon himself put not forth thine hand. So, Satan went forth from the presence of the LORD.

12) **THE BIGGER PICTURE**: There is a lot of evidence that at one time Lucifer and his marauding Fallen angels had access to far away galaxies and other planets and even other dimensions. There is however also evidence that Satan and his Rebellious Band of Fallen angels are currently being restricted more and more.

The picture is that eventually Satan and all of his Fallen angels and resultant many entities will all soon be locked-up in the Bottomless Pit. Eventually they will be cast into the Lake of Fire unless they repent.

12) **EVIDENCE of VISITATION TO OTHER PLANETS**: There are pyramids on Mars that are even bigger than the ones on earth and many claims that they are actually Stargates or dimensional Gateways. There is apparently even a massive Sphinx on Mars, which is over one mile wide – but now abandoned. There is evidence of very tall buildings on the far side of the moon. There are also structures on the moons of Saturn. So tall as to be seen from earth! Who built them? When were they built?

13) The Fallen Angels also apparently long to 'bring back' the so-called 'Golden Age' of the 'Times Before the Flood'- when '*They*' reigned supreme – at least 'over mankind'. Well it might have been the golden age of Atlantis, Lemuria, & the Kingdom of Mu, run by both Fallen angels and their sons the Giants and other hybrids. That is both chimeras and monsters, but the fact is that it was hell on earth for the human inhabitants who were made into slaves and sometimes literally devoured.

14) There is ample evidence that in the times just before the Great Flood that ancient civilizations-built cities under the ground in order to protect themselves from so many hybrid creatures and devouring monsters.

15) It has been noted that God originally only created the animals on earth to be *herbivores* and not *meat-eaters,* so where did the carnivore dinosaurs enter the picture? It has been mentioned on Steve Quayle's website, (and he being an expert in the field of the Giants), that possibly in Pre-Flood times, the Fallen angels, being in total rebellion against God, made the reptilian

dinosaurs, as ferocious meat-eaters in order to try and get rid of many of mankind as possible. Remember Satan's whole goal from the beginning of time has been to totally destroy all of God's Creation, including mankind.

THE GOOD NEWS IS THAT SATAN CANNOT DO ANYTHING TOO DESTRUCTIVE WITHOUT PERMISSION FROM GOD.

16) The Forces of Evil are actually presently largely held back from their destructive purposes until it is the TIME of the END. There is so much evidence of this.

2TH.2:7 For the mystery of iniquity doth already work: only he (Angel of God) who now letteth (prevents) will let (prevent), until he be taken out of the way.

2TH.2:8 And then shall that Wicked be revealed,(Satan in the Flesh -The Anti-Christ along with his band of Fallen Angels), whom the Lord shall consume with the spirit of his mouth, and shall destroy with the brightness of his coming:

'NUCLEAR MISSILE SILOS' PREVENTED FROM FIRING 'HYGROGEN BOMB' MISSILES BY U.F.O's

The Militaries of both the USA and Russia tell us that when upon occasion they have been tempted to order the use of their nuclear big atomic and hydrogen bombs - that immediately UFO's showed up at the missile silos and prevented them for firing the missiles!

THE DEVIL HIMSELF CAN DO NOTHING REALLY TERRIBLE UNLESS HE IS PERMITTED TO DO SO BY GOD HIMSELF!

17) Contrary to what is pushed by Hellywood (Hollywood) and the Satanic agenda of the elite, Evil might appear at present to be winning and getting the upper hand, but it is only allowed by God himself to fulfil a much great purpose – To test those on earth.

REV.3:10 Because thou hast kept the word of my patience, I also will keep thee from the hour of temptation (The Great Tribulation), which shall come upon all the world, to try them that dwell upon the earth.

Those on Earth are being tested to see whom they will follow – the truth – Jesus – the Word of God or swallow the lies of Satan such as Evolution, Global Warming, and the 'dog eat dog' ways of materialism, modernism and unbelief as well as the great deception yet to come: Disclosure!

18) What is *Disclosure*? It is the idea that one day soon Aliens will appear in the heavens in UFO's to declare that 'They' 'seeded mankind' on the planet some millions of years ago, and have now come back to help us 'evolve into the next stage' - some crazy hybrids of aliens and humans. it sounds like more human abductions & alterations.

19) The truth of Disclosure is that it the same thing happening all over again: the return of the fallen angels & the Nephilim now masquerading as aliens

from distant stars. They will again try to rule over the earth as in the original golden age of Atlantis such as before the great flood. According to the Bible their leader the hybrid Anti-Christ will control all peoples on the face of the earth through commerce:

REV.13:11 and I beheld another beast (false prophet) coming up out of the earth; and he had two horns like a lamb, and he spake as a dragon (Satan or one of the fallen angels).

REV.13:12 And he exerciseth all the power of the first beast before him, and causeth the earth and them which dwell therein to worship the first beast (The Anti-Christ), whose deadly wound was healed.

REV.13:13 And he doeth great wonders, so that he maketh fire come down from heaven on the earth in the sight of men,

REV.13:14 And deceiveth them that dwell on the earth by the means of those miracles which he had power to do in the sight of the beast; saying to them that dwell on the earth, that they should make an image to the beast, which had the wound by a sword, and did live.

REV.13:15 And he had power to give life unto the image of the beast, that the image of the beast should both speak, and cause that as many as would not worship the image of the beast should be killed.

REV.13:16 And he causeth all, both small and great, rich and poor, free and bond, to receive a mark in their right hand, or in their foreheads:

REV.13:17 And that no man might buy or sell, save he that had the mark, or the name of the beast, or the number of his name.

REV.13:18 Here is wisdom. Let him that hath understanding count the number of the beast: for it is the number of a man (6); and his number is Six hundred threescore and six. 666 = [False Trinity of Man, The Anti-Christ & Satan]

IX THE FEMALE HOLY SPIRIT

MAT.12:31 Wherefore I say unto you, 'All manner of sin and blasphemy shall be forgiven unto men: but the blasphemy against the Holy Ghost shall not be forgiven unto men.'

MAR.3:29-30 But he that shall blaspheme against the Holy Ghost hath never forgiveness, but is in danger of eternal damnation; because they said, He hath an unclean spirit.

LUK.12:10 And whosoever shall speak a word against the Son of man, it shall be forgiven him: but unto him that blasphemes against the Holy Ghost it shall not be forgiven.

Comment: Why did Jesus make a distinction between Himself and the Holy Spirit here? If God and Jesus and the Holy Spirit were all masculine, which is how they are portrayed by most modern churches, then perhaps Jesus would not have made this distinction!

PROTECTION OF A WIFE COMES BEFORE THE PROTEC-TION OF A SON

A man who has a beautiful wife, whom he both loves and adores, and also has a strong son. If perchance another man comes and gives a blow to his son, it is conceivable that the father will make light of it and forgive the man. However, if the man hits his wife, I guarantee that he would neither forgive him or let him go unpunished. I do think that these above Bible verses prove one thing: The Holy Spirit has got to both feminine and God's wife. Nothing but wrath to those who would hurt and offend her!

GOD THE FATHER, JESUS THE SON & THE HOLY SPIRIT MOTHER.

If you would take all that the Catholics have seen, and heard, and envisioned of Mary, and conceived of her, her glorification as Queen of Heaven, including all the inspired art masterpieces of her etc., I think you would have a pretty good picture of the Holy Spirit as the spiritual mother of Jesus and therefore the wife of God and therefore the mother of the Holy Family, the Holy Trinity. It then all makes sense. In a way, like Jesus is a picture of God, Mary was in a way a picture of the Holy Spirit. That's literally what it means by the Word of God, it means the logo of God, the expression of God, the message of God. We studied that in Greek when I was in Bible college, what a deep meaning there was to the Greek word "logo" which is translated in John 1 as the "word". It was sort of like, the logo was a little bit of God himself, an expression of Him, a manifestation of Him in Jesus his Son.

SOURCE: http://www.peopleofthekeys.com/news/docs/library/Dream+Queen

THE FEMININE HOLY SPIRIT

1) http://www.pistissophia.org/The_Holy_Spirit/the_holy_spirit.html

2) http://www.hts.org.za/index.php/HTS/article/view/3225/html

X THE GIANTS – JOSEPHUS

QUOTES FROM JOSEPHUS CONCERNING GIANTS www.generationword.com

"This notion, that the fallen angels were, in some sense, the fathers of the old giants, was the constant opinion of antiquity, of gods accompanied with women, and begat sons that proved unjust, and despisers of all that was good, on account of the confidence they had in their own strength; for the tradition is, that these men did what resembled the acts of those whom the Grecians call giants."

"These kings had laid waste all Syria and overthrown the offspring of the giants. And when they were come over against Sodom. . ."

"They told them also, that they found at Hebron the posterity of the giants. Accordingly, these spies, who had seen the land of Canaan, when they perceived that all these difficulties were greater there than they had met with since they came out of Egypt, they were affrighted at them themselves, and endeavoured to affright the multitude also."

"For which reason they removed their camp to Hebron; and when they had taken it, they slew all the inhabitants. There were till then left the race of giants, who had bodies so large, and countenances so entirely different from other men, that they were surprising to the sight, and terrible to the hearing. The bones of these men are still shown to this very day, unlike to any credible relations of other men. Now they gave this city to the Levites as an extraordinary reward."

WHY KING DAVID'S MEN MADE DAVID RETIRE FROM BATTLE WHEN HE WAS OLD

"A little afterward the king made war against the Philistines; and when he had joined battle with them, and put them to flight, he was left alone, as he was in pursuit of them; and when he was quite tired down, he was seen by one of the enemy, his name was Achmon, the son of Araph, he was one of the sons of the giants. He had a spear, the handle of which weighed three hundred shekels, and a breastplate of chain-work, and a sword. He turned back and ran violently to slay King David their enemy's king, for he was quite tired out with labour; but Abishai, Joab's brother, appeared suddenly on the scene, and protected the king with his shield, as he lay down, and slew the enemy. Now the multitude were very uneasy at these dangers of the king, and that he was very near to be slain; and the rulers made him swear that he would no more go out with them to battle, lest he should come to some great misfortune by his courage and boldness, and thereby deprive the people of the benefits they now enjoyed by his means, and of those that they might hereafter enjoy by his living a long time among them."

"When the king heard that the Philistines were gathered together at the city Gazara, he sent an army against them, when Sibbechai the Hittite, one of David's most courageous men, behaved himself so as to deserve great commendation, for he slew many of those that bragged they were the posterity of the giants, and vaunted themselves highly on that account, and thereby was the occasion of victory to the Hebrews."

'They had a man who was *six cubits tall and had on each of his feet and hands one more toe and finger than men naturally have.* Now the person who

was sent against them by David out of his army was Jonathan, the son of Shimea, who fought this man in a single combat, and slew him; and
as he was the person who gave the turn to the battle, he gained the greatest reputation for courage therein. This man also vaunted himself to be of the sons of the giants. But after this fight the Philistines made war no more against the Israelites."

XI CHAPTER 6 DEMONOLOGY 101; GIANTS & GOD'S WRATH: https://youtu.be/F24OP2wjNGA?t=2393

MORE ABOUT THE GIANTS: http://www.outofthebottomlesspit.co.uk/411783108

ENORMOUS SKELETONS: http://www.outofthebottomlesspit.co.uk/411784132

XII WHAT DOES THE BIBLE SAY ABOUT CANNIBALISM WHICH WAS STARTED BY THE GIANTS?: https://www.quora.com/What-does-the-Bible-say-about-cannibalism

XIII KING JAMES BIBLE TIME CHART

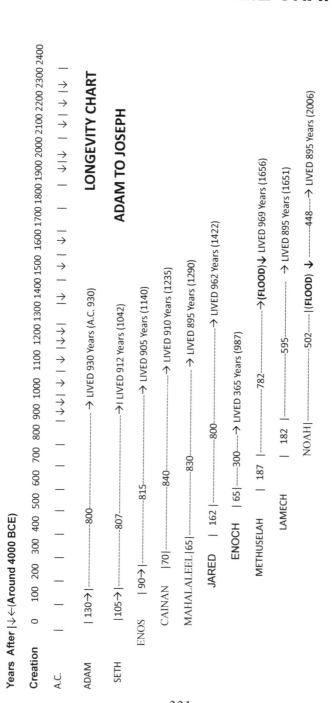

331

ARPHAXAD (FLOOD)↓35| ----------403------→ LIVED 438 Years (2096)

SALAH|30| --------403------→ LIVED 433 Years (2126)

EBER|34| ------430----→ LIVED 464 Years (2187)

PELEG|30|209→ LIVED 239 Years (1996)

REU |32|207→ LIVED 239 Years (2026)

SERUG |30|200→ LIVED 230 Years (2049)

NAHOR |29|119→ LIVED 148 Years (1997)

TERAH |70|135→ LIVED 205 Years (2083)

ABRAHAM |100|75→ LIVED 175Years (2123)

ISAAC |60|120→ LIVED 180 Years (2228)

JACOB |91|56→ LIVED 147 Years (2255)

JOSEPH |110→ LIVED 110 Years (2309)

XIV The Book of Jasher – CONCLUSIONS

C.1 Having studied this Jewish Book of Jasher at length, I would state that much of it is inspired, but not all. Having cross-referenced it to both the K.J.V Bible of the O.T and the Septuagint version of the O.T, the strength of the Book of Jasher is in the amazing amount of Pre-Flood information especially about Enoch, as well as the immediate Post-Flood times with Noah, Nimrod and the Tower of Babel. The rest of the stories are very interesting as well, but it would seem that for whatever reason, someone has tampered with this book as to the genealogies. This is something that is mentioned in the New Testament and tells us to beware of:

1TI.1:4 Neither give heed to fables and endless genealogies, which minister questions, rather than godly edifying which is in faith.

MELCHISADEC IS JESUS CHRIST - THE SAVIOUR – THE MESSIAH

C.2 Unfortunately, it also appears that this Book of Jasher has altered the name Melkisadec to Adonizedec. This Book of Jasher even states that this Adonizedec is Shem. This is plain *incorrect* and is evidence that some-one didn't like the New Testament in the Book of Hebrews explaining that Melchisedec was in fact Jesus Christ who met Abraham at the time just after the 'slaughter of the kings.' Adonizedec is the name given to some of the kings of Jerusalem long before King David made Jerusalem his capital city.

HEB.6:20 Whither the forerunner is for us entered, even Jesus, made an high priest for ever after the order of Melchisedec.

HEB.7:1 For this Melchisedec, King of Salem, priest of the most high God, who met Abraham returning from the slaughter of the kings, and blessed him;

HEB.7:2 To whom also Abraham gave a tenth part of all; first being by interpretation King of righteousness, and after that also King of Salem, which is, King of peace;

HEB.7:3 Without father, without mother, without descent, having neither beginning of days, nor end of life; but made like unto the Son of God; abides a priest continually.

C.3 Some of the Jewish leaders didn't like the early Christians mentioning that it was Jesus in the form of Melchisedec who visited Abraham after his victory in the story of the 'slaughter if the kings'.

Sadly, some very influential people have gone to great trouble to both alter the original scriptures of both the Book of Jasher and the Old Testament part of the King James Bible.

C.4 According to the Septuagint, assembled in circa 300 B.C by 70 learned Hebrew Scholars, Abraham wasn't alive at the same time as Shem or Noah, so why does this Jewish Book of Jasher claim that it was Shem who Abraham met and who was Adonizedec (Melchisedec), if Abraham wasn't alive at the same time as Shem? This is clearly a deception!

C.5 The Leaders of the Jews didn't accept Jesus as their Messiah, and in their hatred of both Christ and Christianity, some of their forefathers had the power to both influence & to alter different passages of excellent original books such as the Book of Jasher and later they made sure that the Masoretic text was used in the Old testament of the King James Bible instead of the much older and Original Hebrew text or even the Greek text of the Septuagint. Why? It was apparently all done to prove that Jesus was not Melchisedec who met Abraham as reported in the Book of Hebrews in the New Testament.

C.6 Unlike in the Masoretic translation of the Old testament which we have in our King James Bibles, I would like to add that the Book of Jasher is not even mentioned in the Septuagint version of **JOSHUA 10:12 &13,** or In **2 Samuel 1:18-27**, but only a reference to the **'Book of Right' in 2 Samuel**. Is it just possible that someone had the references to the Book of Jasher added to the Masoretic Text in order to endorse the Book of Jasher and in particular the story of Melchisedec being Shem?

C.7 In Conclusion: It is sad to see what would have been an excellent book in the form of the Book of Jasher has been corrupted. Why? Because of hatred and spite against both Christ and Christianity. The same goes for the Masoretic text used for the Old Testament in the Bible.

C.8 In order that people don't come to the wrong conclusions, it would be wiser for them to read the Septuagint version of the Old Testament which is more reliable than the Masoretic text, upon which the Old Testament in the K.J.V of the Bible is based.- with the exception of the altered TIME-LINE right after the Great Flood where someone has added 100 years to the lives of the Patriarchs. The question is why someone tampered with the otherwise excellent Septuagint. Read on to find out *why*?

XV BIBLICAL & SEPTUAGINT LXX LONGEVITY CHARTS

C.1 Which is correct? That we are living in circa the year 6000 according to the KJV of the Bible, or somewhere around the year 6700-7000 according to the Septuagint LXX version of the Old Testament?

THE OTHER SIDE OF THE STORy

AN ODD TWIST CONCERNING THE SEPTUAGINT

C.2 The 72 Jewish scholars were living in Alexandria in Egypt, when it was the Southern ¼th Segment of the Greek Empire, at the time that they translated the Septuagint from ancient Hebrew into Greek. The Pharaoh was apparently very proud of the amazing monolithic structures in Egypt including the pyramids and wanted to give Egypt the full credit for building them. But how could he do that?

C.3 What if those who put together the Septuagint LXX were asked to add 100 years to 6 of the Patriarchs from Arphaxad to Nahor? Why? In order to deliberately push back the biblical 'Time-Line' in favour of the Egyptians who claimed to have built the pyramids, but in fact it would seem that the *pyramids were actually built by a super-race prior to the Great Flood from all the evidence.*

C.4 'Is it just possible that 'The Pharaoh' who was apparently financing the writing of the Septuagint, simply asked the 72 men to do him *one favour* and that was to add 100 years to six of the Patriarchs thus *pushing back the annals of time itself,* so that it *would appear that the Pyramids had been built by the Egyptians* around 5000 years ago, which was actually 500 years before the Great Flood in circa 4500 years ago, as mentioned in the K.J.V of the Bible.' The above writing is the inspiration I received when I asked God: Who is right about the Longevity Chart: The Masoretic Text used in the King James, or the much older Septuagint?

C.5 The oldest books on earth are from India and dated as 5000 years old. They describe in great detail the gods and the demi-gods and their 'golden age' before the great Flood. This is when Atlantis and Lemuria and the land of Mu all existed. Cultures with very advanced technology, but technologies that were developed in different ways than our own of today. There are many things that these ancient cultures were capable of doing that even modern man still cannot yet do.

C.6 What I was inspired to receive, shocked me, that those who put the Septuagint together compromised, because of the wishes of Pharaoh, and the fact that the 72 Jewish scholars were guests in his court. Another strange difference in the Septuagint LXX is that it places an extra person called Cainan as the son of Arphaxad instead of Salah. In the Septuagint it states that Salah was the son of Cainan. However, in all the other translations ever found, Cainan is not mentioned? Why would the authors of the Septuagint seemingly deliberately add another person to the TIMELINE? One reason is it would push back the Time-line even further back: But what was the real motive? Why would 72 'Wise men' 'add in' an extra person such as Cainan, apart from to please Pharaoh? What if they actually knew back then that other 'wise men' coming later in time would quickly recognise that something was 'out of place' in the translation of the text? Maybe the 'wise men' who put together the Septuagint LXX were sending a message to future 'illuminated wise men'. Also, why add a person called Cainan after the Great Flood to the Timeline, when there was another Cainan before the Great Flood who was fourth generation from Adam? Sounds a bit out of place to say the least! Perhaps that is why some later translations altered the Septuagint's version on the Longevity Chart? Amazingly, the following confirms this inspiration that I received some 3 months ago:

C.7 'The oldest and most important translation of the Hebrew Old Testament (OT) is the Septuagint (LXX). It translated the Hebrew into Greek in the third century BC in Alexandria, Egypt. The Letter to Aristide tells the story how the Egyptian king Ptolemy II (285-247 BC) ordered his librarian, Demetrius to collect all the books of the world. Demetrius thought there should be a Greek translation of the Torah so 72 Jews, six from each tribe, were sent to translate the Torah into Greek which they did in 72 days *Larsson believes that the translators of the LXX tried to harmonize the Biblical chronology with the Egyptian chronology of Manetho by adding 100 years to the patriarchs ages to push back the time of the flood before the first Egyptian dynasty because there is no record of a great flood.* Early Christian chronologists emphasized the perfect agreement of Manetho with the LXX (Larsson, 403-4). It is interesting to see how they understood Genesis by the way they translated the text.'

SOURCE: https://www.bibleandscience.com/bible/books/genesis/genesisl1.htm

XVI MAPS OF ANCIENT ISRAEL & SURROUNDING KINGDOMS:

MAP OF ISRAEL'S JOURNEY FROM EGYPT TO THE PROMISED LAND:
http://classic.scriptures.lds.org/en/biblemaps/2

MAP OF NATIONS SURROUNDING ANCIENT ISRAEL: Phoenicians, Assyrians, Egyptians, Chittim, Horites, Canaanites, Mesopotamia,Babylon Hittites, Midianites, Land Of Goshen: http://classic.scriptures.lds.org/en/biblemaps/9

MAP SHOWING LOCATION OF AMMONITIES, MOABITES & EDOMITIES: http://classic.scriptures.lds.org/en/biblemaps/1

XVII CONTINUED FROM CHAPTER 34

C.23 Why did God end up judging Israel so strongly In the Diaspora in 70 A.D? It is hardly surprising because they went and **killed their own Messiah Jesus Christ** and God's wrath came upon them in no uncertain terms. The Jews were driven away from Israel for almost 2000 years. That is some great judgement. Why did God judge Israel so severely as he obviously did? The answer is that they should have known better and not killed their own Messiah who had been prophesied by all of the Jewish prophets. So, they were really without an excuse.

C.24 Jesus the Messiah and the greatest of all warriors prophesied that Israel would be judged because they had rejected Him as their Messiah

MAT.23:29 Woe unto you, scribes and Pharisees, hypocrites! because ye build the tombs of the prophets, and garnish the sepulchres of the righteous,

MAT.23:30 And say, If we had been in the days of our fathers, we would not have been partakers with them in the blood of the prophets.

MAT.23:31 Wherefore ye be witnesses unto yourselves, that ye are the children of them which killed the prophets.

MAT.23:32 Fill ye up then the measure of your fathers.

MAT.23:33 Ye serpents, ye generation of vipers, how can ye escape the damnation of hell?

MAT.23:34 Wherefore, behold, I send unto you prophets, and wise men, and scribes: and some of them ye shall kill and crucify; and some of them shall ye scourge in your synagogues, and persecute them from city to city:

MAT.23:35 That upon you may come all the righteous blood shed upon the earth, from the blood of righteous Abel unto the blood of Zacharias son of Barachias, whom ye slew between the temple and the altar.

MAT.23:36 Verily I say unto you, All these things shall come upon this generation.

MAT.23:37 O Jerusalem, Jerusalem, thou that killest the prophets, and stonest them which are sent unto thee, how often would I have gathered thy children together, even as a hen gathereth her chickens under her wings, and ye would not!

MAT.23:38 Behold, your house is left unto you desolate.

MAT.23:39 For I say unto you, Ye shall not see me henceforth, till ye shall say, 'Blessed is he that cometh in the name of the Lord'.

C.25 The fact is exactly 40 years after Jesus prophesied these things to the Pharisee leaders of Israel, Israel was totally destroyed by the Romans as it was the time of the Wrath of God against Israel.

C.26 CONCLUSION: WHAT WAS GOD'S PURPOSE WITH 2000 YEARS OF JEWISH HISTORY from 2000 BCE UNTIL CHRIST?

God's purpose with the nation of Israel was to try to set an example and to teach other nations to follow God. Unfortunately, if we study the entire history of Israel up until the Messiah Jesus, we find that most of Israel's kings were classified by the Bible itself as evil. Very few of Israel's kings were dedicated to God. After 2000 years of its history Israel had become a very bad example to the nations and they topped their crimes by killing their own Messiah which has cost them dearly.

C.27 THE GREAT IMPORTANCE OF JESUS THE MESSIAH

JOH.1:17 For the law was given by Moses, but grace and truth came by Jesus Christ.

Moses and all those leading Israel up until the Messiah took the sword in hand and fought and slaughtered their enemies. When the Messiah came, He taught His disciples something completely different:

MAT.5:43 Ye have heard that it hath been said, Thou shalt love thy neighbour, and hate thine enemy.

MAT.5:44 But I say unto you, Love your enemies, bless them that curse you, do good to them that hate you, and pray for them which despitefully use you, and persecute you;

MAT.5:45 That ye may be the children of your Father which is in heaven: for he maketh his sun to rise on the evil and on the good, and sendeth rain on the just and on the unjust.

MAT.5:46 For if ye love them which love you, what reward have ye? do not even the publicans the same?

MAT.5:47 And if ye salute your brethren only, what do ye more than others? do not even the publicans so?

MAT.5:48 Be ye therefore perfect, even as your Father which is in heaven is perfect.

C.28 Of course all the early disciples of Christ and those who started the spread of Christianity were all Jewish and dedicated ones like Paul. It was difficult from them to unlearn the ways of Moses and the very strict laws such as 'an eye for an eye' 'a tooth for a tooth' etc. Through Jesus the Christians learned about God's forgiveness and mercy. They learnt that it is not by good work that we obtain righteousness and get to heaven. It is all by the Grace of God through his son the Messiah – Jesus Christ.

EPH.2:8 For by grace are ye saved through faith; and that not of yourselves: it is the gift of God:

EPH.2:9 Not of works, lest any man should boast.

2CO.5:17 Therefore if any man be in Christ, he is a new creature: old things are passed away; behold, all things are become new.

2CO.5:18 And all things are of God, who hath reconciled us to himself by Jesus Christ, and hath given to us the ministry of reconciliation;

2CO.5:19 To wit, that God was in Christ, reconciling the world unto himself, not imputing their trespasses unto them; and hath committed unto us the word of reconciliation.

2CO.5:20 Now then we are ambassadors for Christ, as though God did beseech you by us: we pray you in Christ's stead, be ye reconciled to God.

2CO.5:21 For he hath made him to be sin for us, who knew no sin; that we might be made the righteousness of God in him.

C.29 The job of all Christians is to preach the Gospel about Jesus Christ and to also Warn the world of its coming Destruction for its wickedness

MAR.16:15 And he said unto them, Go ye into all the world, and preach the gospel to every creature.

MAR.16:16 He that believeth and is baptized shall be saved; but he that believeth not shall be damned.

C.30 Our job as Christians is also to Warn the world of its coming Destruction for its wickedness

EZE.3:17 Son of man, I have made thee a watchman unto the house of Israel: therefore hear the word at my mouth and give them warning from me.

EZE.3:18 When I say unto the wicked, Thou shalt surely die; and thou givest him not warning, nor speakest to warn the wicked from his wicked way, to save his life; the same wicked man shall die in his iniquity; but his blood will I require at thine hand.

EZE.3:19 Yet if thou warn the wicked, and he turn not from his wickedness, nor from his wicked way, he shall die in his iniquity; but thou hast delivered thy soul.

A **Book of Jasher** that was reliable, otherwise it would not have been mentioned in both the time of Joshua and in the time of King David. As I mentioned in the Introduction of my 2nd Book '**Enoch Insights**' we *must not automatically throw out the Apocryphal Books* just because they are not perfect. Maybe they were excellent books at one time, but some powerful persons have altered the texts at some time or other.

In Conclusion, I would say that most of the Apocryphal books are largely accurate in content with a few mostly 'time discrepancies.

Unlike the Old Testament books, we have *no access to any manuscript of Jasher dating before 100 AD.*

Why that date? *Because the book we have is written in modern, square Hebrew characters without the vowel points.* The earliest manuscripts from this time are also missing the vowel points. *This points directly to Rabbi Akiba and his group's efforts to promote rabbinical leadership over Scripture.* His group, referred to as the Council of Jamnia, wanted to produce a foundation copy of the Scriptures as the original had been burned by the Romans when Jerusalem and the Temple were destroyed in 70AD. They made a number of *changes in the Scriptures* (which have come down to us as the *Masoretic Text*).'

C.3 It sounds to me, like this guy Rabbi Akiba in 100 A.D was very bitter because of the destruction of Israel in 70 A.D, in the which 100,000 Jews were crucified around Jerusalem alone, and millions driven out of the country in the famous 'Diaspora'. That was a direct fulfilment of a prophecy given by Jesus Himself 40 years earlier.

C.4 Jesus warned Israel that because they had rejected Him, as their Messiah, and that they had killed all the prophets that God had sent unto them, that *Israel would be destroyed.*

MAT.23:37 O Jerusalem, Jerusalem, thou that kills the prophets, and stones them which are sent unto thee, how often would I have gathered thy children together, even as a hen gathers her chickens under her wings, and ye would not!

MAT.23:38 Behold, your house is left unto you desolate.

C.5 The Romans came in their full might and fury in 70 AD, in the figure of general Titus, to destroy Israel completely. Normally, throughout history, when an emperor has done something like that, it is simply because that particular nation is being very difficult, rebellious & totally impossible to deal with, and this particular case, being stubbornly unwilling to submit to the Roman Rule. The same thing happened to Jerusalem in the time of Nebuchadnezzar and the Babylonian Empire, some 600 years earlier. It was much worse under the Romans though, as Israel ceased to be a nation for almost 2000 years until 1948.

C.6 What did Israel expect? They murdered their own Saviour Jesus Christ! It looks to me as if *God Himself allowed Israel to be severely judged*, and its people *cast out* for their *blatant rebellion against God Himself and His Son*

XVII 'TOTAL TIME' OF ISRAEL IN CAPTIVITY:

Please read my other book '**JUBILEES INSIGHTS**' which has Charts and exact dates, which actually point out that the '430 years of the Jews being in Captivity' in Egypt, actually started with Abraham having a son called Ismael of an Egyptian woman who afflicted his biological son Isaac. The traditional **AGE OF THE EARTH** Timeframe Chart shows the '430 years of bondage of the Jews' starting when Jacob went down to Egypt. If we take this into consideration and take the date of Jacob entering into Egypt and compare it to the time of Abraham there is a discrepancy of 215 years!

XVIII FINAL CONCLUSION:

It would appear that the K J Version of the Bible is after all more accurate when it comes to the generations born after the Great Flood. After all, God did predict that He would cut man's years short to only 120 years and eventually that went down to 70. If these final conclusions are correct, then the earth is closer to 6000-years old than 7000. With what I hope is all the evidence in, you decide which you think is more likely to be correct concerning this one?

MY *FIVE BOOKS* IN ORDER OF PUBLICATION:

1) OUT OF THE BOTTOMLESS PIT: http://www.outofthebottomlesspit.co.uk/411702511
2) ENOCH INSIGHTS: http://www.outofthebottomlesspit.co.uk/418666481
3) EZDRAS INSIGHTS: http://www.outofthebottomlesspit.co.uk/420942154
4) JASHER INSIGHTS: http://www.outofthebottomlesspit.co.uk/421385649
5) JUBILEES INSIGHTS: http://www.outofthebottomlesspit.co.uk/413438217

USEFUL WEBSITE LINKS:

BIBLICAL CREATION: http://www.outofthebottomlesspit.co.uk/421607713
WORD WARRIORS: http://www.outofthebottomlesspit.co.uk/420555449
THE 4 HORSEMEN: http://www.outofthebottomlesspit.co.uk/412514886
HEAVEN: http://www.outofthebottomlesspit.co.uk/412320663
LIFE AFTER DEATH: http://www.outofthebottomlesspit.co.uk/412645521
BOOK OF DANIEL: http://www.outofthebottomlesspit.co.uk/420616689
BOOK OF REVELATION: http://www.outofthebottomlesspit.co.uk/421238965
MARK OF THE BEAST: http://www.outofthebottomlesspit.co.uk/412733219
SIGNS OF THE TIMES: http://www.outofthebottomlesspit.co.uk/413019004
SIGNS: http://www.outofthebottomlesspit.co.uk/418801558
BABYLON THE GREAT: http://www.outofthebottomlesspit.co.uk/412306605
ABOUT THE AUTHOR: http://www.outofthebottomlesspit.co.uk/413469553
AUTHOR AT AMAZON: www.amazon.com/author/777.7
FACE-BOOK: GROUP: ENOCH INSIGHTS: https://www.facebook.com/groups/323412114853716/

My website: www.outofthebottomlesspit.co.uk

E-mail: strangetruths@outofthebottomlesspit.co.uk

Lightning Source UK Ltd.
Milton Keynes UK
UKHW022048020819
347297UK00008B/424/P